Middle Class Heroes

VOICES FROM BOSTON'S SUBURBS

By Steven A. Rosenberg

To Devorah and Aaron

CONTENTS

CHAPTER 5: Family

CHAPTER 6: Sports

CHAPTER 7: Homeless

CHAPTER 8: Work

CHAPTER 9: Weather

CHAPTER 10: Jewish

CHAPTER 11: Food and Drink

CHAPTER 12: Death

PREFACE

Who likes to be classified? The rich quickly object, the poor do not need another label, and the middle class — which forms the largest economic sector in our society — would rather talk about anything else than accept another categorization.

Anyone who comes from the middle class knows that there's little glamour to that classification. And to begin to even understand their hopes and dreams is to explore a complicated and often contradictory web that encompasses everything from someone's work ethic to a person's will to survive the pressures of debt.

This anthology is not meant to paint a pure picture of Boston's middle class. Rather, it's a snapshot of the early days of the millennium — a time when the country was rocked by two major recessions and the near-collapse of our economy. While many lost their savings during this period, others were left behind as the economy, culture and technology changed.

I wrote these articles for The Boston Globe, where I was a staff writer from 2002-16. (Two previously unpublished pieces are also included in this book, "The Rooming House," and "Arthur and Harris".) The book is sectioned into themes that are woven into daily lives. And so, as a person who grew up neither rich nor poor — and who still falls in that demographic, this collection is as much as about my life as those included on these pages. These subjects — ranging from family to food — are listed as chapter titles, and loosely pull together remnants of vanishing neighborhoods, professions and traditions. They are also dispatches on work, ritual, war, fantasy, poverty, and death.

This collection melds reportage and opinion, two entirely different types of writing. I began writing the personal essays to free myself of the constraints of daily news-gathering and journalism, and to wander aloud on the page, and learn what I was really thinking about at the time. Several of the essays are meditations on growing into middle age, and lessons learned along the way. I rediscovered that walking was a quick way to access my feelings and thoughts; I learned that family and friends are still central to my life, and while my parents have passed, their lessons live on; I sought to understand the relevance of my religion, Judaism; I learned that I am more or less like the adults I remembered as a kid: I prefer a simpler existence with less electronics and more conversation.

During my reporting, I found what I've always known: the middle class is still the most approachable section of society, where people will take the time to answer a reporter's question. And for all its shortcomings, it still provides the backbone of the area's workforce, and forms the infrastructure that plows our streets, protects our cities, teaches our kids, and also volunteers for town boards, PTAs, and sports booster clubs.

In the neighborhoods, I wrote about teachers and veterans and the homeless who still aspired to live up to the values they learned as kids. I met old-timers who sat on their porches and stoops and told stories about food and music and long-gone working stiffs who did what they could to provide for their families.

Tradition still plays a large role in some suburban neighborhoods, but as Boston has grown wealthier, its riches have spilled over to cities and towns — sometimes all but erasing ritual that had taken place for decades or even centuries.

Some of these traditions have been included on these pages — such as the Greasy Pole walk that is still part of the annual fiesta in Gloucester, the Black Picnic that's held every summer at Salem Willows, and the Thanksgiving football game. But some snapshots that I was able to capture are already fading: such as Everett's Line (or Lynde) neighborhood, which will likely be razed by 2019 when the Wynn casino is finished, and the Wonderland Dog Track, which has closed. Chelsea Night, a reunion that I wrote about that once brought 500 Chelsea natives together, is also no longer.

At the Globe, I ventured along beaches and rivers and into woods where I was astonished to find a significant homeless population. I included a section on the homeless because nearly all had come from the middle class and hoped to return to that status one day. Also, their stories reflect a changing narrative among working families — where mental health issues, and often a history of sexual abuse combined with substance abuse — continues to divide relatives.

More than anything, I guess, I was reminded again — while writing these pieces — that everyone has a soul and a story; that people are eager to share their thoughts and beliefs and are mostly respectful of others. And I learned that the American Dream — despite the racism, classism, and wage inequality that has helped divide our country — also still exists, at least in the form of hope or at a minimum, continuity, over the course of each day in most of our lives.

Steven A. Rosenberg
February, 2017

CHAPTER 1

Walking

Play

The late fall sun bathes us in gold as we walk along the railroad tracks. I remember the scene in "Stand By Me" where the four boys saunter along the tracks, and wonder how different the three of us are from them. The kids in the movie were looking for a dead body. We are middle-aged men just out for a walk in the woods, sharing some laughs, seeking meaning from the paths and hills we've traversed.

We walk together, and every few moments I swing around to check for a train.

"The path we want is just ahead," says DT, who went out walking this summer and came upon these tracks, just off a path in Salem. Once a gangly math whiz, he now travels a third of the year and counsels countries on the best way to bring cellular and Internet service to impoverished people.

"This place feels like magic," says Bear, who ambles a few yards ahead of me. I gave him that name when we were 7 or 8 after he picked me up over his shoulders. Now he's a lawyer for a company in Oklahoma.

I snap a photo, capturing their backs as they continue along the tracks. Our friendship, now past the 50-year mark, is not dependent on old stories or reminiscing. But as we walk, I feel more like a child than an older man. I pick up a stone and throw it into the woods and it falls silently into the green.

As I scan the bramble and woods, I continue to walk and slip into a dream state.

We spend hours racing our bikes around the block. I am 5 and we ride in the middle of the street, a quiet suburban road where few cars pass each hour. We are an excited bunch, drunk with speed and determined to pedal even faster. The harder we push, the louder we become. The noise rises up from the rubber tires and asphalt and gives us a sense of collective strength. Everything we talk about ends with a laugh. When we come to a bend in the circle of homes that defines our world, our bikes slant and sometimes my ankles touch DT or Bear's foot or pedal or spoke.

A couple of years later, we take our bikes into the woods and careen down steep paths. Roots, broken branches, and big rocks are our enemy, and sometimes we crash into small trees. Still, when that happens, we get up and ride down the same hill again.

We create a game on bikes called Chase, and race as fast as we can around the circle, through backyards, driveways, and along the worn paths in the woods. Nobody ever wins because there are no rules. Still, everybody wants to be part of the race. No one wants to miss out on a moment.

The only thing we really care about is playing with one another.

"OK, this is it," says DT, leading us off the tracks up a knoll. "It gets steep now."

Five minutes later, we stand on top of a hill overlooking the tracks, woods, and a marsh. All of this is about 2 miles away from the block where we grew up.

We look down at the valley, and breathe the cool musty air of leaves, twigs, and pine needles. DT, who is prone to declarations, suggests that this moment is just another reward for working hard to earn a living, and putting our families first.

"Amen, DT," I say.

We cross the tracks and head up another hill, and pass stone walls that were hewn and placed as markers centuries ago. After another 45 minutes we emerge from the forest, and walk through the town graveyard.

As we wait for DT's wife to pick us up, we sit on a wall outside the cemetery. We acknowledge but do not dwell on the metaphor of three guys in their mid-50s, resting just beyond the graves.

"Hey, at least we've been out walking," says DT.

"Indeed," says Bear.

"Amen," I say.

November 16, 2014
The Boston Globe

Finding the Promised Land at Revere Beach

It's another warm, muggy morning at Revere Beach and I find a spot in front of the Oak Island Bath House. I walk a lot, and it's rare these days that people make eye contact. But here on America's oldest public beach, things are different. A jogger smiles as she runs along the boulevard; a mustachioed man in a beach chair on the sidewalk waves when I walk by.

There are no beach snobs here; even the seagulls come over and sing when I step on the sand. There is nothing pretentious about this beach. There's no fee to park; bathrooms are free; the water's brackish, but clear and warm about 15 yards off shore.

I sink into the balmy granules, close my eyes, and wait for the waves to crash. Somebody like me probably sat here 100 years ago and sought similar refuge. I open my eyes and the small waves rise and fall and start up all over again.

A few yards away, a woman squints and smiles. "Beautiful, huh?" she says.

"Sure is," I say.

Marilyn Hinch is taking a vacation day from work and has come prepared. "I've got my iced tea, my lounge chair, some cheese and fruit and towels," she tells me.

She doesn't like to read at the beach and didn't bring a book. Instead, she listens to the waves, tries to nap, and goes in the water. She describes her technique for dunking: "I walk out and then I wait for a little wave and go 'Oh God, help me!' and do the sign of the cross and then dunk. But this water isn't freezing cold."

Now 60 and living in Peabody, she tells me she started coming here with her parents, cousins, and friends in the 1950s when she was a child in East Boston. She always sits in the same spot, just beyond the bathhouse. "I feel like I know it. It's like a home to me," she says.

Wherever she walks, there are memories from the 1950s and '60s. "The blankets touched from one end of the beach to the other," she says. "Growing up, my mother would pack a cooler and fill it with chicken and potato salad — and you name it — and we'd take the subway and get off at Wonderland and we'd have our supper here."

Hinch closes her eyes and relaxes and I wander off toward a tanned, slim, bald man. He's walking in the surf, carrying a white shirt in his left hand and black shoes in his right hand.

"I'll walk for a little while and then go for a swim," says the man, who introduces himself as John Dineen. He tells me he's been coming here for more than 70 years, first with his parents, who left Ireland for the United States and settled in Cambridge. In these waters he learned to swim, and over the decades he kept coming back. He established a routine where he'd run and swim nearly every day throughout the year for decades.

He says he feels better when he walks and swims and believes there's no big secret about the benefits of exercise. "It makes me feel good," says Dineen, who leaves his Wilmington home every morning to come to the beach.

Winter swimming, he explains, requires common sense. "The water is cold and you only go in for a minute or two. Then you walk out, dry off, get dressed, and go home."

Now he's walking in a foot of water and looking for a cleaner stretch of ocean to swim. The conversation turns to friends and family and he becomes more reserved. He tells me he misses his wife, Carole. They used to walk the beach together and were married for 37 years until she died 14 years ago. His daughters, he explains, are off doing other things. Other old-timers and beachgoing cousins have also passed on.

"So many people have left and gone to the Promised Land," he says in a whisper.

I ask him about the Promised Land and if it exists. "I want to believe it, but I really don't know," he says.

Dineen keeps walking and I step back onto the warm sand. For now, this is the Promised Land and it does not judge or choose a language or care about race or religion. It just gives back, especially to those of us in need.

July 26, 2015
The Boston Globe

Spring Sun

It's 80 degrees and I am walking on a beach and making noise as I move.

I hear the sand being squished by my feet, and in the midst of the first really warm day in more than six months, I actually sigh several times. Warm sand — something that I take for granted in August — seems exotic and otherworldly. I look at the children running into the water, and then look at the sand, and continue my slow gait.

I feel like I am defrosting.

This is what happens to people who were born in this cold climate, I think. This is what happens when people stay in the same place where their parents and grandparents settled. This is what happens when the sun hides for six months each year; when the wind, rain, and chill combine to make autumn and spring a crapshoot. Yes, this is what happens when people who are pushed around by all of that weather are allowed some perspective while absorbing the heat.

I move slowly away from the pounding surf; away from the children throwing wet sand; away from the flirting high school teens. I distance myself from the chatty moms who sip spring water and smoke cigarettes and read hardcover novels.

I am lost in thought and realize that I am not walking in a straight path. Suddenly I feel like my father, who walked the beach nearly every day for years. Like him, I walk slowly, my hands clasped behind my back, looking up, down, with my thoughts drifting between decades.

When I walk to the left, I drift to another era. I am back with my childhood friends on a nearby beach; I am getting ready to go off to college; I am working in a factory on a hot summer day. Altogether, I am fishing, playing baseball, learning to drive, writing my first story, playing in a band in a smoky club, on an airplane headed to a far-away continent; a husband, a father.

I drift to the right and I am aging, listening to close friends who have not worked in months after long, successful careers. I think of my own career and of all the stories that predict newspapers will die. I hear words of advice of close friends who struggle to beat cancer. I think of growing old and look up at the sky and pray that I'll never retire and move to Florida.

I open my eyes and look at the rising tide. I've walked about a mile and decide to turn around. On the way back, I look at everyone. A man who I see frequently sitting in downtown Lynn listening to music on oversized headphones is shirtless and walking extremely fast. Four high school girls kick a soccer ball, smile at two guys throwing around a football, and then run into the water. I eavesdrop on conversations, hoping to hear something profound, perhaps even life-changing, but instead grasp only a few words of sentences.

"Kathy is going tomorrow night," says a girl.

"You can't do that," an elderly woman tells a young child.

"Yeah," says a man covered in green tattoos.

I know I should leave but I stay for another half-hour. I sit in the warm sand. I think of a childhood friend who still lives down the block. I dial him on the cell, and there's an echo when he answers. When I tell him to come down to the beach, he tells me he's in Saudi Arabia.

I look for my car and the seat is warm. I turn on the air conditioner and radio, and then shut both off. I roll down the windows.

Better to listen to the wind.

May 1, 2008
The Boston Globe

Upon Waking in Jerusalem

JERUSALEM — Around 3:30 a.m. the men started shouting on the road below my hotel room.

I couldn't understand what they were saying, but they continued. When that happens, I usually am able to drift back to other worlds, but this morning I lay frozen until the gray light came. That's when I spoke, slowly, my words tumbling out in an unrehearsed rasp.

"What is life?" I asked, surprising myself with such an impossible question, so early, so quiet. I continued on with a bold declaration, which I have already forgotten and to write it as it happened would be a lie. My conclusion was simple: Life should be about finding myself in all that I see; following the clues to more inner discoveries and a balance of giving and taking during the moment.

With this in mind, I looked at my watch: 5:50 a.m. Time for a walk, I thought. Five minutes later I am on the silent streets of Jerusalem on Shabbat; walking in the middle of Rehov Jaffa — the main thoroughfare that brought travelers from Jerusalem all the way to Jaffa just 100 years ago. The road still leads to the highway, but I was walking the other way, toward the Old City. Who is up at 6 a.m. on Shabbat? Mostly men draped in tallit headed toward the Western Wall and drunks rising from park benches and staggering alone. About 500 yards from my hotel I came upon a couple in their 20s. A man was gently trying to move his girlfriend or wife or new friend off a park bench where she was sleeping.

I arrive at the Jaffa Gate, and the Old City nods its own silent welcome. It remembers me, doesn't it? If there is a place on earth that keeps track of all the visitors that walk along its rutted roads it must be this walled box of memories. I've been here during good times, I realize; not in the centuries when people saw fit to burn it all down and build it up again in their own image. I pass a hooded teen speaking a soft Arabic into a cellphone. I don't understand his words, but the gift of not knowing a foreign language in another country allows me to focus on other things, like David's Tower, a massive citadel (in the Middle Ages) standing before me. I follow along the narrow street, away from the Arab Market, and toward the Armenian Quarter, which leads to the Jewish Quarter.

Soon, I pass under small arches, and through a maze of other alleyways that bring me to the edge of the Jewish Quarter. I look at a flier stuck on a wall: "Bass/Guitar lessons by Harvey Brooks." I recognize the name; that guy played with Dylan and also Michael Bloomfield. I heard that he moved to Jerusalem a few years ago. Good for him. Maybe I should take some lessons, I think.

I see myself calling the guy, and jamming with him in some small room probably around the corner from here. That's when I'm zapped back to the present. A tall, slender man in his 60s strolls by me dressed completely in white. He's got a white suit jacket and pants, even a white hat — all to match his long wizened white face, white hair, and white beard.

The walk toward the Wall is a slow descent, and I see a hippie gal in one of those modest cotton skirts that women wore in the 1970s.

There's just the man in white, the hippie, a group of tiny stray cats, and me, all moving together down staircases until the skyline reveals the Wall and gold and silver mosques.

When I reach the Wall, I touch the stones and ask God to heal all of us. My eyes are closed and I feel the cool stone on my forehead, which brings some comfort. Some of the Torahs sit upright; their brightly colored metal encasements tell a long story of Sephardic tradition. I wander from the Mexican minyon to the Iraqi minyon to the Moroccan minyon. There's a group of French men next to the Ethiopians. And the Hasidim are scattered before Torahs in strongholds throughout the plaza.

I listen to them pray, stand near them, and acknowledge that I don't feel too connected to the men. That's OK, I say to myself and let out a little smile. I am part of a tribe that is still in the process of figuring out what it means to be related to one another; that has a shared, tortured history that follows me even in this homeland where I let out a sigh each time I realize that I am part of a majority. It's not a sigh of superiority. It's just a sigh that takes note of this violent but spiritual history that somehow has helped shape my DNA.

Soon I am back up the steps, and as I leave the Jewish Quarter I almost brush up against the man in white. He seems to be on a mission and doesn't even notice me. Perhaps he's returned to his wife, who's making him breakfast now. Or maybe he's lost in further prayer in a small sunlit room back in the Old City. I have to think that he is trying to get to know himself better this morning.

In Kabbalah, white is a sign of purity. I grasp hold of that white color as I walk away from him. It shifts into a brief warm glow that I carry away as the Old City grows distant in the background. Soon, the color disappears, but something happened, right? The man in white gave me his color on Shabbat. Maybe it will return.

August 23, 2015
The Boston Globe

Walking Outside of His Comfort Zone

A suburb can be the kind of place where Ponce de Leon would feel comfortable tying his boat to a dock.

Two days a week, the man may go no further than the corner coffee shop or pizzeria. These are comfort drives that sometimes convince him that life is standing still and that despite the advance of calendar years, his mind and body are unchanged.

As he sips coffee in a corner parking lot looking out at a Swampscott strip mall that he has visited almost daily since childhood, he wonders if this lifestyle has reversed the aging process. Mornings, he stands in front of the mirror and ignores his graying temples, instead seeking out the brown and blond streaks that he recognizes as his youth.

And then one day, the routine is broken when he attends a conference in Manhattan. After several hours of discussion with people 10 to 20 years older — during which he takes note of their sagging skin and slow gaits — he finds a door and decides to search for the sun. A two-hour walk is what he has in mind, a casual stroll that will reconnect him with the buildings he once loved, and the kind of people he is seeking to meet.

But after 15 minutes, his feet tire. With a glance, he looks down at his rarely worn black wingtip shoes and assigns blame.

He eyes a green park, surrounded by chairs and small tables. It appears as a slice of calm and rejuvenation. He sits at the edge of the emerald carpet and wishes.

His feet are still numb when he turns around to look at the city dwellers. An Indian woman with sunglasses talks casually to her Indian boyfriend, who also wears sunglasses. At the next table, a Latina sits alone and smiles while she reads. Behind her, a group of six women laugh and play cards.

All are half his age, and he knows that his observations will have to suffice, and that there will probably be no chance conversation. His weight pushes the legs of the chair into the stone dust, offering some proof of his presence. Otherwise, he is invisible. Perhaps the birds on the green see him. The man does not panic or feel anger. He does think about age, though, and wonders where he belongs.

He searches the faces at the tables for clues, and signs. Perhaps just a few words or even some eye contact will reveal whatever it is he's seeking. As he looks at their faces and eyes and arms, he also looks inward. He decides it all looks unfamiliar.

A strawberry-haired woman in her 20s sits next to a plastic container of pickles at the card table and adjusts her brown sunglasses. The Latina is no longer reading but is writing in her journal. This gives him hope. Perhaps she's trying to figure it out, too? He hears water, and spins around to see a large fountain spouting in several different directions. He lowers his eyes and notices that a red-bearded man in a blue cap is staring into his eyes. He spins back and seeks refuge in the green pasture. He focuses on a pigeon and takes note that he's been seen.

When he turns back toward the man, the connection is no longer. The stranger's face is inches away from a cellphone, and his finger is about to touch the screen.

May 23, 2013
The Boston Globe

CHAPTER 2

Tradition

There Goes Swifty

The entrance fee says $2, but no one here remembers the last time they sold tickets. Walk into the dimly lit Wonderland clubhouse, and it has the feel of a coffee klatch at a local senior center. Here, day after day, around 200 old-timers schmooze about dogs and races that only they remember, lifting them with a buzz that recalls the good old days when the betting parlor was wall to wall with familiar faces who dreamed of a big cash-out.

From 1935 until last September, greyhounds raced around an outdoor track here, chasing a mechanical rabbit named Swifty. But in 2008, Massachusetts residents voted to end dog racing in the state by the end of 2009. The Legislature allowed dog tracks like Wonderland to offer betting on simulcast races until July 31, 2010.

Now, Wonderland workers are gearing up for the day the park goes dark. The copper railing that carried Swifty around the track was cut up and sold for scrap. Brass banisters from the 300-seat Wonderland Dining Room are also set for the scrap yard, and the track plans to auction thousands of seats and other memorabilia once it closes.

Before casinos opened in Connecticut, the 35-acre Wonderland was the mother ship of gambling in New England. Even during the middle of the Depression, 5,000 patrons would line the track's apron each night to root their dogs to the finish line. Some greyhounds, like Rural Rube — who won 19 races in 1939 — were treated as celebrities. That year, the dog attended a dinner in his honor at a Boston hotel where 1,500 fans paid for the right to sit in the same room.

For decades, the track averaged 8,000 patrons on weeknights and 14,000 on weekend nights. Traffic jams along Route 1A were legendary, and for premier events — such as the Wonderland Derby and the Grady Memorial Sprint — cars would be backed up for miles into Chelsea and Lynn. The good times continued in the 1980s, when the track grossed more than $1 million on four separate nights. Attendance and handle fell dramatically in 1992 after Foxwoods opened its casino in Mashantucket, Conn.

These days, the outdoor track lies unused, the tote board is partially covered with plywood, and Swifty is under wraps in the administration office. In the shuttered grandstand, thousands of seats have been undisturbed for more than 15 years. Puddles from the leaky roof sit in front of stations where parimutuel clerks handled millions of bets.

The track opens at noon and people arrive alone and grab a seat at a cubicle that's fitted with a television. Sammy Cain usually is one of the first to arrive and often stays until close to midnight. Cain, 57, first came to the track 40 years ago and served as its announcer for more than 30 years. He still introduces himself as the voice of Wonderland. On this weekday, he marks up a program featuring dogs from Wheeling Island Racetrack in West Virginia. He looks up, smiles when he sees a familiar face, and returns to the dog program.

"I'm a dog person and I still enjoy gambling," said Cain, who called his last race at the track on Sept. 13. Cain, of Chelsea, has spent most of his life at the gambling center. His eyes grow bright and his spirits lift when he discusses some of Wonderland's greatest dogs, such as Downing, Malka, and Rooster Cogburn. If the track closes in July, he figures he'll drive up to the Seabrook Greyhound Park in New Hampshire, which still offers simulcasts.

"It breaks my heart because it was a thriving industry that's in a lot of trouble," Cain said. "The older people are dying off and there's no one to replace them. It's going to be sad when Wonderland closes because it's a way of life, you know?"

Behind Cain, Frank Eon stares at the 30 TVs that line the small betting area. Twenty years ago, there were at least 300 parimutuel clerks to handle all of the bets, but today there are only three. Eon, who is 63 and retired, has been handicapping dogs at Wonderland since 1962. Now he drives from his house in Peabody several days a week, to play a handful of races and reminisce about the nights when wise guys like Bobby the Hat, Jake the Snake, Louie the Lug, and others held court and dispensed counsel to up-and-coming bettors.

"We all come in and remember the old days," he said, standing among losing race and lottery tickets and discarded programs. "It used to be fun here. We'd come in and laugh with our buddies and shoot the bull about what dogs we liked. There's still a thrill of betting a couple of bucks on a dog you like, and if he wins you feel good."

A few yards away, Frank McCarthy lifts his pen and marks a dog program. McCarthy, who is 86, leaves his house in Dorchester every morning and takes the subway to Wonderland.

McCarthy has been betting on dogs at Wonderland for 70 years. These days he spends a few hours at the park betting $2 a race.

"It's a pastime. It breaks up my day. Without it I'd be gonzo," he said.

A retired machine shop owner, McCarthy said most of the research he conducts before each race ends up as wasted time. Lately, he's been bringing dice to the park and rolling them to select a dog number.

He puts his program down, fiddles with his pen, and talks about the touts who used to line the walls back in the 1940s.

"They were something," he said.

McCarthy said he still thinks about a night in 1947 when he almost won a superfecta.

"I had three dogs coming down the stretch. The third dog was supposed to close but he didn't," he said wistfully. "If he closed I would have had 75 grand."

February 14, 2010
The Boston Globe

Salem's Black Picnic

Barbara Barton and the rest of her family will be going to sleep early tomorrow night.

The extra rest will be necessary because she plans to be standing on a patch of green at Salem Willows around 4 o'clock Saturday morning, to secure the spot where her 50-plus family members have been assembling on the third Saturday of July for decades.

Barton and 1,000 others are expected Saturday at the waterfront park in Salem for the annual Black Picnic, which is acknowledged as one of the longest-running African-American gatherings in New England.

At the Bartons' residence in Lynn, and in some other homes throughout the state, the tradition of attending the picnic is considered a required duty among family members, and its very existence is considered almost sacrosanct.

"This is our primary experience of the year," said Virginia Barton, Barbara's mother, who attended her first picnic in 1928, when she was 3 months old, and has never missed an outing.

"To stand in the spot where my mother and relatives used to bring us is an honor," added Toni Cromwell, of Mattapan. Cromwell, who is 58 and works for the Boston Housing Authority, has also never missed a picnic. This year she expects more than 100 relatives to attend.

The roots of the picnic can be traced to a humble gathering in 1741 attended by 26 slaves who met for a quiet daylong celebration on the Saugus River in Lynn. The tradition continued through the 18th century, and dovetailed with another celebration started in Salem by Thomas Paul, a preacher who founded the First African Baptist Church in 1805. At that time, Paul began an annual sermon and picnic in Salem that brought together congregants from his Boston church and blacks from north of Boston.

"It turned out that a lot of people were related, and it became this big event," said Stephen Hemingway, a Salem TV producer who has researched the origins of the picnic.

By 1880, said Hemingway, it had grown into the largest summer gathering for African-Americans in the state, and that year it shifted from south Salem to the lawn at Salem Willows. Toward the end of the 19th century, attendees dubbed it the Colored People's Picnic, and it was held on the third Thursday of July each year.

The picnic accommodated the Thursday day off afforded to most of the African-Americans, who worked primarily as maids, butlers, and housekeepers, said Barton. Barton's family connection with the event can be traced to her aunt Hattie Camps, who began attending the picnic in 1885.

By the early 20th century, the picnic had become an annual event for congregants of Baptist and Methodist churches in Lynn, Boston, Cambridge, Lowell, Worcester, Springfield, and Providence. People arrived early by street car; church choirs performed; track and field events were held, and ribbons were given to the best athletes. A dance was held, and the jazz that flowed from the Charleshurst Ballroom at the Willows was performed by such luminaries as Duke Ellington, Cab Calloway, and Fletcher Henderson.

"It was a place to see and be seen, and to enjoy the company and dance," said Pearl Brown, who remembers her aunts attending the galas in evening gowns. Brown, who is 80, lives in Lynn, and first attended the picnic with her grandmother in 1930. "In those days we went in an open-air trolley. When we got there, there were buses from all over," she said.

During World War II, the picnic was switched to the third Saturday in July — reflecting a shift in the socioeconomic status of many African-Americans, who were then working in factories and defense plants, said Barton.

Hemingway, 70, grew up in Roxbury and first went to the picnic as a child. He believes the event provided a refuge for a minority that regularly faced racism.

"Any time we went out of Roxbury, we were on pins and needles," said Hemingway. "We dressed up because we were concerned about the impressions we made and we didn't want to be stereotyped. Salem Willows was a time when we could let loose, and people in Salem were aware of that, and they understood what was happening."

Virginia Barton, who formerly worked for Lynn Economic Opportunity, said churches took a less active role in participating in the picnic after World War II. She also said the name of the gathering was changed in the 1960s during the civil rights movement. "We recognized Black Power, and people refused to be called colored, so we chose to call it the Black Picnic," said Barton.

Since then, the picnic has evolved into a large, informal event, with no official sponsor or organizer.

But many traditions remain. Some sections of the Willows lawn are still reserved by cities; fried chicken and ribs are still the preferred entrees; swimming, fishing, and basketball are the main activities; for adults, relaxing, eating, and talking with relatives and friends are still the orders of the day.

Other traditions have been modified: Many arrive before dawn to claim their spot; blankets and food baskets have given way to tents and gas grills; big families like the Bartons now rent a truck to bring tables and chairs for family members who travel from as far away as California, Washington, Missouri, Florida, South Carolina, and New York.

For Virginia Barton, picnic planning will occur right up until Saturday. This week she'll be marinating chicken, steak, ribs, and pork. Between now and Saturday, she'll also prepare enough tuna salad, macaroni salad, and potato salad to feed at least 50.

Cromwell brings two vans filled with ham, pork shoulders, fried chicken, ribs, collard greens, and appetizers and desserts to the picnic. She said her family's participation in the event goes back at least 100 years, when her grandmother, Ida Mae Brockett — who worked as a maid in Swampscott and Marblehead — first attended. Cromwell plans to be in her family spot on the lawn by 4 a.m., putting up a tent and balloons to mark the Cromwell area.

In Everett, around midday, James and Edith Lee will begin their drive to the picnic. The two began going with their parents in the 1930s; James grew up in Chelsea, and Edith's father was a deacon at the Zion Baptist Church in Everett. Since getting married, they have attended the picnic nearly every year, and say there's still an inexplicable excitement in the community before the event.

Said Edith Lee, 76, "Even now, if I see somebody on the street, they'll ask, 'Are you going to the picnic?' "

July 19, 2007
The Boston Globe

Living Down the Line

For as long as anyone can remember around here they've called this area "the line" — a small swatch of land that runs along the gritty lower section of Route 99 leading to the Charlestown border.

A century ago when hundreds of Italian immigrants were searching for their piece of the American Dream on these streets, the name seemed innocuous enough. But perhaps today its designators might tinker with the moniker and redub it the gas line, paying homage to its distinction as the center of petroleum distribution in Boston.

Today the line is a place where humanity, electricity, and gasoline coexist, albeit in a delicate yet controlled sense of underlying anxiety. Residents have always complained about the noise and smoke and smell of gas, but have accepted it as part of their neighborhood.

Drive down the narrow streets of the line and you'll find pastel aluminum-sided apartment buildings and single-family homes, festooned with American flags and hand-printed patriotic signs. On nearly every street you can find an auto body shop or a warehouse. Empty lots merge with tomato gardens, Homasote siding with concrete patios; Madonnas rest in the shade of brick transformers; maple trees fuse with aerial telephone and cable television wires.

Until Sept. 11 most residents would have laughed at the thought of a terrorist attack in their backyard. But, while many express a dry fatalism about life, the subject is not far from their lips these days. And for good reason — their homes sit in the shadow of a gasoline village.

Looming above the line are two 12-story, 32 million-gallon liquid natural gas tanks that are refilled by Distrigas almost every week. A few blocks over, Exxon operates its own petroleum farm, with 28 visible tanks containing 56 million gallons of assorted gases. Down the road, another neighbor, Boston Gas, maintains horizontal and vertical tanks that hold an additional 150,000 gallons of propane gas. Also, on the edge of Boston Harbor, Sithe (formerly Boston Edison) is in the process of converting to LNG, which will bring LNG tankers into Everett up to 75 times a year.

Next door in Boston, Mayor Thomas M. Menino has voiced concern over the overall security threat of the shipments, but here, most people just want more guards around the plant. They also want to get on with their lives.

Reading the newspaper on his backyard porch, amid the hum of an electrical generator, Dan Giannelli, at 83, seems content with his little portion of paradise. He's lived down the line his entire life and even went to the Franklin elementary school, which once stood across from his house on Thorndike Street. "We never talked about the LNGs until recently. They never bothered anybody," he says.

His wife, Phyllis, 78, sits on the front stairs with her sister-in-law, Rose, and talks of another time, when the line was bustling with families and children and boccie tournaments. "It was like Little Italy here 50 years ago," she says, waving her hand. "We used to sit out on the stairs every night in the summertime. I used to make the coffee, and people would come over. We would gossip about our problems and lives. It was nice. It's unbelievable that all the people are gone."

While many of the line's elderly residents have died in recent years, a few still carry the same spirit their parents brought to their beloved streets. Louise Boever, 74, calls herself an "old-timer" as she cleans the leaves from the sidewalk.

She was born in the house she still lives in on Robin Street. Her house is directly across the street from the Distrigas LNG plant; her view is obstructed by two concrete walls surrounded by chain-link fence and barbed wire. When she looks across the street she still sees the variety stores and houses of her youth. Beyond the houses was a marsh, which she used to skate on in the winter. After getting married, she returned in the early 1950s to find the houses and stores torn down, replaced by the current wall, which stretches down the entire street.

As 18-wheelers drive by she talks about her mother's "special" potato salad and her father's homemade anisette. She points to the concrete wall and describes a goat pasture that once stood on the site. She says the new residents of the line are just as friendly as the old-timers. Her only complaint is the bumper-to-bumper traffic that comes to a halt outside her front door several times a day.

Her son, Dennis, lives above her and is one of the few second-generation residents who have remained. Dennis Boever believes the threat of the LNG tanks is overrated. Says the engineering assistant,

"People say it's dangerous to bring in the tankers for the LNG. They've been doing it for years. Nothing they've said in the last three weeks wasn't said when they first built those tanks. People say they couldn't sleep at night living across the street from those tanks. I worry more about driving to work on Route 1."

Over on Bow Street, Nam Nguyen, 26, waves to a neighbor coming out an apartment building. Originally from Saigon, he lives with his father just behind the Exxon tank farm. When asked about the quality of life he talks about the civil liberties he has access to here that were denied to him and his family in Vietnam. He seems genuinely fascinated by the melting pot on his end of the line. "I like all my neighbors," he says. "They come from everywhere. They're Spanish, Italian, Brazilian. We barbecue together."

Not all have had the same positive experiences as Nguyen. Kenny Saltman, 20, who lives on the other end of Bow Street, describes his childhood as "rough." He wonders aloud whether man was meant to live so close to industry. He recalls that when he was 4, an older child tossed a lit match onto a generator and he worried that the whole area would explode. He talks about his best friend, an emerging basketball star, who was critically injured after being dragged by an oil truck. Still, says Saltman, the line is the place where he'll probably live the rest of his life. "It's home," he says.

Back on Robin Street, where the concrete wall begins and the human element of the line ends, Mary Boever, Dennis's wife, pats a friend's dog and pulls on a cigarette. Says Boever, "We're in our own little world here. It's our own little place. People are worried about the events in the world. I live it every day."

October 28, 2001
The Boston Globe

Chelsea Night

Leona Grell is in love with Chelsea. That's why she spends most of February sitting in her kitchen in Delray Beach, Florida, coordinating the details of one of the largest annual city reunions in the country. Next Sunday, the 83-year-old retired bank manager will gather with 500 other Chelsea natives in southern Florida for the 21st year in a row. They'll celebrate a city known best for welcoming immigrants over the last 150 years.

"Once you have made a friend from Chelsea, you never lose that friend, and I don't care where they move to," says Grell, who, like almost half of the people attending next week's reunion, spends the winter in Florida and the summer in the Northeast.

Compared with others who will attend the reunion, Grell is somewhat of an anomaly, given that she still lives in Chelsea. Most moved away from their beloved city decades ago, building new lives in suburbs in northern and southern Massachusetts. Like Grell, their vision of Chelsea exists largely in Depression-era memories. Those Chelseans describe a 1.8-square-mile city filled with thousands of first-generation Jewish, Irish, Italian, and Polish families that lived side-by-side in bitter poverty, sharing what little they had. Men were laborers, women raised the children, and children kept busy playing hide-and-seek, hopscotch, kick the can, or stickball.

Grell says Chelsea has rebounded from its low point in 1991, when political corruption forced the city into receivership. Real estate prices have shot up; the school system is being managed by Boston University and has spent $135 million on new buildings. Her only regret is the Tobin Bridge, which split the city in half when it opened in 1950. "This monster's sitting in the middle of the city," she says. The bridge cut through the old Ward 2, where Yiddish, Italian, and Polish were once spoken in the crowded streets.

Today, Chelsea is still an immigrant city. Of its 35,000 residents, more than one-third were born in another country. Downtown, on Broadway, Spanish has replaced Yiddish, and 48.4 percent of the city's residents are Hispanic. While condominiums with views of Boston can fetch more than $600,000, residents still struggle to find their American Dream.

This news did not surprise anyone who attended last year's Chelsea Night reunion in Tamarac, Florida. Poverty, said many, motivated people to dream of a better life. But the congested tenements taught the men and women lessons that money can't buy.

"We're very simple, basic people who grew up with little or nothing, and even though we may have some more now, we're still the same people. Nothing changes," Moe Shaffer said as he stood among the hundreds who had their choice of salmon, brisket, or chicken for dinner.

Inside the stucco banquet hall, across from a group of strip malls, the men and women arrived — some with walkers, some with canes — greeting old friends with hugs and tears. For one night, they were young again, as they searched the hall for old faces from the hard-scrabble streets.

"I guess it's like the birds going back to Capistrano. There's just something that calls you back," said Norman Zagorsky. Zagorsky, 67, is among a younger set of retirees who have embraced the reunion. "You can take the person out of Chelsea, but you can't take Chelsea out of the person."

Yards away, Bonnie Weiner Kerman, now 64, stood with Leona Regnier. The two women clasped hands and talked about their friend-ship, which began when they were 6 years old. They spoke of a time when front doors were left unlocked, mothers looked after neighbors' children, and crime was rare. After the speeches, dancing, and dessert, the lights dimmed, and it was time for everyone to go.

Grell, who wore a teal suede pantsuit, large tortoiseshell glasses, and diamond earrings, took a seat and thought about the evening. "It's the peak time of my life, each Chelsea Night," she said. "And I mean that sincerely."

February 20, 2005
The Boston Globe

In Revere, Soviet Good Times Live On

"Na zdoroviye," the men say, hoisting their shot glasses of Stolichnaya. Tuxedo-clad waiters arrive at long banquet tables with overflowing platters of baked sturgeon, chicken Kiev, and meat pierogies; old friends recognize each other with bear hugs. Grandparents dance with their grandchildren; elegantly dressed couples tango check-to-cheek.

The language is a smattering of Russian, Armenian, Yiddish, and Ukrainian. Amid the smoke and neon lights the visitor is momentarily transported to Moscow, St. Petersburg, or Odessa.

Welcome to the Mirage Restaurant in Revere, the largest Russian nightclub in New England. A bastion of sentimentality and gastronomical exaggeration, the nightspot is a household name to many of the estimated 100,000 Russian- and Armenian-born immigrants who have settled in Greater Boston.

Every weekend hundreds make the trek from Brookline, Watertown, Providence, Worcester, Lynn, and beyond to this former motel and biker bar.

Here they unite under the cultural umbrella of the former Soviet Union, with a melding of food, music, and tradition.

Most are part of private birthday and anniversary parties, which are held simultaneously in the cavernous oval-shaped room. Small children are not left home with babysitters, and teenagers are often front and center next to their parents and grandparents during the celebrations.

Recognizing a need for a restaurant that presented an authentic Russian and Armenian experience, Arik Aronov and Armen Toukmanian opened the nightspot in 1991.

Other Russian restaurants tried to capitalize on the wave of new Americans, but almost all have closed in the last 10 years, a testament to the illusory womb the Mirage has created for its loyal customers.

"When we opened we wanted people to say that this feels like home," said Aronov, a former professional soccer player who arrived here from Lvov, Ukraine, in 1979. He met Toukmanian, a native of Yerevan, Armenia, on his second day in America, and the two have been best friends since. Aronov's first suggestion was to anoint his partner's mother, Cilvart Toukmanian, as head chef.

"She has golden hands and a golden touch," Aronov said.

She's famous for her Armenian barbecue, and other specialty items such as frogs legs and the Middle Eastern staple, hummus.

The Mirage's reputation now extends far beyond New England. On any given night Russian celebrities drop in, such as ballet master Mikhail Baryshnikov or, say, the dozen Russian senators from the Duma who went straight from a Harvard conference to Revere. Then there's Celtic forward Vitaly Potapenko and Bruins stars Sergei Samsonov and Andrei Kovalenko, who usually arrive with a cadre of other Russian NHL players.

Meanwhile, guests indulge in a buffet fit for a Russian royal family. Lynn's Geniya Blackman, a native of Moldova, celebrated her 60th birthday by inviting 40 relatives and friends to her party. They sit elbow-to-elbow; their tablecloth is barely visible, with dozens of plates of red caviar, nova salmon, shrimp, shish kebabs, mushroom julienne, lamb and duck nestled among buckets of champagne, bottles of cognac, and pitchers of Coke.

Soon they move to the dance floor, surrounding Blackman as the band sings "Happy Birthday" in a Russian-accented English.

"It's a small Russian country here," said Peabody's Roman Groysman, who held his own 50th birthday party last month at the Mirage. Groysman became somewhat of a celebrity in the Russian community of Lynn last year, after former Russian leader Mikhail Gorbachev swung by his store to load up on fish and salami before a lecture.

On the other side of the room, Stan Chokler, a Brookline High School senior, marks his 18th birthday, a milestone in Soviet culture. "At 18, in Russia, you can enter the military, get married, and work," said his mother Galina.

She sees the Mirage as not just a restaurant but as an educational experience for Russian-born, American-raised children. The Mirage, she says, is a place where children can witness their parents' culture and absorb a tradition that otherwise may be lost in the transition of becoming an American.

"It goes beyond simply going to a restaurant," she said.

Moscow native Anatoly Mitlin, a software engineer who now lives in Swampscott, agrees. "It's important to have a place like this because it's an educational process for our children," he said. "Here, they listen to Russian songs, and see that there's a place where people speak Russian," and that "it's fully functioning and part of the American experience as well. So they feel better about speaking Russian and being Russian."

As the clock strikes midnight, the live Russian band, "Studio D," strikes up a version of the Yiddish tune "Shalom Aleichem." The families form circles around Geniya Blackman and Stan Chokler, continuing their birthday wishes. An arms length from Blackman is her 10-year-old granddaughter, Luiza Rapoport, who has been dancing with her best friend, Elizabeth Alkhazov, all evening. They seem oblivious to the hour, and reach out to Blackman, who leads them into the middle of the circle.

Armen Davtian and Eddie Gevorkian are just a few yards from the dance floor and are beaming. The 20-year-old men come to the Mirage every weekend, Davtian from Watertown, Gevorkian from Providence. This evening Gevorkian has brought his fiancee, Nenellia Khachatourian, an Armenian immigrant from Isfahan, Iran. Davtian and Gevorkian speak Armenian and Russian fluently, and are part of a second-generation phenomenon that the Mirage has spawned.

"We grew up here, coming on weekends with our parents," said Davtian, an electrician. "All the big celebrations were held here — christenings, weddings, birthday parties."

Gevorkian smiles when asked why he makes the trip from Providence to Revere every Saturday night. Said the Stonehill College student, "My parents don't come as much, so I'm carrying the torch."

September 9, 2001
The Boston Globe

The Stars and Stripes Man

Calvin Anderson was standing and smiling and achieving his goal of getting noticed.

On the day Americans would elect their next president, Anderson had arrived in front of the polling station at North Shore Community College just before 7 in the morning clad in a cotton jacket and matching baggy pants emblazoned with the stars and stripes. Resembling a walking flag, he also had brought a large American flag that he waved to passersby.

Every election day, Anderson dons his flag suit — purchased from an online catalog and carefully hand washed a couple of times a year — and heads to the polls to remind people to vote. "I'm here just to encourage people to exercise their right to vote. If you don't bother to vote, don't bother to complain," he said.

The New Hampshire native likened presidential politics to mother's milk.

"We're weaned on it," said Anderson, who is 56. Anderson casually mentioned that he had met every elected president since Lyndon B. Johnson. Anderson, who moved to Lynn about a decade ago, said he started out the year as a Hillary Clinton supporter but decided to vote for Barack Obama once Clinton withdrew from the race.

While Anderson said he had shaken hands with Obama briefly in a rope line in Manchester, N.H., earlier this year, he feels he's gotten a better idea of Obama's policies by watching the numerous TV debates.

"I almost feel like I know the guy," said Anderson, who took short breaks on a small wooden stool that he also had brought along. Anderson did not leave his post throughout the day, staying fortified on peanut butter and crackers, apples, and a Snickers bar. He had also brought along a small, portable radio that was tuned to a classical station playing mostly Chopin and Bach.

"The music sort of helps make the long day short," he said.

As the sun was preparing to set, Anderson pointed to a spotlight that he had positioned to illuminate himself for the after-work voting crowd.

A horn honked and the driver yelled out "Obama," and Anderson gestured with his flag.

"Nine out of 10 drivers give me thumbs up," said Anderson. "The only scowl I got was from a woman who was a dead ringer for Katherine Harris, you know, the former Florida secretary of state."

November 9, 2008
The Boston Globe

The Virgin Mary Leaves Home

For more than 65 years, the 7-foot-tall statue of Virgin Mary has stood in the center of a grotto — some 20 feet above the ground, hands clasped in prayer, overlooking a small patch of grass and, farther beyond, downtown Salem. On a warm afternoon last week it was suspended in midair, silently swinging as a crane operator gently lowered it to the ground.

The process of removing the statue took an hour, and after it was placed in a truck and driven to a nearby studio — where it will be repaired — the few who watched glumly noted that its removal marked the end of an era for Salem's oldest Italian neighborhood.

"This is like a spiritual death," said Anna Della Monica, whose father headed up a group of Italian masons who built the grotto during World War II to honor the military. It was made from stones collected from nearby Jefferson Avenue, and sat next to the community's house of prayer, the former St. Mary's Church.

Longtime residents and former parishioners like Della Monica say the last 10 years have been some of the most trying times in their lives. First, in 2002, the Archdiocese of Boston closed the church, citing a shortage of priests. The decision sparked an uproar among parishioners, who asserted the church was thriving, had a minister, and more than $100,000 in its bank. In 2004, the archdiocese sold the church and the grotto to a homeless shelter, which now has transitional housing and has changed its name to Lifebridge.

For almost 10 years the former church sat empty. A group of local artists and former parishioners sought to buy the structure and use it as an arts and performance center. But in the spring the building was sold to Gateways of Peace, a Pentecostal church. Gateways infuriated neighbors by painting over the church's elaborate frescos and removing the marble altar. Recently, two men with ties to the Gateways church were arrested after they told police that they broke another statue in the grotto and threw the remains in a dumpster. In addition, police found a blue tarp covering up the Virgin Mary statue, and also saw that the words "Ave Maria" — Latin for "Hail Mary" — had been painted over on a rock.

The grotto area — which has remained largely unchanged in the decade since St. Mary's closed — will be used in the future by Lifebridge, which still owns the property and plans to create a vegetable garden to grow food for the estimated 7,000 meals it prepares each year.

While former parishioners are grateful they have salvaged part of their past, some say they will never get used to a vegetable garden taking the place of an area where they prayed, posed for photos after Communion, baptisms, and weddings, and just felt at home.

"We're losing our cultural Italian footprint in this neighborhood and it's sad," said Bob Femino, a former altar boy at St. Mary's who lives near the old church.

On a nearby side street, Deliana Sanchez paused and watched the statue being moved.

"This is not right," she said, shaking her head. Sanchez has lived behind the grotto for three years, and she made it a priority to walk to the quiet grassy area each morning. There, she knelt and prayed.

"They shouldn't be doing this. It's been there forever," she said. "Now when I walk there it's going to feel weird."

July 8, 2012
The Boston Globe

For Love and Money

Y ou don't have to walk too far in Dock Square to find someone photographing, sketching, painting, or just staring at the red fishing shack that juts out into Rockport Harbor. For artists, tourists, and business owners, there's an ineffable attraction to this reproduction of a simple wooden structure built to store fishing gear in the 1880s, and named Motif #1 early last century by artist Lester Hornby, who recognized that it had become a standard subject for artists.

Since 1950, business owners have celebrated Motif #1 Day every spring — kicking off the tourism season — and this Saturday, they will gather again downtown. Most of the owners of the town's 49 galleries will hold art demonstrations, and the musty red shack — built after the original one was blown down during the Blizzard of '78 — will be open to residents and tourists.

"It seems to kind of ground you," said Donna Hackerott, who drove down from Keene, N.H., to spend the day in the town. Hackerott, who has a painting of Motif #1 hanging in the upstairs hallway of her home, called the structure timeless. "It's part of everybody's past who's ever lived on the seacoast. You could pull it out of here and stick it on the coast of Maine and it would still look right."

For the last 70 years, the shanty has been Rockport's postcard to the world. The exposure began when the US Navy used to anchor ships off Rockport's shore, with tourists embarking for tours on the ships from the shack's granite wharf. In 1933, Rockport's business owners saw an opportunity to promote their town to middle America. That year, artists Aldro Hibbard and Anthony Thieme oversaw the design of a 27-foot replica of the motif, which was driven to the Chicago World's Fair. Along the way, 18 Rockport businessmen held tours of the float, illuminating the motif at night, as they passed out brochures describing their seaside town.

In Chicago, it was entered into an American Legion parade with 200 other floats. The parade lasted 10 hours and passed by an estimated 2 million people. It won first prize, and national acclaim, and returned to the cheers of 4,500 Cape Ann residents.

Just how much money the building brings into the town these days is at issue. According to town administrator Michael Racicot, there are 225 businesses in Rockport — including inns, galleries, restaurants, and boutiques.

"We don't have any other businesses besides tourism here," said Janice Ramsden, the former executive director of the Rockport Chamber of Commerce.

Ramsden, like other business and gallery owners, believes the simplicity of the building, and its quintessential New England coastal setting provide the perfect photo opportunity.

It's not just the high-end galleries and photography studios that dot Bearskin Neck and the downtown area that pay homage to Motif #1. Inside nearly every store in town, the red icon has found its way onto postcards, magnets, sweatshirts, T-shirts, salt and pepper shakers, mugs, cups, shot glasses, towels, and tote bags.

"I think it's more popular than ever," said Katie Cahill, who owns Katie's Gift Shop in Dock Square. Cahill estimated that up to 20 percent of her business was Motif #1-related. "It's our calling card. It's what people come to Rockport to see," said Ramsden, who first painted Motif #1 or the Motuf (as it's know to locals) at the age of 9. She estimates that she has drawn the structure more than a hundred times, and is particularly attracted to its double converging roof. When she paints she often thinks of her grandfather, who emigrated from Sweden. "He was a lobsterman for 65 years, and as a child I'd go to the harbor and wait for him to come in," said Ramsden.

It's a 40-yard walk from the beginning of Bradley Wharf past the stacks of green and black steel lobster traps to the 48-by-21-foot red building. On the harbor side, dozens of old wooden buoys hang on the wall, and a weathered American flag that was strapped to the building by an unknown person shortly after Sept. 11, 2001, flaps quietly in the breeze. The 20 fishermen who use the building regularly, must stand on a cinder block and a large stone to enter the sliding door. Inside are seven chicken wire booths filled with buoys, fishing line, rods and reels, and boat parts. There's also a workbench and shop for fishermen, and in a large room at the end of the pier, there's a harbormaster's storage area, also filled with buoys. Twelve steps up on the second floor is a small room filled with tools, fishing rods, buoys,

and 11 pictures of Motif #1.

"I like to go up there in the middle of a howling nor'easter and feel the elements," said Jack Burbank, who has rented the second floor of Motif #1 for the last 35 years. "You feel at ease up there and I don't know why."

Burbank, who is 80, still works as a commercial lobsterman, and spends most of his time in his studio repairing lobster traps, and painting buoys. On occasion, he'll invite friends to sit and talk, and listen to Red Sox games.

Burbank watched the wind blow down the old Motif #1 in 1978, and helped raise $22,000 in "nickels and dimes" to reconstruct the shack. "It's a lot sturdier," he said. "The old one had quite a lean to it. We tried to get the carpenters to put the lean into it but you know how carpenters are — they wanted everything level."

May 15, 2003
The Boston Globe

CHAPTER 3

War

Remembering Pearl Harbor

Black smoke filled the sky above Pearl Harbor, and black oil spread across its waters. Robert Antell steered his Navy patrol boat through the harbor and saw lifeless bodies that had been blown from ships and men swimming through burning oil slicks trying to reach the shore.

On the morning of Dec. 7, 1941, Antell knew his country was at war.

"Everybody was on their own, and it was just mass confusion," the Amesbury resident said.

Now 86, Antell is part of a shrinking group of Massachusetts veterans who were stationed at or near Pearl Harbor in Hawaii in December 1941. According to Don Tabbut of Winthrop, commander of the state's Pearl Harbor Survivor and Friends Association, there are fewer than 60 left.

On a recent afternoon, Tabbut spoke at a Pearl Harbor commemoration at Faneuil Hall in Boston, and today he plans to toss wreaths into Boston Harbor to remember men who died aboard the battleships USS Arizona and USS Utah.

Tabbut had arrived at Pearl Harbor in November 1941, and worked as a Navy radioman, helping to guide pilots around the island of Oahu. The night before the attack, he drank beer and talked with friends he had met at Navy radio school in San Diego.

"The next morning, I awoke with a terrible hangover," said Tabbut, who is 83.

Hearing the barrage, he ran out onto a porch overlooking a Navy airstrip and saw a Japanese plane drop a bomb on the runway. "I could see the red rising sun on the bottom of the plane's wings."

Tabbut ran downstairs, but an officer prevented him from leaving the barracks. Just 150 feet from the harbor, Tabbut watched the attack unfold.

"I can remember watching the USS California get hit with torpedoes and sink to the bottom of the harbor. It didn't get completely covered with water, as the depth of the harbor wasn't that much. Then I saw the Oklahoma keel over and sink on her side. Now came an awful explosion; its location wasn't known to anybody. It turned out to be the Arizona blowing up."

Peter D'Andrea is 86 and lives in Saugus, not far from his boyhood home in Everett. D'Andrea, one of four brothers to serve in World War II, doesn't have any plans to mark Pearl Harbor Day, and said most of his friends from the war have died. He had kept in touch with an old Army friend in San Antonio, but now that man can't write well enough to return his letters.

"Army life was good before the war; it was like you had a job. Hawaii was paradise," said D'Andrea, a retired General Electric welding inspector.

At Fort Shafter, near Pearl Harbor, Army Corporal D'Andrea had expected to work his regular shift as an antiaircraft observer for the 64th Coast Artillery. But instead of searching the skies for enemy aircraft, he was given the morning off.

"I got up and showered and was getting ready for breakfast. I never made it to the mess hall. All I could see was a big red ball on the planes," said D'Andrea, who grabbed a gun, loaded it with ammunition, and started firing at the sky.

Emery Arsenault was also part of the 64th Coast Artillery and just a half mile from Pearl Harbor that morning. Shortly before 8 a.m., he looked at his radar screen and saw trouble.

"All of a sudden, the scope on the radar filled up with blips, and about two minutes later, all of the Japanese planes came over us at treetop level and they started strafing the beach," said Arsenault, who took cover under a tree.

Arsenault, who is 85, and resides in Peabody, spent another two days near that tree before he was allowed to leave his position. "Everybody was afraid that they were going to invade us after the attack," he said. He left Pearl Harbor in 1943 and went to work in the maintenance department of Trans World Airlines.

Arsenault also has no plans to mark Pearl Harbor Day. He had hoped to attend the 65th anniversary ceremonies this week in Pearl Harbor but said health and financial issues prevented him from making the trip.

"I wanted to go," he said. "I think this is going to be the last one they have; there's not that many of us left."

In Amesbury, Antell will meet with other retired police officers and reminisce. Antell, who served as an Amesbury police officer for 37 years, said he frequently thinks about Pearl Harbor Day and the impact it had on his life.

Two weeks before the attack, Antell had dinner aboard the USS Arizona with James Landry, a friend from Amesbury High School. It was the last time the two men would talk — Landry died aboard the Arizona, which is still underwater at Pearl Harbor.

On the morning that the war began, Antell awoke aboard a 40-foot motorboat used by the USS Chester that he helped maintain. After a wave of Japanese planes flew over his head he was summoned to put out a fire caused by a downed Japanese plane at the Pearl Harbor Naval Hospital.

He spent the rest of the day in his motorboat ferrying officers from dock to dock; at night, he patrolled the harbor with Marines, expecting a Japanese invasion.

"Everything was in the water, oil, mostly oil; things floating and bodies .... There was fire all over the harbor, just debris all over the place," Antell said.

Reminders of the war are throughout his modest house in Amesbury. Over his bed is a framed picture of the Chester. Antell was aboard the heavy cruiser on Oct. 20, 1942, when several of his shipmates were killed by a Japanese torpedo.

He was aboard the USS Aaron Ward on May 3, 1945, when several Japanese planes crashed into the vessel, killing 42. Antell received the Purple Heart for injuries in the attack. "I was in the engine room when the bomb exploded; my clothes were blown off of me. All I had was a belt, a knife, and my shoes."

Antell said that despite the years, he has not forgiven the Japanese for the attack. When asked about what he learned during the war, he replied, "I guess to be hard-hearted."

December 7, 2006
The Boston Globe

A Belated 'Merci'

In the European fields, cities, and beaches where much of World War II was fought, the two teenagers were surrounded by death at every moment. While many of their friends were killed by Germans, James Gabaree and Merrill Feldman survived and returned to Massachusetts to begin life all over again.

Nearly seven decades after the war ended in Europe, the men will be honored by France for their bravery on the battlefields and receive that country's highest award, the National Order of the Legion of Honor medal.

"The Legion of Honor recognizes eminent service to the French Republic, and I cannot think of a more eminent service than the one they gave to us. France will never forget," said Francois Gauthier, France's consul general in Boston.

Gabaree, of Newburyport, and Feldman, of Swampscott, are pleased to receive the medal, but both said they will be thinking about friends and fellow soldiers they left behind in Europe.

"All the guys who are still back in Europe under crosses and stars of David probably deserve it a heck of a lot more than I do, but outside of that I feel very, very honored," said Feldman, 83, a Dorchester native who served as an Army medic and went on to become the chairman of radiation medicine at Boston University's School of Medicine.

Gabaree, who underwent brain surgery last week, said he would still attend the ceremony and planned to accept the award in honor of the Army Rangers he fought alongside. "I don't think it's an honor to me; it's an honor to the Rangers," said Gabaree, 83, a former Boston Fire Department lieutenant.

After growing up in foster homes in Quincy, Gabaree became an Army Ranger in 1943 when he was 18. By the spring of 1944, his Ranger battalion was sent to Scotland to train for the Allied invasion of Normandy, France. On June 6, 1944, he boarded a small boat 12 miles from Omaha Beach at Normandy. His mission, along with the other 559 soldiers, was to capture Pointe du Hoc — a strategic cliff over the ocean — and destroy the large guns the Germans had placed there.

"It was like entering the Valley of Death," said Gabaree, who remembers Germans shooting Allied soldiers even before they could leave their boats. "I dropped into water up to my waist and by this time blood was everywhere. The water was like wine."

Armed with a Bangalore torpedo, Gabaree stepped onto the beach and fired dynamite from the long metal tube, blowing up barbed wire and mines, allowing 22 other Rangers to run past the beach toward a cliff. When he reached the top of the cliff, he had a panoramic view of the battle.

"You'd actually see bodies flying in the air," said Gabaree. "I looked down at that beach there and lost my religion. I wondered where God was. I said to myself, 'If there's a God why would he let this happen?' "

Gabaree and his fellow Rangers went on to capture Pointe du Hoc but found that the Germans had moved their big guns away from the point. The next day, after going more than 24 hours without food or water, Gabaree and six other Rangers headed back to the beach. On his way down, Gabaree was shot by a German sniper.

"I started crawling," said Gabaree, who eventually reached an open field. Sensing danger, he said he turned around, reached for his rifle, and shot and killed a German soldier who was standing in a foxhole.

He crawled to the foxhole and sat alongside the dead soldier. "I was hallucinating. I saw Mickey Mouse and Goofy in full color," said Gabaree, who thought he was dying and decided to kill himself if the Germans approached. Eventually, he heard soldiers speaking English. They brought him back to the beach, where he was evacuated by ship to England and underwent surgery on his hip and stomach.

Feldman also joined the Army in 1943. By that time he was a premed student at the University of New Hampshire, having graduated from Boston Latin School at 15. Soon he would face death every day, and as a medic, would be responsible for the medical care of his 70-man platoon. Armed with just a pistol and wearing a Red Cross armband, Feldman would run into the middle of battles to treat soldiers.

"There were all kinds of battle wounds: gunshot wounds in various parts of the body, mortar shell wounds, immersion foot disease for guys who stood in the foxhole all night in water up to their knees; frostbite up in the snow in the Battle of the Bulge," said Feldman.

Feldman calmed the injured and also helped administer last rites to soldiers. "You try to comfort them as much as you could to make them comfortable, and say, 'You're going to make it, don't worry; we're going to get you back.' "

Feldman wasn't supposed to fight, but in 1945, he led an attack on a German farmhouse and captured more than a dozen soldiers. He was also wounded twice — the first time in 1944, during a key battle near Metz, France, and the second time in Augustdorf, Germany. In Augustdorf, Feldman raced to save his best friend who had been shot. Before he reached his friend, Feldman was shot in the hand.

"He was dead by the time I arrived," said Feldman, who bandaged himself up and refused to accept evacuation. He would later receive a Silver Star for his actions.

Feldman and Gabaree, who both oppose the current war in Iraq, said survival is foremost on a soldier's mind. "You live to survive, so that means you learn how to use Mother Earth to protect you, by crawling, and creeping, and running, and ducking, and learning how to recognize sounds that may be dangerous," said Feldman.

Both men have returned to Europe since the war, and Gabaree said a return visit to Omaha Beach brought him comfort. "We had a picnic and everybody was having a good time, and I went into the woods and I had a little cry for myself," said Gabaree. "That kind of did the trick. It was kind of like closure."

July 13, 2008
The Boston Globe

Marty Doesn't March Anymore

Marty Robichaud used to march in Memorial Day parades, but Monday there will be no flag-waving, cemetery visits, or reminiscing about Vietnam. He'll spend the day with his wife, daughter, and son, and plans to hold a cookout to celebrate his twin grandchildren's birthday.

It took Robichaud years to discuss his time in Vietnam. Maybe it's because when he returned, his fellow Americans turned their backs. It was an undeclared and unpopular war back home, and hippies and yippies got as much attention for their protests as the soldiers who were fighting a war most wanted nothing to do with.

"We were a handy whipping boy," said Robichaud, a retired Lynn firefighter, now 69. "Americans had no idea what we were doing over there. We were called baby killers. We were tagged with that for quite a while: baby killer. That tears you up."

He was an Arlington guy, fresh out of high school and assembling computers in Brighton. Four days before Christmas in 1967, his Army draft notice arrived.

"My mother told me there was some mail for me on the counter and I knew what it was. I didn't open it for an hour. My mother was going nuts," Robichaud said.

He was 21 when he shipped out for Vietnam on Father's Day in 1968 and arrived at an Army base in Cha Rang Valley. He didn't mind driving and was put behind the wheel of a 5-ton cargo truck.

He worked seven days a week on a supply convoy that stretched for more than a mile along Highway 19. They brought clothes, food, and weapons to soldiers four hours away in Pleiku.

It was a daily 12-hour run on a road he will never forget.

After five months, they handed Robichaud a machine gun and told him to hop on the gunner truck that protected the convoy. On Jan. 15, 1969, he heard someone say there was a mine in the road. It exploded, and the Americans came under fire. One of the drivers, John F. Kapp, a 21-year-old from Pennsylvania, was found dead with a bullet in his head.

"I got shrapnel in the head and shoulders and face," Robichaud said.

After Kapp was taken away, Robichaud and the convoy rolled on to deliver its shipment.

A month later, on Valentine's Day, Robichaud and one of his close friends, Roger D. Lewis, a 20-year-old from Ohio, were standing in the gunner truck they called Sergeant Pepper, since it was the '60s. One minute they were talking and then Lewis was dead, killed in another ambush.

"I just continued on and made the delivery," he said. "The convoy didn't stop."

He would later receive a second Purple Heart for another round of shrapnel injuries to his head and face.

Robichaud came home in January 1970. He drove a cab in Arlington for a while and then moved to Lynn to be with his fiancee. One day he headed over to the VFW to become a member. He was told that he had fought in a conflict and not a war, and was ineligible to join.

He never mentioned Vietnam around his family. He only told his son that he had fought there after his boy asked about the war.

These days, he still has his Purple Hearts. They're tucked in a drawer that he hasn't opened in years. Sometimes in his dreams, he's back holding a gun on Highway 19, staring into the bush.

"I wake up sweating because it was hot and sometimes it can be intense," he said over a coffee.

He's not bitter about the experience and harbors no anger toward the enemy soldiers who killed his friends.

One thing he has learned in life is that politicians should think a lot harder about the impact of war before sending people off to kill.

"We don't need wars," he said. "It's not good for any living beings. To me, there's got to be another way of doing it. Diplomacy has to work somehow."

May 27, 2016
The Boston Globe

Seabrook Foes Took a Stand

About a mile from the Atlantic, the Seabrook Station nuclear power plant rises up from hundreds of acres of auburn clam flats. From a distance, the 6.5-foot-thick steel-reinforced concrete dome has the look of an amphitheater, but within the gray sphere atoms are split, using uranium and in the process creating enough electricity for more than 1 million homes every year.

For as long as most people in this working-class town of 8,000 can remember, they've called this place the Nuke. Tucked about a half-mile within a narrow road off Route 1, it's easy to miss. Thirty years ago, however, on April 30, 1977, the plant was hardly anonymous. With helicopters hovering overhead, hundreds of State Police and National Guard troops spread out over the 900-acre site, and then-governor Meldrim Thomson Jr. walked the grounds in army fatigues.

Thomson told the news media he had expected violence from the 2,500 demonstrators who walked onto the dusty construction site to protest the plant's construction. Instead, police faced a group that practiced civil disobedience, and within 24 hours they had begun the largest mass arrest in New Hampshire history, taking 1,414 antinuclear protesters into custody.

Tomorrow, there are no demonstrations planned. More than 650 full-time workers are expected at the Seabrook plant, just as on any other workday. But for the founding members of the Clamshell Alliance, which spawned more than a dozen similar organizations nationally, the day is remembered as the beginning of a shift in the country's energy policy, when public opinion turned against nuclear power plants.

In the following years, 2,000 more Clamshell Alliance members would be arrested during protests at the plant. Although its owners declared bankruptcy in the 1980s, the plant was finally finished — at a cost of $6.3 billion — and went online in 1990. Still, Clamshell members say the protests brought a new public awareness that stopped the government's plan in the 1970s to allow hundreds of nuclear power plants to be built. Since Seabrook opened 17 years ago, just two nuclear plants have followed.

"Maybe we lost this particular battle here in Seabrook, but I think we won the battle because of the impact we had on a national scale," said Kristie Conrad, who, along with her husband, Renny Cushing, helped create the Clamshell Alliance.

The couple still live just 2 miles from the plant in Cushing's childhood home in Hampton. Like more than a dozen other former "Clams," Cushing went on to serve in the state Legislature and is now the executive director of Murder Victims' Families for Human Rights. Conrad works to promote literacy. Tomorrow they'll both be working, and they don't have any particular plans to commemorate the 30th year of the occupation. But the years have not softened their views on nuclear power plants.

"People may want to pretend that it can't happen here, but the lesson of Chernobyl is that they should never have built an atomic plant anywhere," said Cushing.

At Seabrook Station — now owned by FPL Energy — a plant spokesman, Alan Griffith, called Seabrook a "top-rated power plant" that has not experienced any major problems since opening. "There's absolutely no danger in terms of radiation or security. It's an extremely safe environment at Seabrook," said Griffith.

But Seabrook has not been incident-free over the years. Seabrook Station has been fined twice during the last 10 years by the Nuclear Regulatory Commission, which oversees the plant. In 1999, the plant was fined $55,000 after the government ruled it had discriminated against an electrician for raising safety issues. In 2006, the NRC fined the plant $65,000 after identifying a security issue at the plant. NRC spokeswoman Diane Screnci declined to comment on the security violations and fine.

"We don't want to reveal any potential vulnerability," she said.

In June of 1976, about 25 people from coalitions throughout New England gathered in Rye Beach for a meeting about the proposed Seabrook plant. They included representatives from the People's Energy Project, the Granite State Alliance, the Wampanoag Tribe, and anti-nuclear groups from Cape Ann, Western Massachusetts, and Boston. At the meeting, they decided to name their group the Clamshell Alliance — a nod to the clam flats that the nuclear plant owners had planned to flood with water from the plant.

"The strength of the whole Clamshell Alliance was our organization," said Jay Gustaferro, a Gloucester lobsterman who was one of the alliance's founders. Gustaferro and Isabel Natti had created the North Shore Alternative Energy Coalition in Gloucester and held alternative energy science fairs in Cape Ann in the early 1970s. They said they joined the Clamshell Alliance because they could see Seabrook, which is 14 miles from the shores of Gloucester.

On Aug 1, 1976, the first protest at the plant was held, and 18 people were arrested. On Aug. 22, another occupation was held, and 180 people were arrested. Then, on April 30, 1977, more than 2,500 people walked onto the Seabrook site from four directions; others were ferried by boat to the site by local fishermen. Most had spent the night at campgrounds provided by sympathetic area residents who opposed the plant.

Surrounded by hundreds of police, the protesters pitched tents, sang no-nukes songs, and discussed the use of alternative energy such as wind and solar power. With drugs and alcohol forbidden by the alliance and the group sticking to its philosophy of civil disobedience, no major injuries were reported, and there were no scuffles with the police.

"I think it was the power of nonviolence that really energized the Clamshell Alliance," said Cushing.

"I think the nonviolence and civil disobedience aspect was extremely powerful because it was so peaceful," added Sam Lovejoy, who led a contingent of antinuclear protesters from an organic farm in Montague.

After the group refused to disperse, protesters were arrested and held in five National Guard armories throughout the state for 13 days. Most declined to post bail, which helped their cause, said Guy Chichester of Rye, N.H., who served as a spokesman during that time and appeared on national TV. "We were getting news all over the country and all over the world. Why would we move out?"

The alliance's dedication to nonviolence would be short-lived. By 1980, a rift had developed with the Boston chapter, which advocated using violence. Still, over the next decade, the alliance held regular protests against the plant, and in 1989, shortly before it opened, more than 600 were arrested for trespassing.

Lovejoy went on to create Musicians United for Safe Energy — which produced concerts and a movie by Jackson Browne, Bonnie Raitt, Bruce Springsteen, and New York Congressman John Hall, cofounder of the band Orleans. He said Seabrook served as a model for the antinuclear movement. Local protests, combined with court challenges and publicity, could effect change, said Lovejoy, who helped set up antinuclear groups based on the Clamshell's philosophy.

While most of the former "Clams" have moved on to other social and political causes, several say their biggest concern now is the nuclear waste stored inside the Seabrook plant. Many said they would resume their protests if more nuclear plants are approved by the government.

"If the industry starts new nukes, they're going to be surprised. I think people will come out of the woodwork," said Peter Natti, who lived on the same Montague farm with Lovejoy and other activists in the 1970s and took part in the Seabrook protests.

Griffith, the Seabrook Station spokesman, said the plant's nuclear waste is stored in a pool at the plant, where spent 12-foot-long fuel assemblies containing radioactive uranium pellets are placed to cool. That pool will be filled to capacity in a couple of years, said Griffith. At that point, the company plans to open an onsite dry fuel storage facility where the fuel assemblies will be encased in concrete.

April 29, 2007
The Boston Globe

Arthur and Harris

Memories of happiness or heartbreak have no linear order. I'll see or hear something that triggers a memory and the event is immediately considered for analysis. This first investigation may or may not always be an honest search, where thoughts leading to the event are reviewed, and intent — of all who may be involved — is established. Then the incident is played over and over in my mind, until I reach what I believe is an honest assessment that invariably totes along deep feelings of joy or sadness.

These first reviews are always the most sober remembrance, and from then on the story is told and retold to compress the pain or amplify the joy. While the memories are compartmentalized and sectioned into categories that are triggered during different moods, I'm rarely aware that I've altered the truth — even so slightly — when I retell these stories even decades after they happened. In essence, the literal truth is lost immediately and our history is subject to our own interpretation.

Those of us who have come to peace with our past by altering it in order to fit our idealized persona would undoubtedly dispute any assertion that we're essentially liars. In our culture, chronic liars are recognized as deeply-troubled individuals. Yet, in the unlikely event that we were challenged with indisputable evidence of all that has occurred in our lives, we'd have to admit to reshaping our past. We could argue that the blur between truth and fiction is part of the human condition and is necessary for our survival. But what happens if other liars — who fabricate different events for different reasons — say the same thing? A man I met recently by the name of Arthur Foster would argue that lying is, more of less, part of the foundation of a person's truth.

Arthur L. Foster is a carefree, unfailingly polite Korean War veteran who has spent the last quarter of a century sleeping in furnished rooms, homeless shelters, parks and train stations. At 77, he's sharp-witted, and surprisingly energetic given his long-standing fondness for panhandling, and working odd jobs while roaming the country. While he appears mild-mannered and shy, he's patient — and can even turn garrulous — if someone asks him a question or a favor. Still, he'd rather not know anyone's business, and would prefer if people don't inquire about his past. "One of the secrets to life is to respect other people's lives and not be nosy," he told me one gray afternoon earlier this month. Since 1985, he has lived, successively, in Seattle, Spokane, Las Vegas, Ogden, Utah, Dilworth, Minnesota, Boston and Lynn, Massachusetts. While his white hair is thinning, and his gait is slow, he professes to be in good health and doesn't take any medication. He is 6 feet, 150 pounds and his back slopes forward when he walks or sits.

Foster is ruddy faced and well groomed for a man who doesn't mind sleeping in a different cot or patch of lawn each evening. His face is always clean shaven, his teeth are bright and immaculate, and his clothes — everything from a spotless red windbreaker down to his neatly pressed and hemmed beige chinos — look like they recently hung on a department store merchandise rack. His eyes are sad and blue, and when he talks about his life he speaks with a certain unquestioning authority that makes you believe that all of the heartbreaking and solemn events that he says led him away from the clean, country air of rural Minnesota to the boozy flophouses and asphalt beds are really true.

I first heard about Arthur while researching an article on homeless veterans. I was looking for an itinerant World War II or Korean War vet and after a few calls to Boston-area shelters, I was told to drive to a grim-looking, yellow-bricked building in downtown Lynn around 4 p.m. — just when the homeless guests begin checking in. After a couple of minutes, I spotted Arthur pushing his slim frame down the sidewalk. He gripped a smudged purple cane and seemed aloof when I mentioned that he was the oldest homeless veteran in the city.

I have spent enough time around the homeless to understand that their path is often a multilayered, tragic journey that almost always involves a considerable amount of lying. Extensive reports on the US homeless have shown that more than two-thirds experience mental health issues and substance abuse problems. As I stuck out my hand to greet Arthur, I was on guard to discern truth from fantasy.

Unlike the other guests, who shot mistrustful looks my way, Arthur couldn't have cared if I stayed or walked away. When I mentioned that I was a newspaper reporter he seemed relieved that I wasn't another hustler looking to shake him down for his Social Security or VA check. I told him I was there to ask about Korea and what it's like to be homeless at 77.

"Korea," he sighed, "was one big place of death."

"Oh Pop," said a tattooed, Hispanic man in his 20s who had come over to greet his new bunkmate. He had a wide smile and broken teeth and patted Arthur on his shoulder. "It couldn't have been worse than this."

"Now you shush," he told the man. "I know what I'm talking about when it comes to Korea."

The man's face went limp and he apologized. "I don't even know what Korea was," he said.

Arthur shook his head disapprovingly. He batted his eyelids a couple of times, swallowed and took a deep breath. "It was a war," Arthur said, gently pivoting around to face the broken-toothed man. "They called it a police action but it was a war, and I was there for 18 months. If I live to 150, I'll never see as many dead people as I saw in Korea. It was a no-win situation."

I asked him about the dead and the battles. I wanted to know the impact it had on his life.

"I think about it all the time," he said. "They massacred us and we did the same to them. You remember Lieutenant Calley from what-tayacallit, My Lai? We had those kind of things all the time. We'd line people up and shoot 'em down and move on to the next town. Our lieutenants told us to kill everybody we saw, whether they were Chinese or farmers. It was either kill or be killed. I was a medic over there. I had come from a little town in Minnesota, Harris. You probably never heard of it, right?"

The tattooed man had stopped listening and had successfully bummed a cigarette out on the sidewalk. Arthur didn't seem disturbed and turned toward my pen and paper. "In Harris, I grew up on a farm and didn't know anything about treating wounded but in Korea, they told me to just run out and grab the wounded and pull them back in. Well, after I got shot at a couple of times, I wised up and started carrying a pistol. The Red Cross said that was against the rules — but damn the rules. The first guy I killed, I remember very well. The guy I was treating said 'look out doc' and I looked up and saw a Chinese running at me with a bayonet. So I took out my gun and shot him and he fell on his face."

The door opened and the stale air of old bedding, cigarette smoke, and sullied clothing nearly knocked me over. We quickly moved past several cheerful women in their twenties who were checking guests in and settled into a quiet back room.

I already had much of the story, and just needed to call the VA to verify that Arthur had served in the war. I wanted to know how he became homeless.

"Since I was a kid on the farm, I always worked. Even before I went into the service I went door to door selling Bibles. Then, the accident happened with Joanne and the child," he said, and his eyes quickly filled with tears.

"What happened?"

"It was after the war, and things were going real good. We had a farm up in Harris, and I was selling computers for IBM and my wife Joanne was working as a nurse and Esther was 12 and in school. They were riding back from a dance recital in St. Paul. It was a 60 mile ride, and just when they got on the road they got hit by a drunk driver. Both of them were killed right away."

"I'm so sorry," I told him.

"My life ended right there and then. I lost my job, the farm, and I took off. It was around 1985. I had a nervous breakdown and I've been on the road since. If you write this just tell people that all I want to do is go home to Minnesota."

I dutifully wrote down the names of Joanne and Esther and made a note to confirm the accident. He told me he had only been in Boston for a month and was out of money. He expected his VA check to arrive any day and he didn't seem too upset about staying in the shelter. During his visit to the VA, he said he had been diagnosed with post-traumatic stress disorder.

"So this is the first time you've been to Boston?"

He nodded his head earnestly and shrugged his shoulders. "Yeah, never been here before. But I did become acquainted with one of your people in the war."

"Who was that?"

"Oh, it was Ted Williams. I never heard of him, coming from Harris. We were so busy doing chores we had no time to play baseball or listen to the radio. Anyway, when he crash-landed in Korea, I was one of the medics at the airport who rushed out and pulled him out of the cockpit."

I was familiar with Williams' accident and it had become the stuff of lore. But I remembered where I was, and was reminded that lies and stories in homeless shelters are a natural match. Often, below the subterfuge, there are some truths — deep and obfuscated within the time, place and event. Life stories are also pliable and expand or contract depending on a person's mood or the weather. Summer days tend to stir the memory of a person's noble and heroic deeds. Once on a hot humid June morning a homeless man who was collecting aluminum cans from garbage bags explained to me that after he won the New York State Lottery he had to bring his entire winnings, $14 million in cash, to a plane at Kennedy airport where a Mossad agent collected the money and gave him a receipt.

I couldn't rule out the Williams story but there was no way to confirm it. Nearing deadline, I snapped a quick photo of Arthur and rushed to my car.

I wrote the short profile in 70 minutes and during that time I did an extensive search of national newspaper archives to determine if Joanne or Esther Foster had been killed in an accident in the 1980s. Nothing came up. The US Department of Veterans Affairs did confirm that Arthur had served in Korea. And, I found a reliable database which verified that he had lived in Minnesota during the 1980s.

On the Sunday when the story was printed, more than a dozen people called the shelter and offered to buy Arthur a plane ticket to Minnesota. Arthur accepted the one-way ticket from a married couple in their fifties. He would leave on Tuesday morning and they planned to have dinner on Monday night to get acquainted. I was intrigued by the generosity of the couple and their interest in Arthur. I agreed to meet with them for dessert that night.

Meanwhile, I couldn't get Arthur's story out of my head. Like all homeless stories, there were holes in the timeline and the facts were sketchy: A battle-tested Korean vet scarred for life by a senseless family tragedy rambles across the country to Boston for no apparent reason and lands in an old factory town with no money; yet, he is well groomed and suddenly eager to return home to Minnesota. In my article I attributed everything to Arthur and I was careful to only include facts that I had verified — "In September, he said, he boarded an Amtrak train in Minneapolis, and came to Boston to try his luck," I wrote.

Yet after spending a couple of hours searching and cross referencing databases I began to question much of his story.

When I called the town of Harris — a farming community of 1,200 where everyone seems to know everyone else — the clerk told me there was no birth record or marriage certificate of an Arthur L. Foster. Nor had anyone had ever heard of his beloved parents, George and Beulah Foster. The public relations man from IBM told me he couldn't find any work history of Arthur Foster with the company. And, a quick Internet check revealed that Ted Williams had crashed-landed in Korea on Feb. 16, 1953 — at least a year after Arthur had left the country. By the time I arrived for dessert to meet Arthur, and his new patrons, Anthony and Debra Freelove, I was convinced that Arthur probably had local ties, and had been deeply affected by the war.

In the sunken dining room of the restaurant, I found the Freeloves and Arthur chatting and smiling. Arthur was waving his hands and telling stories and they leaned forward to listen and laugh. Just 12 hours earlier, Arthur had crawled off of his lumpy shelter mattress with $1.25 in his pocket — he had bummed $10 from me for cigarettes a couple of days before. Now, a sense of ease fell over his face and his blue eyes brightened as he sipped clam chowder and held court with the Freeloves.

The Freeloves are a sensitive and attractive couple who share a deep respect for the elderly and veterans. Both work in sales, and are devoted family people. Anthony, who has bushy eyebrows and a wide forehead, served in the National Guard in the 1970s and his brother died after being exposed to Agent Orange in Vietnam. He tells me his family has lived in Massachusetts since the 1600s and the Freeloves have served in every American war.

Debra spent much of the last decade caring for her father in Las Vegas and a cousin in Florida. She wore a brown sweater and jeans, and smiled continuously at Arthur during the meal.

"I need to thank you for fighting for our country and being over there," Debra told Arthur. He nodded, pressed his lips together in a tight smile and fidgeted with his clam chowder. "I think it's sad how this country treats senior citizens and the homeless. We take care of the rest of the world but not our own."

Arthur ordered a cheeseburger and declined a glass of red wine. "I haven't had a drink since 1952," he said, as the Freeloves sipped their Merlot.

The couple wanted to know his plans once he landed in Minneapolis. Arthur seemed confident. As soon as his plane landed, he would hop on a bus toward Deluth and get off at Harris. There, his old friend "Crozzer" would be waiting. Crozzer had a farm and plenty of rooms. "It'll be a quiet winter; just what I need," he told the Freeloves.

He talked of the sometimes brutally cold Minnesota winters and his penchant for bear-hunting. Maybe, just maybe, he might find a job — perhaps in sales. "You gotta like sales. You gotta be motivated. You gotta know your product — that's the number one key. I was great at IBM until the accident," he said.

The Freeloves nodded sympathetically, and Debra reached out to touch Arthur's arm.

"Arthur's told us all about the accident," Anthony said, as Debra welled up with tears.

"Could you believe that man got only six months for killing my wife and daughter?" Arthur said, pounding the table with his fist. He raised his voice, as the couple listened intently, open-mouthed.

"Six months! That was before the drunken driving laws were put in place up there. For years I went from bar to bar throughout the state looking for that man. I carried a pistol and wanted to kill him. An eye

for an eye. That's what I say, and that's what he deserved," Arthur told the Freeloves. His face was beat red; suddenly he seemed exhausted as he sunk into his chair.

From a distance, he looks youthful — especially when he smiles — but if you sit close to him you'll notice deep wrinkles that form a grill-like, horizontal pattern across his forehead. His bulbous nose rises up like a berm, and his sagging, gaunt cheeks and chin are filled with deep creases.

"That's what he deserved Arthur but we know it's a good thing you didn't do it," Anthony said.

Arthur was silent when his cheeseburger arrived. The couple sipped some wine and then Anthony wanted to know how long it would take for him to gather up his clothes at the shelter.

"Oh, about ten minutes," Arthur told them.

"Why don't we go back to the shelter and you pick up your bags and you can come and stay with us for the night? You'll get a good night's rest and in the morning I'll take you to the airport," Anthony said.

"Sounds good," Arthur said.

The next morning Arthur boarded a flight to Minneapolis. The Freeloves had given him $200 in spending money, and he was wearing Debra's father's black shiny leather jacket. As Arthur went through security I casually mentioned to Anthony that Arthur may have been lying to us. That didn't seem to bother Anthony. "Whether he's spinning a yarn, or whatever the case is, he's still an elderly man and I'd like to see him in a comfortable place," Anthony told me.

I felt better about Arthur's fate and almost forgot about him until three days later. That's when my cell phone rang and identified the incoming call from Washington. It was a familiar, high raspy voice that seemed to have a twinge of a Boston accent.

"Yeah, Steve, it's Arthur, I'm in Seattle at the train station. You gotta help me. I got mugged in Minneapolis, and then a conductor allowed me to ride the train to Seattle. But I don't know anybody here anymore. All the people I knew here are gone and I gotta get back to Boston."

"Boston? I asked. "I thought Harris was your home."

He told me he hadn't eaten in a couple of days and that he had seven cents in his pocket. His voice was surprisingly calm for a person who had willed himself across the country.

While I realized that I had been taken — even before he got on the flight — I had hoped that Arthur would stay in Minnesota. I pictured him falling back into his old habits of working Minneapolis sidewalks and charming the locals for spare change. I thought he'd find a cold-water flat and lay his head down and eventually die one day. But now, I was more intrigued and furthermore, felt partially responsible for him leaving the shelter for the road. Something bad might actually happen to this man, I thought. Arthur was no longer a story. He was a responsibility.

Over the next several days he called me more than 25 times — mostly borrowing cell phones from gracious commuters. I insisted that he stay in a shelter until I could get him a ticket home. In the meantime, I was determined to find out who Arthur Foster really was.

———————————

Somerville, Massachusetts is an old working-class city of about 80,000 that borders Boston and Cambridge, and served as a base for George Washington's troops in 1776. According to state and city records, Arthur Leroy Foster was born in this heavily Catholic city on June 2, 1932 to George and Beulah Foster. He was the youngest of four children. His oldest brother Stanley died several years ago, but his brother Charles and sister Mary are still alive. Mary lives in Florida, and is 85 and disabled. Charles is 81, lives in Chelmsford, Massachusetts and has dementia.

After I mentioned that I was calling to get some information about Arthur, Mary seemed suspicious and almost hung up. "I've done all I can for my brother," she said, in a weary and drained voice. She caus-ally mentioned that she hadn't seen her brother in more than 40 years.

There was a long pause and then she started to talk. "Arthur was normal until the war." Mary told me. "The only thing different about him was that he was a very sick child, an Rh negative baby. The first year they never thought he would live. And, because of that he was spoiled horribly by my mother. If we played games we had to let him win. And he got his own way, he had to be waited on completely."

Donna Foster is 78, and first met Arthur in 1947 at the Grace Baptist Church in Somerville. She remembers him as a chatty and enthusiastic boy who liked to dance. "When he was 15, we elected him as president of our church youth group," said Donna, who met Arthur's brother, Charles, that year at a Billy Graham rally.

In 1948, Arthur's mother fell ill and suddenly died. A year later, George Foster, a Boston meat cutter and porter, signed army papers allowing Arthur to go to Korea.

"He went over there and what they put him on was burying the dead and that's pretty rough on a 17-year-old. After he got out I talked with the Army doctor. I was a registered nurse. The doctor said Arthur had a lot of problems."

After the war, Charles and Donna frequently brought Arthur to Fort Devens — a former Army base 40 miles west of Boston. "We asked the Army to do something for him. He was just foggy, and always coming and going and making up stories. He came back a different person and we wanted them to do something. But they said they couldn't do anything. Maybe it was different then than it is now."

In the mid-1950s, Arthur moved in with Mary and her husband in Hopkinton, a town of 13,000 best know to locals as the starting point for the Boston Marathon. In the quiet town west of Boston Arthur took odd jobs — such as a short order cook and landscaping positions — but rarely was able to work for more than a week at a time. In 1956, he met and married Judith Adams — a 16-year-old high school student. Within a year, Judith gave birth to a daughter. Months later, their marriage ended.

"I'd give anything to know where that baby is," Mary said.

Over the next five years, Arthur bounced between Boston, San Francisco, Reno and Las Vegas. Every few years, he'd arrive unannounced and penniless at his siblings' homes. Over time, Mary noticed that he had become a prodigious liar and felt that the war had a lot to do with it. "He became totally unreliable. He'd be with you and everything would seem fine and then he was gone. I'd never hear from him until he'd show up again a few years later."

In 1964, he landed in St. Paul, Minnesota and told a young nursing student, Joanne Nelson, that he was an architect.

"He said he was an architect but I saw some of his drawings and they were made with crayons," said Howard Kanis, who attended Arthur and Joanne's wedding reception in 1964. Kanis is Joanne's uncle, and used to host Joanne at his St. Paul home while she was in nursing school. The wedding had taken place just two months after the couple had met, and the two flew out to Reno where a justice of the peace conducted the ceremony.

Harris, Minnesota is 55 miles north of Minneapolis and its economy has been driven by dairy, corn and bean farming for more than 100 years. Another 10 miles north, sits Almelund — a sprawling unincorporated town filled with soft, rolling hills and comprised of dozens of square miles of farmland and about 200 people. The area was first settled in 1850 by Swedish immigrants and nearly all of its residents still claim Swedish ancestry. Today, the downtown looks much the same as it did in the 1950s — there's a gas station, grocery store, a bank, an antique store and a Lutheran church.

Joanne Nelson was an only child who grew up in a two-room house on a 60-acre farm in Almelund. While there were 10 Holsteins in the barn, her childhood was marked by poverty and tragedy. Nearly all of the farmland was sandy and not suited for crops. Inside the farmhouse there was no electricity or running water, and the family slept in two beds in the tiny living room. In 1953, when Joanne was eight, her mother was committed to a mental institution for six months. Two years later, her father died after he fell off a roof during a carpentry job.

Book smart and studious, Joanne seemed to be the opposite of Arthur Foster. Joanne had jet black hair, buck teeth, and found solace in taking care of the sick. She landed a job at a nursing home in Forest Lake, Minnesota while Arthur pitched the idea of building homes to locals. A month after they married, the couple purchased a large farm on Highway 61 in Harris.

"They bought a farm and furniture and a Ford and I don't know how they did it because he seemed like a fast talking con artist," said Howard Kanis.

Myrtle Peterson, a cousin of Joanne's, recalls that Arthur was frequently spotted walking long distances away from the farm. She last saw him 45 years ago walking along a highway. "I know he walked a lot. He used to walk all the time from his place in Harris to his mother-in-law's in Almelund. It must have been 10 miles each way," said Peterson.

Several months after they purchased the farm in Harris, creditors started knocking on their door.

"I never met the man but I know he caused a lot of aggravation for me and my husband," explained Lavonne Foster. Foster's husband was also named Arthur, but he worked as a janitor for the county school district. "Because of Arthur L. Foster our credit got loused up for years. One night a big, burly sheriff came and wanted to arrest my husband and realized he had the wrong Art Foster."

Nine months after their Reno wedding, and just as they were settling into their new farm, Arthur and Joanne disappeared. "They left the coffee pot on and a fridge full of food," Lavonne remembers.

Howard Kanis also recalls their sudden departure. "They drove to the airport, left the Ford in the parking lot and got on a plane to God knows where," he said. "We didn't hear from Joanne for eight years."

In 1971, Joanne returned to visit her mother Evelyn who was ailing. She had divorced Arthur and moved to Kelso, Washington. In Minnesota, she had been a nurse for less than a year; in Washington, she became a regional sales manager for Stanley Home Products. She remarried, divorced, and was childless when she died in 2008 of ovarian cancer.

Russell Haskin, Joanne's ex-husband still lives in Kelso and said Joanne rarely mentioned her first marriage. "She never talked much about him. I heard he was a gambler. She figured that the mob had killed him," he told me.

Jamie Foster is Arthur's niece and the daughter of Charles and Donna Foster. A school secretary, she is now 52 and survived cancer last year. As a child, Jamie was enthralled by her eccentric uncle's whirlwind visits and stories. "At Christmas time he would miraculously call. We would go and pick him up and he would be so excited that he was home. It was a big treat and he would tell us about all of his adventures. One time he came home and told us he was working in the Midwest riding Brahman bulls. The truth is he probably worked in the rodeo and wanted to be one," she said.

During his short visits in the 1960s and 1970s, Jamie's parents lent him money, purchased clothing, provided housing, and helped him find menial work. But the stays grew shorter, and each time he seemed more desperate. On one occasion, in the early 1970s he arrived unannounced at his sister Mary's house in Billerica, Massachusetts and told her he had tuberculosis. She drove him to the VA hospital in Boston.

Several members of his family suspect that gambling exacerbated his mental illness. "We knew he liked to gamble," explained Jamie, who last saw her Uncle Arthur in 1984. He had come to town to visit her parents and asked if she would drive him to a bank so he could deposit a $6,000 insurance settlement check. But he did not deposit the money. Instead, he came out of the bank clutching a wad of hundred dollar bills and hurriedly dropped a crisp $100 note on Jamie's passenger's seat. "He said, 'Go ahead, you take it, Jamie. You've been nice to me.' I tried to argue with him but there was a green light and some cars behind me and he just started to walk away. That was the last time I saw him."

Jamie's mother, Donna, says he took the money and went straight to Nevada. "He talked about gambling and he liked Reno and Las Vegas. He took all of that money and thought he would make a killing in the casino. But he lost it all. He just didn't have any perspective," she said.

———————

Every year, more than 1 million rail passengers leave the King Street Station in the Pioneer Square section of Seattle. From King Street, a person can take a direct train to Vancouver, Portland, Los Angeles or Chicago. "Put me on that Chicago train," Arthur told me one late night "and I'll connect there to Boston, and be home in three days." Three days after he started calling me from Seattle, I acquiesced and purchased a non-refundable ticket to Boston. Arthur had a VA check waiting for him at the Lynn shelter, and he insisted he would pay me back.

But before I bought the ticket I wanted to make a deal. "When you come back you have to agree to stay in the shelter until we get you permanent housing," I said.

"Yeah, sure," he told me and there was a long pause on the line. During his previous calls he had seemed desperate, describing sleepless nights of crouching in alleys next to the station, and going without food. Now the thought of a ticket in his hand, and a cross country ride in a warm train car had lifted his spirits. He sounded like the guy you run into at the corner coffee shop. "So, how are you? What have you been doing with yourself?" he asked.

In just a short week, I had become nearly obsessed with Arthur Foster's story. But why? Drifter, loaner, bluffer, storyteller extraordinaire, he had been on the road so long that this latest cross-country jaunt fell within the boundaries of what he would consider a normal week. He was, by all accounts, an old flim-flam man who had stepped over the edge at least five decades ago. What kept him going? Was it disorder that somehow forced him to create a routine for coping, and led him to walk miles along back roads and dark highways? Had it been easier for him to continue on, as he retold, and reshaped the stories of his life while creating a utopia in Harris, Minnesota? Did he attain a certain comfort level through isolation and distancing from loved ones? And, was the pain of repeatedly witnessing death on the battlefield still too great to forget after almost 60 years?

When I spoke with Paul Smits, associate chief consultant for VA's Homeless and Residential Rehabilitation and Treatment Programs in Washington, he explained that post-traumatic stress disorder can stay with someone forever. Smits mentioned that about 10 percent of America's 131,000 homeless vets have been diagnosed with post-traumatic stress disorder, and without treatment — such as therapy, medication, and housing — people like Arthur could ceaselessly drift in a perpetual state of fear and fantasy. "There could be recurrent re-experiences of the trauma, avoidance to the point of having a phobia of places and people, and chronic physical signs of hyper-arousal, including sleep problems, trouble concentrating, irritability, anger, poor concentration, blackouts or difficulty remembering things," he told me.

The morning after his train arrived from Seattle I ventured over to the senior center near the Lynn shelter. During the day, the hall is a haven for the homeless and I had a hunch he'd be there. I found him standing on a porch smoking a USA Gold cigarette and chatting with an affable woman in a wheelchair.

"Well, I'll be darned," he said with a confidence and swagger of a returning hero. He had made it back from Washington in three days and had stories to tell.

There were no marks on his face or hands to suggest that he had been mugged. His clothes were still clean, and he quickly mentioned that a woman had insisted that she treat him to breakfast, lunch and dinner each day on the three-day ride.

While this was just our fourth meeting, I was elated to see him and had many more questions.

"Come on in and I'll find us a place where we can sit in quiet."

More than 200 seniors stuffed the small hall, and sunlight fell on women in dusters and floral dresses and men in faded jogging suits and mismatched shirts and pants. He took a seat by the large storefront window, and seemed upbeat and ready for his next phase.

"How was your trip?

"Oh, just fine. Nice to be back here. Next step is to get me a room."

He took out eight twenty dollar bills and handed them to me.

"We're square now. Thanks for the ticket."

He seemed alert, focused and curious about why I had suddenly taken an interest in his life.

"I care about you Arthur," I said.

He seemed amused by my intentions of goodwill and our eyes locked in unspoken debate. When I asked him why he had told so many stories so many different ways he smiled, shrugged his shoulders and stopped me before I could continue.

"Let me ask you something. If I drop dead now, would it make a difference to you?

"Of course."

"You say that but you really don't mean it. I'll tell you why. I don't think anybody cares what happens to me because I'm not worth anything. What good have I done?"

"Well, you fought for this country."

"A lot of people did. But when it comes down to it after you die if you don't have a will or property or anything to pass on, people will forget about you right away."

"You don't think real emotions pass between people?"

"I used to when I was a young teenager. The war changed everything."

It's easy to give a homeless person a buck; a little more strenuous to lend an ear to somebody who has been forever luckless; much harder to help correct a wrong in someone's life and make their pain go away — if, just for a moment. I had wanted to help Arthur but how sincere was I about my intent? By bringing him back I had hoped to clean up a messy situation and clear my conscience. But now that he was back before me was he really a friend? Besides my fascination with the details of his life, what did we have in common?

I had reached out to his family, and received long, sobering e-mails from relatives who lauded my efforts to help and longed to see him again. I had huddled with the shelter director and created a strategic plan to get him subsidized housing and psychiatric treatment at the VA. This type of plan had been prepared countless times for him, no doubt, though. To believe that Arthur could conform to a standard of living he had rejected more than 40 years earlier was fantasy.

I knew he was right. After his death I would quickly move on. We had not even really become friends yet; we had opposite intentions. I wanted to learn all I could about him so I could cobble together the truth and help him live with dignity. But I knew that he considered his stories sacred.

He had carried and told them countless times while sojourning across the country and was not going to let a newcomer wrest them away. For Arthur, every word of each tale was true. There was tragedy and joy; deprivation and sustenance; murder, conception and loss. The only solace could be found during long, silent walks and in the quiet, rolling countryside of the Midwest — in towns like Harris, Minnesota.

November, 2009
Previously unpublished

CHAPTER 4

Music

Get Back

Late Saturday evening, Winthrop's Laurie Mansfield plopped herself down in an overstuffed chair in the lobby of the Sheraton Ferncroft Hotel in Danvers, and started to sing the words to the Beatles song "Help."

Mansfield, who is 72 and a retired financial analyst, sat on the edge of her chair and smiled. She joined 15 others who strummed guitars, played piano, and did what they enjoy most in life: sing Beatles songs.

The closest the Beatles ever came to playing music north of Boston occurred on Aug. 16, 1966, when they played at Suffolk Downs in East Boston, but last weekend thousands made their way to the Fest for Beatles Fans, at the hotel.

They arrived wearing sweatshirts and blue jeans; jean jackets and Merrells; and as they approached middle age, they walked, and did not race from exhibit to exhibit. Mansfield, who wore a blue sweatshirt with a peace sign engraved with the names of John, Paul, George, and Ringo had already viewed the CDs, LPs, books, videos, T-shirts, buttons, towels, Nehru jackets, and posters on sale. She had seen the photo shows by Robert Freeman and Paul Saltzman, who captured the Fab Four on albums and in India; and had strolled from the Beatles karaoke booth to the Beatles puppet show to the performance by Liverpool, the Beatles cover band.

Sitting and singing, Mansfield was reminded that the music of the group she has adored since 1964, is timeless. "I think they were the song track for my life. They pretty much told me what to do," she said, crediting the Beatles for pushing her to participate in the peace movement in the 1960s.

Thirty feet away, Neil Innes sat at a table signing autographs. Innes, of the Monty Python comedy troupe, and a friend of George Harrison and Paul McCartney, has become a cult figure for some Beatles fans. Innes wrote the music and starred in the Rutles, a parody band. Innes, who later in the evening would perform Rutles favorites "Cheese and Onions," "Hold My Hand," and "Piggy in the Middle" has been attending Beatles conventions since 1994. He does not disappoint fans, accommodating them with Beatles stories, including the time he proclaimed "Hey Jude" "a dirge" to McCartney, after the Beatle had performed the seven-minute song for him — before even playing it for John Lennon.

As he paused and listened to a sing-along of "Imagine," he tried to explain the unexplainable — just why thousands of people are drawn to memorabilia weekends. "[The Beatles] were the real thing — four guys writing incredible songs, singing incredibly well, keeping together really good beats. That's why these people are here now singing their songs. It's people music. It's Mozart. It's good stuff, and it lasts. It lasts forever."

In a nearby room, George Keller, who goes by the stage name Jorge, was lip-synching "I Saw Her Standing There," as his mother nodded in approval. Karaoke Karen, who ran the video booth, also gave him high marks, as she asked the Malden man how many copies of the video he wanted. "I've had thousands of people, and he's in the top 5 percent," she said.

Down the hall, in a darkened room that is used as a bar during weekdays, 25 people sat in silence in the transformed cathedral, watching John Lennon videos. There was awkward clapping after "Instant Karma" finished. Some sipped beer, others reached for their cellphones as the video dissolved into "Jealous Guy."

Inside the vendor's area, Richard Gray had finished his shopping for the night, settling on another John Lennon T-shirt.

Gray, who is 52 and lives in Everett, has been hooked on the Beatles for nearly 40 years, and listens exclusively to their music. "I wake up to Beatle music, listen to them all day long at work, and put their CD on when I go to bed," he said.

He still mourns Lennon's death, and said on Dec. 8, he'll commemorate the date by lighting candles and listening to his music. He also holds on to his brush with fame when he bumped into Lennon and Yoko Ono on Beacon Street in Boston in 1972.

"He said he was looking at apartments in that area," said Gray, remembering that he had no questions for his idol. "It was like Moses coming out of the desert and you see God. And what do you say, 'Let's go to lunch?' "

November 13, 2003
The Boston Globe

Forever Young

In Douglas Gilbert's Amesbury darkroom, the black-and-white silhouettes slowly emerge, revealing images of a person and a time that changed the face of rock 'n' roll history. The person is Bob Dylan, the time is the summer of 1964, and the photos were hidden from the public for four decades.

Gilbert took over 900 pictures of Dylan over a seven-day period during the summer of 1964 in Woodstock, N.Y., Manhattan, and at the Newport Folk Festival. Most of the photos were taken at Dylan's retreat in Woodstock, which was owned by his manager, Albert Grossman. The photos show a 23-year-old Dylan at ease with his music, and his friends who included poet Allen Ginsberg, writer Terry Southern, and musicians John Sebastian and Ramblin' Jack Elliott.

The photo shoot was Gilbert's first assignment as a 21-year-old staff photographer for Look magazine. He remembers driving while Dylan played the harmonica and Sebastian sang "Mr. Tambourine Man"; Ginsberg holding a large tree limb over his shoulder and laughing hysterically; Dylan placing an empty picture frame around his neck at the Kettle of Fish bar in New York, and saying, "Take one now, the picture's already framed."

But Look never published the photos.

"The editor just thought that he was not fit for a family magazine, and Look prided itself on being a family magazine," said Gilbert, a psychotherapist who continues to work as a professional photographer.

"He said he thought the photos looked too scruffy."

A year later, Look ran a major story on Dylan but did not use Gilbert's photos.

When the magazine folded in 1971, Gilbert was given the negatives from the shoot. He kept them under wraps during his moves to Chicago, Newburyport, and Amesbury. Unsure of who owned the rights to the pictures, Gilbert was content to let them go unpublished. He never bothered to print and frame a Dylan photo for himself. He went on to win photography awards for other work and published a book on writer C.S. Lewis.

"There were long periods when I forgot about them," Gilbert said.

But two years ago, another former Look photographer, Douglas Kirkland, told Gilbert that he did, in fact, own the rights to the photos. A year later, when PBS began work on a Dylan documentary, Gilbert's daughter asked the producers if they might be interested in the photos.

Then came the call from Dylan's office in New York. They wanted to see the entire collection.

Gilbert printed 31 contact sheets, and sent them to New York. Soon afterward, Gilbert learned that several had been chosen to run in a booklet included in the recently released CD, "The Bootleg Series Volume 6: Bob Dylan Live in 1964."

"I think they're remarkable. They were all amazing. We were just floored," said Geoff Gans, Dylan's art director.

Gans was a week away from finishing up the artwork for the CD when he saw the photos. He quickly pulled 11 photographs that had been scheduled to run and replaced them with Gilbert's pictures.

Gans called the photographs "technically beautiful," and lauded Gilbert's perspective and depth of field. He said Dylan is a fan of the photos.

"One of the things Bob really liked is you can see the furniture, which to him really dates the time. He also liked the photos of him sitting around with a bunch of people because they weren't just focused on him," Gans said.

Chelsea Hoffman, an associate producer for the PBS documentary on Dylan that is being directed by Martin Scorsese, said she expects several of Gilbert's photos to run in the film.

"They're very candid, very innocent, and not posed," she said.

Gilbert's instincts told him to focus on Dylan's interactions, but not become a participant in the conversation. The one time he asked Dylan to pose for a photo, the musician declined.

"I was trying to set up an interaction with him and someone else, and I said, 'Could you do this because I would like to make the situation look real?' " Gilbert said. "And he stopped and he looked me right in the eye, and said, 'Nothing's real, man.' So I didn't do anything more after that. And the point was really clear. It was more than the words.

"I knew that just my presence changed a few things, and I tried to be as inconspicuous and quiet as I could be. I believe he appreciated that. He never asked me to stop photographing. He would let me wander around where he was and we got along fine."

The photos, of Dylan sitting with friends, playing music, writing, and standing in New York City, tell the story of a young poet and musician enjoying life. Gilbert, who is now 62, has not identified a theme from the collection, but believes it reveals a vulnerable side of Dylan that's rarely seen in photos after 1964.

"I knew that it was a pretty rare experience, even at that point," Gilbert said. The pictures were taken before Dylan produced much of his seminal work, such as "Like A Rolling Stone," "Just Like a Woman," and "Lay, Lady, Lay."

"It wasn't long after that when he began to be much less accessible," Gilbert said, "and I really felt as if I was able to spend some time with him when he was not as guarded, not as private, and it's part of what makes the photographs unique."

Gilbert, who chose a 35-millimeter Leica rangefinder camera for most of the shoot, used available light and did not use a tripod. His photos rarely seem rushed and reflect a relaxed, sometimes pensive Dylan.

One picture shows him drinking red wine and watching late-night TV alone. Many were taken in a Woodstock cafe, where Dylan wrote on a manual typewriter in a second-floor office.

The writing, said Gilbert, was part of Dylan's routine, lasting about 15 minutes at a time. Once, when Dylan left, Gilbert read the words on the typewriter paper. Months later, in 1964, when he purchased the album "Another Side of Bob Dylan," Gilbert recognized some of the poetry on the liner notes and realized that it had been written during the photo shoot.

Gilbert has read Dylan's recent book, "Chronicles: Volume 1," and still listens to the musician, who, he says, has influenced his life.

"He worked on my thinking," Gilbert said. "His work was really helpful to me in clarifying a lot of what I was sensing, and feeling, but didn't have words yet to put it all together. When I would hear his work it would kind of come into focus."

January 23, 2005
The Boston Globe

Yup ... Joe Smith signed Jimi Hendrix, James Taylor and the Grateful Dead

LOS ANGELES — Some 3,000 miles away from the hardscrabble streets of his native Chelsea, Joe Smith stood next to his living room stereo in Beverly Hills and thumbed through a row of CDs.

"Dylan, Streisand, Paul McCartney, Artie Shaw," he said aloud, holding them together like an accordion. "I got them all to talk. Well, that's pretty good."

Smith, a former Boston disc jockey who went on to lead Warner Bros., Elektra/Asylum, and Capitol/EMI, was responsible for signing the likes of the Grateful Dead, Jimi Hendrix, Van Morrison, Garth Brooks, and the Eagles. But one of his biggest projects occurred outside of the studio in the mid-1980s. Smith wanted to learn more intimate details of the artists' lives and spent two years recording over 200 hours of interviews with over 200 rock and jazz luminaries for a book he wrote 25 years ago.

Smith recently donated the tapes to the Library of Congress, and this month the library will post the first 25 hours of his interviews on its website. The initial batch features 24 artists, including Paul McCartney, George Harrison, Mick Jagger, Ray Charles, Steven Tyler and Joe Perry of Aerosmith, and David Bowie. Eventually, more than 230 hours will be available on the site for historians, music buffs, and anyone else who may be curious about popular music in the 20th century.

"The Joe Smith Collection is an invaluable addition to the Library's comprehensive collection of recorded sound," said Librarian of Congress James H. Billington. "These frank and poignant oral histories of many of the nation's musical icons give us unique insights into them as artists, entertainers, and human beings."

Smith's interview cassettes sat in a bunch of boxes in his garage until earlier this year. That's when former Grateful Dead drummer Mickey Hart called up Smith and suggested he donate the tapes to the national library. Smith agreed and sent the tapes to Washington, where the library quickly digitized the treasure trove of voices.

Hart, who credited Smith with nurturing the Grateful Dead during the band's early years, said he was aware of the collection and didn't want the tapes to decompose.

"We were just talking and I just realized that these things, you know, this history would be lost," said Hart.

James Taylor, who lives in Western Massachusetts, also praised the donation. Smith signed Taylor in 1969 just before Taylor released "Sweet Baby James" — an album that went triple platinum. Taylor's interview with Smith will also eventually be posted on the Library of Congress site. "Joe was of huge importance to me in the early days of my career. It takes me back to a time when record companies and their executives had a real connection with their artists and felt a responsibility to us," said Taylor, in an e-mail.

Al Kooper, who founded Blood, Sweat & Tears, believes some of the history of rock 'n' roll has been incorrectly reported in articles and books, and said the collection could correct some of the inaccuracies. "It will be closer than before because it's all first-hand," said Kooper, who lives in Somerville.

During his interview, Kooper detailed the studio recording of Dylan's "Like a Rolling Stone," where he had hoped to play guitar but deferred to Mike Bloomfield. During a break, he hopped in front of an organ, played along, and then listened along during the playback when Dylan told the engineer to turn up the organ.

The collection grew out of a promise Smith made to John Hammond, the record producer who helped fine-tune everyone from Benny Goodman to Dylan and Bruce Springsteen. Ailing, and in his hospital bed, Hammond insisted that Smith — a music insider whose friendships ran from Frank Sinatra to Frank Zappa — visit artists and supergroups and hear their stories.

Smith accepted the mission. Armed with a cassette recorder and a microphone, he traveled throughout the United States and Europe in search of the backstory to artists' careers. "I was known and had no problem getting to anybody," he said.

Smith, who was once a Globe newsboy in Chelsea, said he corralled in the giants of the music business simply by making a phone call or two. He said he learned most of his early street smarts on Chelsea's gritty streets.

The son of an insurance salesman who moonlighted as a bookie, Smith went on to Yale, and worked in radio, becoming one of Boston's first disc jockey's to play rock 'n' roll. By the late 1950s, he wanted a new challenge and set out for Hollywood, where he made a name for himself by signing comedians like Allan Sherman before shifting to rock acts.

Most of his interviews were done in person, lasted at least an hour, and often resulted in a confession, with the famous sounding more like regular working stiffs than carefully primped stars. Jagger told Smith that the Rolling Stones hadn't made a good record since 1972; McCartney acknowledged that his songs were not the same without John Lennon's touch; Little Richard recalled feeling an "electric charge" run through his body after he first heard "Tutti Frutti" on the radio at his home in Georgia.

"I got caught up in hearing these stories, and the importance of knowing all of these people — even if it was only for the two hours that I was with them," said Smith.

The interviews took two years to complete, and in the midst of his conversations with Streisand, Roger Daltrey, and Tina Turner, Smith became president of Capitol/EMI, where he stayed until retiring in 1993.

Meanwhile, in between launching acts — such as Garth Brooks — he carried his tape recorder and squeezed in interviews when he could. George Harrison showed up one day at his office in Burbank and confided that his favorite cover of "Something" was recorded by James Brown. In New York, Streisand answered his questions in her bathrobe in a hotel and admitted she doesn't read music or do much to take care of her voice: "I don't pamper it, I don't use humidifiers or special sprays, I don't vocalize, and I don't sing in the shower."

In Beverly Hills, Ella Fitzgerald asked Smith to fix her stereo before the interview. In London, Van Morrison said he'd agree to an interview only if they met in a hotel lobby and was addressed by Smith as Mr. Johnson.

Outside of Palo Alto, Jerry Garcia tried to explain the increased popularity of the Grateful Dead and the proliferation of "Deadheads": "We represent something like hopping railroads or getting out on the road. It's not supposed to be done anymore, but being a Deadhead means you can get in your van and cross the US. We ponder the thought of these people daily. It's become our life, really."

Smith also got to meet some of his childhood idols, such as Artie Shaw, who told Smith he quit in the middle of his career because he was tired of playing the same songs every night. "I got to a place where they said, 'Stop, don't grow anymore,'" Shaw told Smith.

Smith believes that insecurity, the desire to stay on top after writing a hit song, and the will to perform before thousands of people, are the common threads that link the artists together. "Some of them were absolute perfectionists," said Smith. "But insecurity, at the bottom of it all — that may be the one emotion that registered through everybody."

There are other threads that help define the music, the era, and its overall impact on society. Some like Hart, the Grateful Dead drummer, said the tapes reveal a time when art met drugs and business and how the mediums learned to coexist. Hart also said it was an era when record executives had great patience with artists, who sometimes took years to record and mix an album.

"That was a big part — nurturing, mentoring — because artists sometimes don't appear unless they're produced or manufactured, which you see today," said Smith.

Smith now spends most of his time with his wife and family. He used to go to Chelsea reunions but most of his friends have passed, and he now rarely gets back to his hometown. He said today's music business is the antithesis of the industry he helped develop some 50 years ago. He said it would be unlikely that record companies would sign acts like The Grateful Dead, Neil Young, and Joni Mitchell if they were starting their careers today.

"First of all, the corporate would want a business plan. They'd hear the Grateful Dead and they'd say, 'What's this about? How many do you expect to sell, what kind of profit can we make on this?' " he explained. "This is a different business altogether and different kinds of artists make it, and there are still great artists, obviously, but nowhere near the numbers, nowhere near the creative world that was out there during that period."

November 26, 2012
The Boston Globe

Play Those Bells, Marilyn

On Tuesday nights up in the highlands of Portuguese Hill, there is clinging and clashing; car horn-honking and solitude; prayer and meditation; humming and napping.

Such is the life here on this hill. At its base, in the blue, stucco towers of Our Lady of Good Voyage Church, 31 bells sit in testament to the night of July 23, 1922, when these carillon chimes were officially played for the first time.

Marilyn Clark, a former Gloucester schoolteacher, began playing the carillon years ago, and has reached a level of mastery of the instrument that few have attained.

On Tuesday nights in July, Clark plays a recital after passing out programs to concertgoers who remain in their cars, and wait for the music. After each tune, there is silence, and then the horn honking begins. At that point, Clark says, she knows she's connected with her audience.

In addition to the July concerts, Clark can be found most Sunday mornings in the small room below the belfry playing the instrument after Mass; she also practices during the week.

"I try to be expressive in my music and think about what I'm playing," said Clark, 74, who added that she was hooked when she first touched the awkward wooden keyboard.

The church's instrument is the oldest, properly tuned carillon in the country.

It's a complicated device to play; musicians strike a note by pounding on the keyboard with a fist, and pushing down on levers just above the floor. The keys are connected to wires and "clappers," which strike the bells.

The carillon bells have a long and proud history on Portuguese Hill, beginning with their controversial arrival from England. After they were unloaded from a ship, the bells were seized by US Customs officials, who demanded the Gloucester church pay a $40,000 tariff. It took an emergency act of Congress to release the bells, and on July 2, 1922, the bells were blessed by Cardinal William O'Connell.

Off and on through 1975, summer carillon concerts were held on Portuguese Hill, with as many as 10,000 jamming the small square around Prospect Street.

During that period, John D. Rockefeller Jr. listened to the bells, and was inspired to commission the world's largest set of carillon bells for New York's Baptist Riverside Church.

Years later, in 1944, President Franklin D. Roosevelt heard the bells from aboard a boat in Gloucester Harbor. Martin Gilman, a local musician, and Rev. Eugene Alves played the carillon from 1946 through 1975. Then, after 10 years of silence, Clark began her tenure.

When Maria Brum hears the bells on Tuesday nights, she opens her backdoor, and takes a seat on the cramped porch, just one street behind the church. The 94-year-old Brum has lived on Portuguese Hill since 1949, when she left the Azores for Gloucester. For her, the bells are a symbol of her great devotion to the church.

"I love the bells and the church," she said. "In the Azores every day at noon time I would hear the bells and bless myself. When I first came here I'd hear the fog horns, and I thought they might be bells, so I'd bless myself."

At the top of Ledgemont Avenue, George Doherty stood in the same spot that artist Edward Hopper chose in 1923 to view the church for one of his paintings. "It's beautiful; I know most of the songs they play," said Doherty, 12, who calls the hill "Mount Hurtalot" because of its steep decline and difficult sledding paths.

"They played 'Ode to Joy' this morning," Doherty said. "I was sitting in front of the church listening."

Over on Sadler Street, Vivien Manning sat on her lounge chair outside of the house she was born in 86 years ago. She said that while the neighborhood has changed, the church has been a constant reminder of the way life was for Portuguese families.

"Please play for me that sweet melody, called 'Doodley Doo, Doodley Doo,' " she sings, revealing a rich, soprano voice.

Her song is all that's left of a time during the Depression when her neighbors used to meet at the top of the street to play guitar and sing Portuguese and American songs.

As Manning listens to the carillon bells, she closes her eyes and says a prayer: "It makes you sit there and think, and say to yourself, 'Thank God I'm still here on this earth.' "

July 21, 2002
The Boston Globe

Drummer Man

There's always a jazz tune playing on the lower end of North Shore Road. If you've stopped at a red light down by the General Edwards Bridge, you might hear the music of Oscar Peterson, Stan Getz, or Gene Krupa emanating from a white saltbox.

Inside, a drummer sits and listens and marvels at the music that has transformed his soul and brought deep meaning to his life.

At 75, Norm "Scotty" Scott is the dean of salesmen at Boston music stores. Now a drum consultant at Jack's Drum Shop on Boylston Street, he's the last of the old-timers who worked at the original Jack's Drum Shop (now the site of the Four Seasons Hotel), E.U. Wurlitzer, and the short-lived Drummer's Image. Over the years, he's sold thousands of drum sets, counseled many promising drummers, and has become known as the man drummers seek out when they arrive in Boston.

Scott's admirers include "Tonight Show" drummers Marvin "Smitty" Smith, Ed Shaughnessy, and Louis Bellson; Anton Fig of the CBS Orchestra and the "Late Show" with David Letterman; Ginger Baker, formerly of Cream; Peter Erskine of Weather Report; Randy Jones of the Dave Brubeck Quartet; and Alan White of Yes.

"He's like 'Father Drums' in the Boston area," said drummer Fred Sargeant Jr., who has worked with Scott for the last 30 years.

Scott got hooked on drumming when he was 13, and despite a scholarship offer from Bowdoin College, walked out of East Boston High School to drum professionally and never looked back. He fashioned his first drum set from old chairs and cymbals from pawn shops, and started playing big band music in the '40s.

It was a chance meeting in 1942 with Krupa, his idol, that solidified his career choice. "He had just finished a gig at Canobie Lake Park in New Hampshire, and we talked about drumming all night," said the white-haired Scott, who demonstrated Krupa's legendary style, tapping his palms on the table, as a cigarette burned in the corner of his mouth.

Scott recalled 20 years of nightly gigs at Route 1 roadhouses and Revere Beach clubs. "We called it cocktail jazz," said Scott, reeling off the names of long-vanished clubs such as Carl's Duck Farm, the Checker Lounge, Bali, Mickey Mouse, Lindy's Lounge, and Frolic.

Scott also spent five years as a member of the house band at the Route 1 Hilltop Lounge before former trumpet player Frank Giuffrida expanded his watering hole into a steak restaurant.

In 1963, he joined the staff of Jack's Drum Shop, during a time he described as a golden era of music in Boston. "The place was jam-packed every day. Everybody thought they were going to be like the Beatles," he recalled.

It was at Jack's that he struck up a friendship with the late Buddy Rich, and cymbal-maker Avedis Zildjian. "Buddy was a perfectionist who demanded 100 percent from his band," said Scott, who spent many nights as Rich's guest at the historic Paul's Mall and Lennie's on the Turnpike in Peabody. Zildjian, who would corner the market in cymbals, later included several of Scott's designs.

Jack's closed in the early '70s, and Scott settled in at E.U. Wurlitzer's on Newbury Street, before moving to the new Jack's Drum Shop in 1978.

Scott called the E.U. Wurlitzer staff a dream team of Boston musicians.

In the cavernous, smoke-filled display area where rock stars mingled with teenagers, the salesmen — Scott, Eddie Cooper, John LaMont,

Bob Cavanough, and Phil DeLeo — worked the floor, offering advice, encouragement, and old war stories about past gigs as they developed loyal customers. Scott reserved particular praise for Cooper, the late Chelsea saxophone player. "He was an excellent sax player," said Scott. "He could sell you the Brooklyn Bridge. He was a top salesman."

Scott still counsels Berklee College drummers, and occasionally teaches them how to play a merengue or a tango. He plays at least one hour a day, and plans to record in the studio this spring with his son, Jay, who is a blues guitarist.

He's also one of the last craftsman who can tuck calf-skin drum heads. He's fielded requests for his expertise from all over the world, and recently finished work on a Civil War drum sent from a collector in Arizona.

But, it's the connection with other drummers that keeps him coming to work, he said. "Have a good gig," he tells drummers as they leave the store.

They listen to the man who is their link between the past and the present, and who can still sit in and beat the drums with the boys.

February 10, 2002
The Boston Globe

Blood, Sweat ... and Fred

In a small narrow room at Berklee College of Music, Fred Lipsius moves his fingers effortlessly over an upright Yamaha piano, leaving dreamy suspended major seventh chords to drift into the visitor's subconscious, creating a moment of grace.

For Lipsius, it's always been about grace and music. Forty years ago, he was a New York sax virtuoso who went on to lead the horn section of the group that originated fusion, Blood, Sweat & Tears. For the last 20 years he's been a professor of music at Berklee, and since 1991, he's lived in Brookline.

Lipsius, who is 60, looks considerably younger, and with his trim fit and Bronx accent, he hardly conjures the image of a '60s rock star who played at Woodstock. The fact is, says Lipsius, he was an accidental rocker. "Something happened and I decided I wanted to be a jazz musician," says Lipsius, of his teenage years when he played tenor and alto sax in the Bronx and Harlem.

By then he was hooked on the melodies of Charlie Parker, Cannonball Adderley, John Coltrane, Sonny Rollins, Benny Goodman, and Sonny Stitt. To tighten his chops, he transcribed his favorite songs note by note. "I wanted to know what the mystery of what they were doing, what the phrases were," he says.

In the late fall of 1967, he was hired over the phone by drummer Bobby Colomby, who, along with Al Kooper, wanted to start a band that combined horns with rock 'n' roll. "There wasn't a name Blood, Sweat & Tears yet. It was a concept. And it was basically a rhythm section and me," says Lipsius. Two days later, Lipsius joined Colomby and Blues Project players Al Kooper and Steve Katz onstage at the Village Theatre (which later became the Fillmore East). In early 1968, they released their first album, "Child is Father to the Man."

By March 1969, their second album had reached number one in America and included three gold singles, "Spinning Wheel," "You've Made Me So Very Happy," and "And When I Die." That year Lipsius won a Grammy for his arrangement of "Spinning Wheel." "That was the first rock arrangement I ever wrote," says the soft-spoken Lipsius. "I told my wife the other day as we were listening to a bunch of cars honking their horns and I said, 'That's where my idea for the introduction for Spinning Wheel came.' It reminded me of traffic in New York City where everybody's honking their horn at the same time."

After the Grammy, Lipsius stayed on for two more albums, which also went gold. There were gigs at Woodstock — "it was kind of just another gig for us" — and at the London Palladium, where the band members were told the Beatles were in the audience.

Lipsius left the band in the early '70s to arrange his own music, and compose for radio and TV. In 1982, he met his wife, Setsuko, while touring with Simon & Garfunkel in Japan. She came to Boston in 1984, at the same time Lipsius began his tenure at Berklee. Since the early '80s he's written five books on tools, techniques, and improvisation for musicians and released two albums.

Lipsius does not dwell on the past, but on the occasion when he does listen to his old band he is satisfied with the music. "When I listen to it, I always say, 'Is it my imagination, or does this band sound great or what?'"

June 13, 2004
The Boston Globe

Dark Side of the Charles

Picture a tiny island in the Charles River where the '70s survived. Throw in a light show, rock music, and a crowd united by a longing for that era, and you have a party forever frozen in time.

Since 1982, laser beams, star projections and Pink Floyd's "Dark Side of the Moon" have been combined at the Hayden Planetarium at the Museum of Science. During that time, the estimable British rock ensemble has released new CDs, toured, broken up, reunited and disbanded.

But its legions of fans have remained faithful, especially to the lingering magic of "Dark Side of the Moon," which, since its 1973 release, has continuously stayed on Billboard's top 200 list.

On a recent Saturday evening, 169 people — mostly students and aging hippies — waited in line for the 10:30 show to begin. They chatted quietly, challenging each other with Pink Floyd trivia, gossip and conspiracy theories — including the "Wizard of Oz" hypothesis, which claims that when played together, the music and lyrics of "Dark Side of the Moon" synch perfectly with the plot of "Oz."

Sabrina Iannarelli, Jack Frost, and Chris Daly listened to the album New Year's Eve and decided to take the train up from Attleboro for the laser show.

Frost, 21, a computer science major at UMass-Amherst, said he first heard Pink Floyd when he was a baby. His parents would ride around in the country, playing Pink Floyd 8-track tapes until he fell asleep.

"My father is an electrician and the stereo in the car had Christmas lights wired to it that went around its interior. It would react to the waveforms of the sounds, so different sounds would produce different colors from the Christmas lights," said Frost, who says he has listened to the album over 1,000 times.

At the front of the line stood Jay Polsky, formerly of Swampscott, now of Providence. At 48, Polsky said Pink Floyd has been a continuous presence in his travels, from the Merchant Marines to a stint in South Africa to his present job as a chef in a Rhode Island hospital. "I flew to London to see 'The Wall' concert at Earl's Court in 1981," he said, referring to Pink Floyd's 1979 album of that name.

The show is based on a computerized palette created by Laser Fantasy International, and is directed by laserist Bruce LeBlanc. As the crowd shouted "I love you" and "Bruce," LeBlanc did not disappoint. With the soft background of the solar system shining on the dome of the planetarium, he pulled nearly every fractal, double helix and spirograph out of his bag of tricks.

At times it worked, and other moments it seemed like a random sampling of screensavers. At the conclusion, during "Eclipse," 38 special-effects projectors combine with the lasers to produce a simulated nuclear explosion of a panoramic image of Boston.

Whether or not that was Pink Floyd's original message seemed almost irrelevant to the crowd. "I'm going to see it again," said Frost as he disappeared into the darkness.

January 13, 2002
The Boston Globe

Air Apparent

When an Allman Brothers tune booms out of a dark corner of the Old Timer's Tavern in Gloucester, Samo Frontiero and James "Turk" Matthews instinctively move away from the bar, raise their imaginary guitars, and start picking.

Frontiero and Matthews may not be as well known as such air-guitar luminaries as Tom Cruise and Jerry Remy, but for locals the two are in a different league. While the men do not play guitar, they are considered local rock gods who have participated in one of the longest air-guitar contests in the United States, and helped inspire a couple of generations of wannabes.

"It's dexterity and choreography," said Frontiero, 49, who has worked as a fisherman for 32 years. "I just feel the music; every note and every riff I know from the songs."

This week, the air guitars will be pulled out again for the tavern's annual competition. About a dozen acts are expected to perform. The winner earns $100 and bragging rights for the year.

In Gloucester, there's a long tradition when it comes to pretend guitar playing. But air guitar is big business all over the country these days, as the subject of video games, instructional books, American and international contests, and even a film documenting the ascent of working-class men to rock stars. For Frontiero and Matthews, all that seems impossible to believe.

"We do it because we love music," said Matthews, who is 47 and helps select fish for a local market.

While no historian has stepped forth to tell the story of the movement, one day a chronicler of air guitar will undoubtedly make the trip to the Old Timer's, down by the docks on Gloucester Harbor. It was inside the tavern in 1978 that a group of fishermen, carpenters, and builders participated in what aficionados believe was one of the first air-guitar contests in the country. And, these days, the contest is still going strong.

"This town is big on tradition," said Mike Favazza, who owns the Old Timer's. As children, Favazza and his friends would peek in the back door of the bar to see performers take the stage during the air guitar contest. "It was a good time then and it is now. It links generations," he said.

For locals, the air-guitar contest is the unofficial kickoff for St. Peter's Fiesta, an annual Sicilian tradition that began in Gloucester in 1927. Initially a religious event, the Sicilian festival ran from Thursday through Sunday on the last weekend in June, and included an outdoor Mass, a blessing of the fleet, and a procession of the statue of St. Peter through the city.

By 1978, some city residents, like Peter Asaro, were eager to put their own spin on the fiesta. Asaro, who helped manage Old Timer's, also was the bar's disc jockey, and would end each night standing on the bar and pretending to strum a guitar while listening to Pablo Cruz.

The music helped transform the tavern, which had been known as a fishermen's bar for decades. "It was your typical old-style fishermen's bar, and they would put a bottle on the table with glasses, and you would drink as much whiskey as you wanted," said Asaro, who spoke by telephone from his home in Hawaii.

A few weeks before the fiesta that year, Asaro asked some friends to participate in an air-guitar contest at the bar. On the night of the first show, he showed up wearing a pink sports coat, red sneakers, and sunglasses. With over 300 people jammed in the tavern, and a line around the block, he hopped up on the small stage. "It looked like a small little arena; the people were stacked up on top of one another," said Asaro, who is 54 and still works as a bartender.

There were 12 acts that night, which ended prematurely when the sound system's speakers blew. Asaro was not surprised that so many people wanted to be part of the contest. "Everybody aspires to be a rock star. You can be up there for five minutes and be king of the world and the next day you can go back to being yourself without the trappings of fame," he said.

In the contest's early years, most of the guitarists were fishermen, who saw the event as a way to relieve the pressures of life at sea. It was also the only weekend of the year that they would not be working. As part of the fiesta's tradition, the fishermen would paint their boats and spend several uninterrupted days with their families, awaiting the blessing of the fleet — often by Boston's Roman Catholic cardinal.

Some fishermen, like Frontiero, used to polish their air-guitar moves at sea. "Back then, we had cassettes, and when I was at the wheel steaming home, I'd be practicing my song, getting my dexterity in line. It's an incredible vibe. I'd feel like Jimmy Page," said Frontiero, who advises aspiring air guitarists to choose a song no longer than five minutes that's dominated by lead-guitar solos.

Matthews still practices occasionally on the job. "I've got a shovel at work, and I'll pick it up if I hear a good tune on the radio. I'll just crank the music and I'll go crazy with it," he said.

At the bar, Frontiero, wearing a Jimi Hendrix shirt, said he is considering performing a song by Hendrix or Stevie Ray Vaughn. Frontiero, who won the contest in 1982 and 1988 with performances of songs by Humble Pie and Jimmy Barnes, predicted a third title this year. He said the key to winning is not to lose the crowd.

A few stools away, Vinnie Scuderi and Jon Gaipo talked about their own dream of repeating as champions. The two men, who graduated from Gloucester High School in 1995, have won six of the last seven contests. Unlike the early acts, the men perform a farrago of tunes, mixing bands such as the Beastie Boys, Run-D.M.C. and Rage Against the Machine, and don't rely solely on their air-guitar skills, incorporating break-dancing and other steps.

The two plan to practice once or twice in the coming days; they never reveal the precise medley they'll sing before the event.

"A lot of people get bored. When they're in this atmosphere they don't like to pay attention — they like to be moved and captivated and you have to be in their face," said Scuderi, 30, who wants to be a police officer.

Frontiero considers himself an air-guitar "purist" and abhors the idea of doing anything onstage besides pretending to play guitar. "Air guitar is not lip-synch," said Frontiero, who also helps carry the St. Peter statue during the Sunday procession through the city.

Matthews said he prefers a stark stage with no props.

"I'm a left-handed guitar player," he said.

"All I need is an empty mike stand or maybe a pair of headphones."

June 24, 2007
The Boston Globe

CHAPTER 5

Family

On the Road to Camp

The sun splashes gold on the ocean as we leave the North Shore at 6 in the morning. We are a family of three, and my wife and I already have lumps in our throats before we hit the Mass Pike. Nothing is wrong. Actually, everything is right: We knew that a day like this would come, when our 11-year-old son, Aaron, would go off to overnight camp.

A perfect summer day. A long drive into the mountains to fresh air, a bunk room of happy kids, a panoply of fields and swimming holes. This was another defining moment-to-be in a lifetime of memories now accessed in a nonlinear timeline, where recollections become more selective; years can be remembered and described in a handful of sentences. Milestones are anticipated and cherished, but also ineffable.

There is beauty and awe that can be lost in the moment of separation. Our ride is simple. Devorah, Aaron, and I play word games, laugh at the rhymes and riddles we create, and marvel at the Berkshires. Aaron, who is 4 feet 10 inches and likes to wear Big Papi T-shirts and Tom Brady game jerseys, multitasks, working his Nintendo as he formulates a "think it-link it" rhyme while trying to harmonize with a Beatles song.

"Was it John or George who played lead guitar," he asks, as we roll into a Berkshire town I have never heard of. There are emerald meadows, and farms, and Devorah and I discuss the terrain as Aaron hums a Green Day song. "It looks like Italy," she says, pointing to the sloping farms.

We drive and look at the country, and try to imagine what it's like to not live near a big city. And then, as we sense our ride is about to end, there are more suggestions to Aaron about how to live like a grownup while he's on his own. He listens, and we wait for questions, but there are none. We drive down a wooded road and see kids on bicycles, rocky roads and tennis courts.

We are greeted by the camp director, a woman who has spent more than 30 summers at the camp. She extends her hand to Aaron, and he makes eye contact. There are more counselors to meet, and it is both pleasant and awkward.

As a journalist who asks questions for a living, I am tempted to begin my querying. But as a father, I resist the urge, and just trust.

It's time for Aaron to go off to his new bunk, and his life for the next three weeks.

We get a hug and a kiss from our son, and stand and watch as he walks up a pebble-filled path with his counselor. They head up the hill, and he does not look back at us. This is a good sign, I think.

The two continue to stroll, and we stand until they are no longer visible. We enter the car, and Devorah notices the blanket Aaron forgot to take. She gives it to a counselor, and we are assured he'll receive it.

The corn and the farms and the hot summer winds greet us again. I pull over for a moment, and take it all in before returning to the road.

July 30, 2006
The Boston Globe

The Economic Stimulus Check

Dear American economy:

The other day I heard the economist Martin Feldstein telling people on the radio that the best thing they could do for the country is to spend their economic stimulus checks. He was saying that the rebate program hasn't worked out too well because too many people are saving the money.

Last week, my check finally arrived. It's colorful and brushed with yellow and green, and screamed out "spend me." So, in order to fulfill my duty as a good American consumer and to help big business, I started thinking of ways to spend the $1,500 and made a list of possible purchases that I submit to you:

1. Go on vacation

It's a time-honored tradition for American families to go away on summer trips. Why shouldn't my family? What we need is some good country air, mountains, sun, and silence. Although I have never been to Lake Winnipesaukee I quickly research rentals, and spot a two-bedroom unit that's only $1,200 for the week. The ad says it's not on the lake but there are views of the water. And there's $300 left over for gas and food!

2. Go to Foxwoods

Take a chance make it happen ... The TV commercials make the big gambling house so inviting that it's hard not to believe that if I drove down there and plopped down my stimulus check I would win big ...

Pop the cork, fingers snappin' ... Soon I'd be dancing in a dinner jacket with no financial worries; another new millionaire ... Spin the wheel, round and round we go ... all the while humming along with everyone on the dance floor ... Let's live for the wonder of it all.

3. Buy the wide-screen TV

Yeah, it makes so much sense. Big Papi, Tom Brady, and Kevin Garnett already spend a lot of time in my den. As their virtual coach, and motivator, I need more details. I want to see the dirt on Big Papi's batting gloves before he slams them together; I need a better view of Brady's posture, especially if his shoulder might be acting up; I need to see exactly how much sweat is on KG's face three minutes into a game.

4. Get the Gibson SG

You've wanted that electric guitar since the 1970s and now here's your chance. It's a heavy, brown double cutaway instrument that sings with its dual humbucking pickups and Grover machine heads. George Harrison played an SG on "Revolver," John Lennon picked up an SG during the White Album, and Pete Townshend was on the stage at Woodstock with an SG. What are you waiting for?

5. Paint the house and fence

This is a decidedly unsexy choice, but it's time. I've held out for a year or two too long, and as a homeowner, I've gotta keep up with the Joneses. But in order to bring the job in on budget, my wife and I gotta do it ourselves. My wife likes watercolors, and I embrace the Jackson Pollock method. Together, we will laugh, fight, and cry, and possibly fall off a ladder. But nobody ever said home improvement was for the weak.

6. Buy a dog

I've wanted a dog since I was a kid. I liked the TV show "Lassie," and I even had a dog for a few days. When I was 8, a collie came to my backyard and stayed. My grandmother fed it corned beef and I begged my parents to let me keep him. They said OK, but eventually the owners located the collie and took it home. Now, after all these years, I can right a wrong. All I have to do is go to the pet store or go online, and I can have my dog in a matter of hours. Then, I will take on a new identity and be known in my neighborhood as "Steve, the dog walker."

I should do one or all of these things. But soon, after I deposit the check, I will sit down and write a big check to Visa or MasterCard. I will feel relieved for about five minutes. And then, I will realize I've let the economy down. I'll take out my credit card and happily give it to cashiers in as many big box stores as I can find.

Your trusted servant,

Steve, the future dog walker

July 27, 2008
The Boston Globe

Fare Thee Well, Mom

It's beige and it looks like a TV remote, and I've picked it up several times over the years to press the nurse's call button. My discovery that it also controls the light above my mother's bed seems like a little victory. I finally realize that I don't have to bother the nurse and can shut the light off all by myself.

I push the button and the tension from the fluorescent light eases, and there is calm in the corner of a quiet hospital room. All of the life-sustaining drugs to control blood pressure, heart rate, and fluid build-up have been discontinued. There's just morphine now, the drug of choice when someone is about to die in the hospital.

My mother, Ruby Rosenberg, is 75 and has spent at least 12 out of the last 36 months in the hospital.

Her problems began three years ago when she underwent unsuccessful back surgery. During her recovery, she picked up an infection that kept her in the hospital for four months. Two years ago, her kidneys failed after a heart attack, necessitating dialysis. There were several more infections, and she was forced to give up her apartment. With chronic back pain, she ended dialysis and gathered all of her children in a nursing home for a final goodbye.

But a very funny thing happened four days after her announcement. She woke up, realized she hadn't died, and called us together to make another declaration. "I tried to die and that didn't work," she told us. "So, I'm going to live."

And live she did. She went to physical therapy and learned how to stand and walk again. A former business owner, she counseled her three children on the economy and the stock market. Even two weeks ago, when she was brought to the emergency room with a collapsed lung, she quickly studied the number of employees in the room and determined that they could get by with one-third fewer.

But now the morphine had slowed her words, and she wasn't talking anymore. She was asleep, and the doctors had said it would be days, maybe even hours.

We were called into the intensive care unit, where the doctors had advised us that she had just a few hours to live. Atrial fibrillation was causing her heart to beat more than 150 times a minute. My mom had declined to have her heart shocked, and did not want to be intubated.

And then, after a rabbi was summoned, and her children and grandchildren bid her goodbye, she did something not unexpected: her heartbeat and her blood pressure returned to normal.

This is the roller coaster that children of aging and sick parents ride as we balance work, home, relationships, and personal goals. Years of caregiving go by and we begin to forget what our parents were like before they became sick. We are suddenly medical experts on their condition; advocates when they are ignored; and ethicists when we are told they should live no more.

My mother opens her eyes, and flashes a quick smile, acknowledging my presence. Our eyes lock, and we beam together. I hold her hand, and I then remember that I spent nine months in her body. We continue to smile; I try not to cry but am unsuccessful. We know that we will soon separate. She squeezes my hand.

Her smile grows bigger, her eyes brighter. This is unconditional love, I think. Her smile is familiar, and I realize that this must have been how we communicated before I could talk.

Three nights later the phone rings at 3:50 a.m. My sister tells me my mother has passed peacefully.

In an hour her funeral will begin. I try to make sense of the last three years. But there are no epiphanies as I prepare to bury my mother, just gratitude. My mother brought me life, and I will forever remember her kindness.

May her name and memory always be a blessing.

December 21, 2006
The Boston Globe

Satisfaction

It's 5 p.m. and I've just picked up my son Aaron from his after-school program. He informs me that he's finished his homework and is hungry. I steer the car toward the supermarket to pick up dinner, and the cellphone rings. It's my friend Ben, who tells me he's leaving for the Rolling Stones concert in 30 minutes. "It's not sold out. You can get a ticket," he says.

I begin to decline the invitation, and start to explain that it wouldn't be right to take my 11-year-old son to see the Rolling Stones. Then I realize that what I'm saying is a lie. This would be a fine educational experience for a kid who already knows much of the Beatles catalog, I realize. I tell Ben to hold on, then look back at Aaron. His homework is done, and he doesn't look tired. He also knows about the Stones, and has a bunch of their songs on his iPod.

"Aaron, you want to see the Rolling Stones?"

A big smile spreads across his face. "Let's go!" he tells me.

Thirty minutes later Ben swings by my house. He is a good friend, and has had a difficult year. Tomorrow, he'll face another round of chemotherapy. But tonight, he'll savor his 10th-row seats with his wife, Rebecca, and sister Debbie.

My wife is working and begs off from the road trip. As we pass through Boston, Debbie hands us a couple of pastrami sandwiches. "We figured you'd be hungry," she tells us.

During the ride I think about my decision to take Aaron. I couldn't have imagined going to a Frank Sinatra concert in 1970 with my dad. "My Way" was a nice tune but not something I'd want to turn up full blast on my record player. Also, I wouldn't have felt right wearing a suit to a concert.

More than 40 years after first playing stadium events — including an abbreviated gig at the old Manning Bowl in Lynn — the Stones still sound great with the volume turned up, and my generation still embraces their lyrics like anthems. We've been told that if you try some time you might just find that you get what you need; reminded that we were all responsible for the Kennedy assassinations; advised that sometimes our heart is beating louder than a big bass drum; consoled that even if you try you may not get any satisfaction.

I look at Aaron and he grips my hand and smiles as we head toward the gate, seeking to buy tickets. It's the fifth time the Stones have been to Boston recently, and the scalpers are selling for below face value. We quickly execute a deal with a man in his 20s. He wants $100 for two tickets that he says he bought for $750. Seconds later, we are inside the big stadium, and smiling.

Inside, there was no talk of Altamont, or "Gimme Shelter," or the night Kevin White sprung the Stones from a Rhode Island jail. No, the Stones would be the geriatric remedy that would bring solace to this crowd, and transport them back to an era when anything seemed possible, and when things like obesity, addiction, disease, and just plain bad luck happened to old people.

A few aging hipsters approach Aaron and ask him what he's listening to these days on his iPod. A couple insists that he pose with them in a photograph. They tell him he's about to see the greatest rock group ever, and that one day he'll tell his kids about it.

Deep down, I also know they want to tell him that their generation wasn't all about drugs and rock 'n' roll; that American society changed in the '60s and '70s, and civil rights were advanced. More than anything, I think they want to impart to my son that their culture mattered.

We reach our seats, just 19 rows from the stage, and soon Mick Jagger is telling us to "Paint it Black." Aaron eats a pretzel and photographs Jagger and Keith Richards. We stand and rock to the 21 songs that include "Brown Sugar," "Sympathy for the Devil," and "(I Can't Get No) Satisfaction."

Like everyone else, Aaron sings along with "Satisfaction." I take note that an 11-year-old is singing a song that was a Number 1 hit in 1965.

When the show is over I await Aaron's review. He thinks for a moment, and says, "I liked everything." We regroup with our friends and pile into the car, and a minute later my son is asleep.

October 1, 2006
The Boston Globe

Moving Day

It was supposed to be easy and unemotional. A routine transaction. Just like an e-mail, or electronic bank transfer or a drive to the coffee shop.

After almost 15 years, we sold our house and were downscaling to an apartment a couple of towns away. The move had been in the works for a while. Our son had been pleading to move to Marblehead for years, and had never embraced the spirit of city living we had sought out when we chose our home by the ocean in Lynn.

In 1994 we knew nothing about owning a house. Devorah and I had lived in and around Boston for over 20 years and had always rented. But she was pregnant and our apartment had three floors and too many stairs. And so we looked at a few dozen homes in search of a place where we could start a family. After a couple of months we still hadn't found the right house and were resigned to staying in our apartment.

And then, a close friend called and mentioned that his next-door neighbor was selling a ranch house. "It's got ocean views," Fred told me.

A few hours later we pulled up to the brick house and turned around and stared at the Atlantic. After the realtor opened the door, Devorah set foot in the hallway and looked at the sunken living room, pink marble fireplace, and large living room. She began to cry. "We're moving here," she announced.

Two months later we did.

That winter was particularly cold, and by late January, 1995 it was frigid. My wife, who is a chiropractor, had decided that she would have our child at home and to heck with a hospital birth. She assured me that a couple of midwives — not even nurse midwives — could handle the delivery and all I would have to do was just be there for moral support.

As someone who really does faint at the sight of a lot of blood, this decision brought about great anguish. But before I could talk her into a new-aged styled hospital birth, she woke at midnight one Sunday and was convinced she was having contractions. I ran to the kitchen and pulled out a big book on pregnancy. I flipped open the book and the first page I saw was a heading "Signs of Labor." I raced back in the room, and informed Devorah that she was going to have the baby soon.

How ironic that a person who knows nothing about science can become an attending physician at his son's birth. It occurred in our bedroom at 3:33 p.m. that day.

Until that house, I had taken most of my living arrangements for granted. Never before had I depended on a dwelling to provide certain necessities — such as heat, and later that summer during a brutal stretch of humidity, air conditioning.

About a year after Aaron's birth I realized how perfectly the house suited us. A large living room and dining room with ocean views, two bedrooms with even better views of the Atlantic and then a master bedroom that was so quiet you'd never know you lived in a city with more than 90,000 people.

All homeowners quickly learn that each house has its own personality. This house exuded ease and sturdiness. Its large rooms lent a focused and uncluttered look; its impressively huge heater and air conditioner worked seamlessly when called upon; its windows were sometimes hard to open and didn't quite close all the way.

Sometimes you move so many times that lifecycle events occur in a string of places, and lack a sense of continuity. Now, as we leave, we realize how lucky we were to stay in one place so long. Yes, the house represented a certain stability. But, inside our house we became a family and shared all of the intimate milestones together. Besides coming into the world in our bedroom, Aaron's first steps were in our living room; I learned of my mother's death over the telephone in my bedroom; Devorah healed many people in her home office.

Our footsteps echo as we walk through the empty house. We are now a sentimental middle-aged couple, and find ourselves politely thanking each room. Having given away my record collection, I grab my last LP, Sgt. Pepper's Lonely Hearts Club Band, and walk out the front door. We each take our own cars and drive to the new apartment. In the back seat, Aaron's first nightlight with a built in wind-up music box plays a note and stops, and begins again.

The music is "Twinkle, Twinkle Little Star."

July 12, 2009
The Boston Globe

The Rooming House

I believed it when my father used to say that the rooming house would kill him. What he really meant to say was that all of the aggravation that came from the people who lived at 8 Rogers Avenue would kill him. "If I had all of the tea in China, I wouldn't have owned that place another minute," he told me a few years before his death.

It had started out as a simple investment. On Nov. 28, 1961 — nine years and one day after they married — my parents, Sam and Ruby Rosenberg, purchased a rambling, three-story, 16-unit rooming house in the heart of downtown Lynn, Massachusetts for $14,000. Its grim, gray clapboard exterior, with austere cornices and sad, warped mansard roof, matched the cheerless nearby streets. One hundred years earlier, the city had been a center of shoe manufacturing, and thousands of Irish and Eastern European immigrants headed to Lynn to work as unskilled laborers. By the time the rooming house was constructed in 1910, it was just one of dozens of makeshift inns that served employees of the downtown factories.

My parents were the building's seventh owners. They saw real estate as an honest, American business practice and believed that buying and selling property would ultimately bring security, and possibly wealth. Both had known abject poverty. My dad had left Lithuania with his family as a child in 1924 and had grown up with an alcoholic father and a blind mother. My mother's father worked, but still they had gone hungry often, and nearly every year — after coming up short on a month's rent — they moved to somber two-room apartments.

The rooming house or Rogers Ave (in generous moments my father expanded the name to Rogers Avenue), was their eighth real estate venture. By the time they signed the papers and purchased it from an elderly widow, Mildred Glover, they had made more than $25,000 in their fledgling new field, and also owned a home. "At the time, it seemed almost too good to be true," my father explained one day when he wasn't too upset to talk about the building.

For most of the 1960s, the rooming house was run by Mrs. Gleason, an even-tempered, streetwise widow who had lived there for more than 20 years. In exchange for free room and a $5-a-week stipend, Mrs. Gleason assumed most of the responsibility for the house's day-to-day management. During her tenure, there was little vacancy and she hand-picked most of the residents. Many were widows, others were retired factory workers. Several were gainfully employed men who had been put out on the street by their wives and were hoping for another chance. Just a few were alcoholics. Rooms were $12 per week, and tenants were required to stay at least one month. The units were simply adorned. The walls were beige, and rooms were assigned a twin bed, a drab dresser and a hot plate. Tenants were also given fresh linens, and shared a bathroom at the end of each floor.

Each week, my mother would visit Rogers Ave to collect the rent. "I remember mom used to schlep us to the place," my sister Phyllis told me recently. She also recalls Mrs. Gleason as an unfailingly polite employee, who wore a hearing aid. I remember that she was a kind woman who requested that we stay out of the hallways in order to give guests privacy.

Still, I pranced throughout the building stealing glances of mustached women and men who stank of what I thought was foul-smelling perfume. I did not dare make eye contact with them and sensed that their lives were too complicated for children to understand.

One morning in the spring of 1967, Mrs. Gleason died of a heart attack in her first floor room. After my parents help bury their manager, they set out to hire someone of the same ilk — an upstanding retiree who could keep order and collect the rent.

Until Mrs. Gleason's passing, my parents had little day-to-day involvement with the building. It had proved to be an important source of income, with each weekly $12 room check going toward the mortgage and paying for our family groceries. My father made a modest income owning a deli in nearby Chelsea, but it was not enough to cover all of the bills; my mother sold real estate and played in high stakes poker games. At the end of each month, it was the rooming house revenue that put them in the black.

John was the first manager to succeed Mrs. Gleason and he convinced my parents that running a rooming house would be easy compared to fighting the Germans at Normandy on D-Day. He had been a tenant on the third floor for a month and mentioned to Mrs. Gleason that he was a disabled veteran with a pension. During his interview he showed his wartime medals to my father, and also pointed to his prized 1958 red Packard.

During the first week on the job, he hired a 12-year-old boy to work on the weekend to help clean out the basement. Days later, John called one night from the Lynn Police Station. "It's a trumped up charge," he told my father, who learned at the station that John had been arrested and charged with raping the boy. John needed $300 for bail but my father didn't believe his story. Finally, John convinced my father to give him the money in exchange for the Packard.

John skipped bail and left his medals in the room. While the Packard was immaculate, it had engine problems and could not start. My dad took $50 from a junkyard and tried to forget about John and the car.

For the next two years, my parents managed the building themselves and watched as the old-time spinsters and cheating husbands died off. Still, they seemed satisfied with filling the place with alcoholics and manic depressives. "They're people, too," my mother often said.

In the social circles that divorced men, drunks, petty thieves, and tramps ran in, Rogers Ave had developed a reputation as a four-star flophouse.

In 1969, my parents decided that the building could use two managers. A new breed of tenants had arrived. They were drug users, house thieves, and pickpockets. To stem the tide, George and Melinda were hired. They were a couple in their late fifties who had met in the building and promised a return to the days when just drunks and depressed people rented rooms.

By then, my parents talked a lot about selling Rogers Ave. My mother had become pregnant and given birth to my sister Sheri in 1968. I rarely saw her — most nights she played poker, and mornings she either slept or went off to show properties, leaving the child-raising to my grandmother.

During the next year, my father visited Rogers Ave several times a week. It had become increasingly difficult to find rent-paying tenants, and the people who took rooms often became unruly. One time, my father was called by a woman who claimed she had been beaten by her boyfriend. When my father arrived, the man tried to strangle him. Another time, a tenant instructed his German shepherd to attack and my father ended up breaking a chair over the dog's head.

George and Melinda were pasty-faced, barrel-chested drunks who relished the opportunity to get into management. They moved from the high-ceilinged, isolated third floor down to the ground level. Melinda took over Mrs. Gleason's room and George accepted the room on the opposite side of the hall. They swore they would put out the word among their friends in the close-knit rooming house community that old-timers were welcome.

Shortly after they took over, I sensed something was wrong. I was supposed to go to a baseball practice but my mother said there was no time to drop me off. In the middle of the afternoon, we hurried to Rogers Ave and found the couple in George's room sitting on wooden chairs talking and drinking. My mother wanted the rent money but the couple seemed confused. "Where is the money?" my mother patiently asked.

George had a puzzled look on his face and finally spoke.

"That, I do not know," he told her.

My mother left the room and immediately started knocking on doors. Some tenants handed her cash, others launched into sob stories.

I was intrigued by George's response. Steady in his chair, cradling

a juice glass filled with whiskey he recited the words with a lyrical inflection that suggested a background in drama. Melinda nodded earnestly. I knew then that they would be living somewhere else in another week or two, but I was curious about their backgrounds.

Melinda said she had come from an old Lynn family, and had a big house nearby that was being renovated. George had worked in a shoe factory and said he had moved to Lynn after the war.

I wanted more specifics. "Which war, the first or second?" I asked. He paused and his answer surprised me.

"That, I do not know," he said with a crooked smile.

I asked him a few more questions — about work, family, the rooming house — and his response was always the same. After he'd answer, he would take a sip of whiskey and stare at the wall. He had a cave of brown teeth and gums and rubbed his belly as he listened to my questions.

Melinda seemed on edge and moved closer to the slender whiskey bottle. She was a former cleaning lady who wore her black greasy hair in a pony-tail, and had just a couple of badly stained top and bottom teeth. She could hear my mother in the hallway, and every few minutes yelled out compliments like, "You're too good to me, Ruby."

On our ride home, I asked my mother what she thought about George's phrase. When she didn't answer I started to imitate his low voice, and said aloud, "That, I do not know."

As I sat in the front seat of the station wagon imitating George, she was silent for a while. I took this as a bad sign since she also was amused by the rooming house crew. I expected a lecture, or a reminder that money didn't grow on trees. Perhaps it would come in the form of a story that served as an emotional default when she felt too much pressure. It was one she carried around with her since she was 18 and considered the root of her underachievement. It was one that she told in tears that had few facts and barely made sense to a suburban kid like me: she was 18, a math whiz, offered a college scholarship to Bentley and forced by her parents to decline the award and go to work in order to help pay their rent. To repeatedly hear the story seemed like a punishment. It got to a point where I started to believe all parties were wrong: my grandparents, my mother, and even the college. The single lesson I learned was that regret is easily passed down to a younger generation, who can wallow in a relative's sorrow without using it as a motivational tool.

At that moment, the only thing I was motivated to do was to go back to George and Melinda and ask more questions since I was actually enjoying my visits to the rooming house. To a suburban kid, Rogers Ave was a kind of theater and interaction with a segment of society that the middle class had come to avoid. There were no drunks, vagrants or thieves in our placid neighborhood. On our circle, there were kids on shiny, fast bikes, mothers who attended PTA meetings, and fathers who came home at 5 o'clock, and were handed a drink and the evening paper by their wives.

I was bored by my daily routine and wanted to do more than study after school and ride bikes. I had stumbled into an adult world that I didn't know existed and I wanted to learn more. Besides being sad, poor and sometimes hungry the tenants didn't seem like bad people. Some had even earned college degrees and had once lived in towns like mine. While I couldn't articulate it then, I realized that they were not horrible nor totally benevolent souls. They were ordinary people who did good and bad and stood out because they were poor.

After George and Melinda packed their bags, my parents understood that the old days of mannerly alcoholics and quiet spinsters were gone for good. By 1970, a whole new class of rooming house lodgers had developed; nearly all had served time in prison. They were heroin dealers and addicts who regularly stole cars, TV sets, jewelry, fur coats and anything that could be hawked for dope. My parents did not fight the rising tide, deciding instead to vest the management of the rooming house to seasoned criminals. They knew that much of the rent would never be collected, but some money was better than none. They also understood that there was almost no chance of selling the building since few people would buy a flophouse populated by thieves and addicts.

Mr. Hartigan was the first manager during the drug reign. He was a fast talking, bald-headed, moody man in his early thirties. "I'll get this place in order, Ruby," he told my mother one summer day. "You have nothing to worry about."

As Hartigan pushed a broom down the hallway of the first floor, my mother whispered into my ear. "Once someone says you have nothing to worry about, you should run," she told me.

Hartigan lasted about six months and during that time, the rooming house was about half-occupied. Once, when I volunteered to help clean out the basement apartment he paid me $5. That day, he bought me a hamburger at a dirty luncheonette around the corner. When "Hey Jude" came on the radio, he grew animated and instructed me to listen to the lyrics. I knew the song well. It had been on the radio already for two years.

"OK, this is the most important part of the song," he said. As the counterman cooked my greasy hamburger in the cramped restaurant, I sat at the table and wondered what all the fuss was about. Meanwhile, I heard Paul McCartney sing on the crackly speakers:

> "Hey Jude, don't be afraid.
> You were made to go out and get her.
> The minute you let her under your skin,
> Then you begin to make it better."

"That's it. That's it right there. Do you know what they're singing about?" he asked.

"Not being afraid," I answered.

"Well, not exactly," Hartigan said. His face had turned red; he was sweating and excited and I suddenly felt uncomfortable. "The song is about heroin. They're telling the world about how great heroin is. When they sing, 'The minute you let her under your skin, then you begin to make it better,' it's about shooting up."

He had an elbow on the table and flexed it back and forth as he spoke. I didn't know anything about heroin but tried to be cool. I took a couple of bites of the burger and made up a story about having to study for a test and waved goodbye. I got on a bus, and headed home shaking.

I never told my parents about Hartigan's interpretation of "Hey Jude" and hoped that he would find another line of management. One night he took off with the week's rent receipts and my parents never talked about him again. They did not realize that their next manager, Donald Conzano, would make Hartigan look like a bar mitzvah boy.

Donald "Donny" Conzano was a career thief and strongman who made no secret of his occupation. His presence was disturbing — scars ran up and down his cheeks and when he spoke his sentences leapt out like garbled growls. My parents weren't aware that he was one of the most dangerous criminals in the city. He had rented a room with a swagger and appealed to my parents' soft side when he mentioned that he had a Jewish mother. Surely, my parents decided, a Jewish neshama or soul could help in this situation.

After Donny set up shop, the Lynn police began to call our house every week. The place filled with junkies and whores, and it became a one-stop center where you could buy drugs, stolen merchandise or sex at all hours of the day. At first, my parents tried to convince Donny to leave quietly. He gave them a fraction of the rent he collected, and started sending over items that he deemed the equivalent of rent money — such as a beaver coat, a guitar amplifier, a gold ring, and over 100 boxes of pantyhose still sealed in original plastic.

"I wore that beaver coat to a Thanksgiving football game," my sister Phyllis said recently after I asked her about Donny. While I would brighten up just at the mention of the rooming house, Phyllis stayed as far away from the place as she could. She was interested in dating and applying to colleges while I was eager to eavesdrop on as many wise guy conversations as I could.

During Donny's management, my mother seemed even more distraught than her usual nervous state, and my parents — who fought regularly about money, my mother's obesity, my father's low-paying job and nearly every thing else they were charged with making a decision about — started to argue daily about the rooming house. At times, I expected my mother to have a nervous breakdown. As for my father, he expected to simply die from all the aggravation. "That place is going to kill us, Ruby. We have to get rid of it," my father would yell.

For a while, he stopped going to Rogers Ave and left all of the maintenance to my mother. One day, when she had little money to buy groceries, my mother confided that she had not received rent in more than a month from Donny.

I suggested we sell Donny's pantyhose door to door. I quickly changed into my Boy Scout uniform and loaded the merchandise into the car. I was a scout in good standing and knew a lot of people in the neighborhood. Surely, they would contribute to a good cause. My mother played along with my plan: we would drive house to house as I presented homeowners with an opportunity to buy discounted pantyhose. What I hadn't realized was all of the hose was plus sizes, much too large for most women. After visiting 10 houses, I sold only two pairs and seemed discouraged. My mother smiled, shook her head and gave me a big hug. "Gedilla," or my joy, she said in Yiddish. "It's going to be OK." We made enough from the sales to purchase two hamburgers at McDonalds.

By then, I wanted them to sell Rogers Ave. I had seen enough rough characters and feared for our safety. Still, my mother was optimistic and felt the neighborhood would turn around — a district court had been built nearby and a Navy recruiter had inquired about renting all of the rooms. None of it panned out and soon after my failed effort to sell the pantyhose, the Lynn police politely informed my parents that the coat, guitar amp and ring had been stolen (curiously, they

did not ask about the pantyhose). No charges would be brought if the merchandise was immediately returned. The items were rounded up and dropped off to Donny, who had made a deal with the police. Somehow, for a while he was able to stay out of jail.

We learned of Donny's arrest in the newspaper. His picture leapt from the front page of the Lynn Item, and the report detailed charges of kidnapping, assault and battery, larceny and rape. According to the police, he'd placed a nylon stocking over his head, and had broken into a woman's house. As he was leaving with a bag of jewelry and cash, the homeowner confronted him. She told the police that he tied her up, carried her out to his car and raped her.

My parents seemed relieved and started making plans to sell the building. "It's going to take time, Sammy," my mother told my father. "We have to find the right buyer."

In 1972, a lanky, pony-tailed, bearded man in his twenties rented out the rooming house's basement apartment. Jerry explained to my parents that he was a recovering alcoholic and heroin addict, and was looking for a fresh start. He offered to become the manager.

While he was able to stay away from heroin and alcohol for a short period, he smoked marijuana frequently and on occasion snorted large amounts of cocaine. For six months, the building was quiet. He listened to Elton John and extolled the virtues of meditation. Little revenue was generated but the police were no longer calling our house. Jerry likened my parents to guardian angels, and insisted that my father serve as best man at his wedding. He was the son of a police officer from Long Beach, but was no longer welcome in California. An old motorcycle accident had left him with a limp. Like so many of the managers, he was moody and vacillated between cerebral moments and violent outbursts.

Just before he returned to drinking and shooting heroin, Jerry started doing odd jobs at our house. My father didn't want anyone from Rogers Ave near our house but Jerry owed my mother money. The two times he entered our home things ended badly. After he cleaned the basement during his first visit, my mother brought my father downstairs for an inspection. When he reached a small room where an old desk had stood for years, my father began to panic.

"Where's the desk, Ruby?"

"Oh, Jerry took it away. Doesn't the room look good?"

My father's face grew pale and he found a chair. For years, he explained, he had been saving silver dimes in the desk's bottom drawer. "There must have been 3,000 dimes there," he told my mother. Jerry said he never looked through the desk before he took it away but I once saw it in his apartment.

The other occasion he came to clean was the last time my parents saw him. It was just before Passover and he was vacuuming the house and polishing the modest chandelier that hung in our dining room. That's when my grandmother, a stern woman — then in her late seventies — confronted him about her missing ring. It was gold and it had been in her family for 100 years and if he wanted to stay out of jail, he would hand it back to her and leave, she told him.

Jerry pleaded innocence but my grandmother held firm. Finally, he insisted that he did not have the ring and challenged her to call the police. He was right. After the police arrived he submitted to a body search and they did not find the ring. What he hadn't counted on was a thorough examination of his windbreaker, where the police found a couple of joints. He was promptly arrested, handcuffed and led away. My grandmother watched him leave and several hours later announced that she had found her ring.

A few months after Jerry left, the phone rang at one in the morning and my father was told that the rooming house was on fire. He lit a cigarette and we drove in silence to Rogers Ave. At that moment I prayed that no one would die in the fire; that my parents would never have to go back to the place. When we arrived, the blaze was out and a window was being boarded up. "It was a close call," the fire captain told my father. "You got lucky."

In February of 1973, my parents found a buyer and quickly sold the rooming house. The deal was consummated in 72 hours and had been sealed after my parents agreed to hold part of the mortgage. Helen Cittadino paid $16,982 for the building. After 12 years, my parents had made $2,982 in profit. Two years later, Ms. Cittadino made a final payment of $6,982 toward the mortgage, and my mother and father were overjoyed.

After the sale, there was great relief in the family but slowly, a historical revision of Rogers Ave began to take shape. It was a moneymaker and then it all turned to shit, they'd say. What they refused to admit seemed obvious, even to a teenager like myself: They weren't hardened business people, willing to throw people out on the street and flip the property for new investments. Somewhere along the way they had lost the desire to buy and sell properties. Instead, they had become saddled with a boarding house that seemed to have a will of its own and a desire to teach the same lesson over and over again: bad things happen when bad people live together.

And so, with the rooming house dispatched to some poor soul, it seemed easier for my mother to rectify the whole mess of a decade with the building through a weird nostalgia and benevolence. I thought that the new owner would, perhaps, show up one day at our house demanding a full refund or drop dead one week after asking for a rent check from a tattooed felon who ran teenage girls out of the rooming house basement. But that never occurred, leaving my mother to occasionally drop hints about why she stayed with a losing proposition so long. Eventually, the reason, she said, could be traced to my parents' upbringing. They had been poor; had known people like this all their lives and couldn't turn their back on the needy. When prompted, my mother would rattle off the names of dozens of people she had helped. Those former tenants formed the backbone of a new and gentler narrative. About a year after they sold the rooming house my mother decided that her favorite tenant was a teenage girl who had nursed her newborn in the back room on the first floor.

My last contact with anyone from the building came in 1975, when Jerry spotted me hitchhiking. He was driving a tow truck, and embraced me when I hopped into the cab. He still had his ponytail, and showed me a picture of his baby girl. As he fumbled with the picture he failed to see a red traffic light near the edge of town. The tow truck slammed into a car that had stopped at the light and my head smashed against the windshield. He told me to leave the car. I walked away, dazed with a light concussion. The next day, the Lynn Item reported that a driver of a tow truck had been arrested on charges of reckless driving, and driving without a license. The article also reported that a teenage passenger in the truck was spotted leaving the scene of the accident. I never saw Jerry again.

Up until my father's death in 2001, he rarely talked about the rooming house. But, as real estate prices jumped in the 1980s, my mother began to believe what she suspected all along — that the rooming house had returned large profits to its subsequent owners. My mother died in 2006, and afterwards I checked the records at the Registry of Deeds. She was right: people had made a lot of money on the property since 1973.

According to the records, Ms. Cittadino sold the building in 1981 for $45,000. In 1987, it sold for $225,000, and after the property was foreclosed in 1999, it sold for $175,000.

As I grew older, the long-gone characters from Rogers Ave seemed to fade. I moved on to college, where I took an interest in writing, and working for the school paper. I realized that the interview process in journalism brought an intimacy that I had relished back in the days of the rooming house. If I did not fear felons like Donny or Jerry, then asking tough questions to people in authority — like politicians or police chiefs — would be a breeze. Eventually I landed at the Boston Globe, where I spent years covering the suburban poverty beat.

While at the Globe, I went to Rogers Ave to interview the mother of a gang member. She was in rehab herself, after spending most of the previous decades on heroin and cocaine. The woman lived in a tiny room in a brick building adjacent to the rooming house. After the meeting, I left by the back stairs, opened the side door, and found myself standing at ground level with the building that my parents had worried about for a decade. I took a quick glance at the structure, felt a chill run down my arms and legs, and moved quickly to my car.

Over the last year, I stumbled upon the address while writing a piece about drug addiction and recovery. I learned that one of the area's most successful women's sober houses was located at 8 Rogers Ave. I called Marie, the director of the program, and explained my family's history with the building. She invited me over, and said the women were friendly. "All of them have stories to tell," Marie said.

I had plenty of reasons not to enter or even look at the rooming house again. But the lure of more stories was too strong to resist. What would I learn? Were these the children or even grandchildren of the hustlers and whores who had stiffed my parents and had entertained me with tales of larceny, decades-long benders, and general debauchery?

People return to long-forgotten locations sometimes to confirm that events really occurred. I wanted to see the site that my parents had spent so much time trying to polish into something. They were now dead and could no longer warn me to stay away. Was I also coming back to the building to prove that it hadn't killed all of us? Or, that my presence was a sign that we had survived our tenure as custodians?

While the outside walls boasted newly installed gray vinyl siding, the windows and cornices and roof looked as dark and foreboding as ever. I climbed five wooden steps and stopped in front of the door. Under the number 8, a two-foot-high cutout of Frankenstein's head had been taped — presumably to honor the Halloween holiday. I pressed a circular, rusted doorbell.

A somber-faced woman introduced herself as Marie. "I run this place," she said, and I sensed a no-nonsense lady who knew from demons.

"A little different from the last time you were here, I bet," she said. "I just gotta finish this phone call. Look around. The girls know you're here."

She hurried into her office, the first room on the right. Mrs. Gleason had lived there a half-century before.

I stood in the cramped hallway and recognized the long, brown stairway that led to the second floor. On several occasions I found tenants sleeping off a drunk on those stairs. They were freshly swept and a sense of order that my parents could never quite introduce — no matter whom they hired to run the operation — filled the place.

The room doors, once dirty white and often filled with stained fingerprints of long-lost tenants had been painted purple and a list of house events and reminders were stapled to a bulletin board outside of Marie's office. Next to the door the house rules were displayed prominently. Almost all were prohibitions: No drinking, drugs, smoking, overnight guests, sexual activity, stealing or violence. Guests were allowed during the day but only in common areas, such as the kitchen and living room.

Women giggled in the hallway, and I smelled bacon being fried in the kitchen. It had the feel of a tightly-run sorority house.

George's old digs had been converted into a community room. I pushed open the old purple door and stepped inside, and half expected to see George pouring himself an afternoon cocktail. Four smart brown corduroy couches formed a rectangle. The old brown paneling had been covered with a fresh coat of white paint. Japanese Shoji lamps dotted a few end tables. Next to a framed print of the Golden Gate Bridge, an enthusiastic Oprah spoke from a large screen TV. I sat down on a couch, next to a glass coffee table that held an overflowing bowl of gum, peanut butter cups and mints.

Marie explained that the transitional house allows women to stay for up to two years as long as they remain sober. Drug tests were given three times a week, and women were required to work and attend 12-step meetings. "Six out of seven women stay clean while they're here. Our model is if they relapse they have to go," she said with little emotion.

———————————

A woman in her mid-twenties moves slowly into the room. She wears a black shirt, black pants, and a small black apron. She breaks into a hesitant, tiny smile.

"I'm Cassandra," says the attractive, pockmarked woman with bright blue eyes, straight brown hair and wide hips.

She had heard that I had some connection with the house a long time ago. I briefly describe my parents, and some of the old tenants like George. She sits a few feet away from the spot where I had first heard George utter the phrase "That, I do not know."

"George would have loved living here now, I bet," she says.

I ask her why she likes it so much.

Her face grows serious, and she digs into her pocket and fishes out a key. "See this? I never had a key of my own before I came here. This place is my home. I've never been around so many loving and supportive people in my life," she tells me.

She had grown up in Medford, a city outside of Boston — now best known as the home of Tufts University and the birthplace of former New York Mayor Michael Bloomberg. Her father was a Hell's Angel who never married her mother and had seven children with seven different women.

She had grown up around bikers and until she started attending school she believed that all children had parents who used heroin. "When I was little I would fit in and feel comfortable at a bar, but I didn't fit in the classroom," she says. By 13 she was sniffing heroin; at

16 was shooting it several times a day. The money for the drugs came from stripping and prostitution. Now 24, she explains that she has been sober for 18 months.

Cassandra looks at her watch and hurries away. She needs to head out to her waitressing shift.

I climb the old stairway where thousands of guests carried modest bags and suitcases upon their arrival and departure. As a child I couldn't have possibly understood what this drab, steep walkway must have meant to some of the residents. I had been charmed by their colorful personalities but tended to lump the souls together as part of a collective underclass. If I had met them now, I would have understood that each person — like Cassandra — needed structure, and a reasoning to break their addictions.

I walk into a vacant room, sit on the bed and stare at the beige walls. The building is silent. This is the type of quiet that my parents always hoped for here — tenants off to work, others minding their own business. All those years ago, they wanted the guests to be responsible so they could find a way to ascend from their misery. While the stories hadn't changed over the decades there were now rules and consequences. For a long time, shelter had been an afterthought for paying guests and freeloaders. Now, obtaining a room was a privilege that had to be earned; a successful stay meant that they would be held accountable for their actions.

I walk downstairs, pass an educational poster about sexually transmitted diseases and reach the end of the hall. A door is open. It's a familiar room: Donny Conzano once stocked stolen merchandise here.

The room is now a kitchen where a clean white stove and fridge stand side by side, next to new brown cabinets; a granite counter supports a coffee maker and toaster. A steady breeze gently lifts white lace curtains. A woman with long black curly hair and blue eyes sits behind a brown wooden kitchen table painting her fingernails.

"Hi! We've been waiting for you," Leanne says, patting a chair and gesturing for me to sit.

I blush and wonder why I'm considered a big deal to the women. Perhaps, it's because I'm interested in their lives?

Leanne is 5 foot 4, 34, and looks a lot like the suburban mothers you see on gym treadmills and behind the wheel of mini-vans in front of elementary schools. That impression is washed away within a minute after she describes decades of cocaine and heroin abuse — drugs that she says she cared about more than her children.

"My son was born blind because I smoked crack almost all of my pregnancy," she tells me.

The boy is now 17, and has been with her sister-in-law since he was a few months old. He has never formally been introduced to his mother. "He met me once but he thinks I'm a friend of his aunt," she says.

She insists that I see a picture of her son and leads me across the hall. She now lives in the same room that my mother had allowed the

teenage girl with the baby to stay. She points to a photo of a young, happy girl with brown hair and blue eyes on her dresser.

Leanne stands in front of an oval mirror that hangs on a white stucco wall just above a tired gray radiator. A white, brown and pink striped comforter covers her bed, and brown and red teddy bears rest below her pillows. She says she wonders about all of the people who lived in her room over the years. She often thinks of the last woman who resided in the room.

"There was this girl who lived here a couple of years ago. I never met her but her name was Keisha and a lot of people loved her. She died of an overdose. I just feel her in this room. I think her spirit comes back here," she tells me.

I allow for a last glimpse of the front hallway. If spirits exist then they must be floating in these hallways, whispering old stories, making plans and checking in on the new residents, I can only conclude. Perhaps they have found some calm and peace. Perhaps my parents have been here, too, touring the newly painted rooms, rooting on the women who have so much to reclaim. And, perhaps — as I stand in a place where time seems suspended — I have been summoned here as some kind of witness, to observe that change can occur when there is respect and love.

And, I wonder, is the structure not some kind of semipermeable membrane, allowing molecules and ions entry? The building does not talk or judge. It accepts all who enter and provides shelter when asked. It flourishes when given attention and grows sadder when it falls into disrepair. And it does not remember history. Because if it did, it would fill its rooms and hallways with so many tears that it would float away.

January, 2012
Previously unpublished

CHAPTER 6

Sports

Today, I Am Everyman

I am pretending to run on a field filled with football players one-third of my age. I am supposed to be doing a lap or two, but after 20 yards my steps slow and before long I stand in the middle of the field and groan.

Logic says that I don't belong here. Watching a game on a large-screen TV might be more age-appropriate. But if you watch football long enough, you can be pulled into a dream that suggests a man can rise up from a couch, prance onto a field, and even quarterback a team.

At fifty-something, I am everyman.

On the cushy synthetic turf at Manning Field in Lynn, age is suspended for at least a few hours. Like everyone else, my focus is on getting ahold of the football. As I shuttle from drill to drill, I realize I am walking in a circle. I wear a black helmet, white football pants that don't quite fit, and a jersey sporting the number 7. The movement of the players, the tackling, the shrill of the coaches' whistles all form a mantra that feels right.

The longing to get up close and become part of an art or sport is not an original idea. George Plimpton, the co-founder and editor of The Paris Review, had also created the genre of participatory journalism: sparring in the ring with boxing great Archie Moore; standing on a pitcher's mound where he somehow retired Willie Mays on a pop-up, and among other adventures, spending a pre-season as a last-string quarterback for the Detroit Lions.

Who couldn't relate to Plimpton's dalliances with greatness? Also, I had yet to come to terms with a failed tryout for my high school team decades earlier. I had planned to show the coaches my kicking skills, but before I had a chance, I had the wind knocked out of me by a beefy lineman and nearly crawled back to the locker room.

The desire to return to the field had resurfaced last summer, after I took a walk with my wife and son and strolled through the same park where I last wore a uniform. We had spotted a Nerf football, threw it around, and my son held it steady before I kicked it through the uprights.

The dream had not died.

And so, after I began working on an article about semipro football, I inquired about playing.

"Sure," said Kevin Donahue, who owns the North Shore Generals, a team of former high school and college players based in Lynn that competes in the New England Football League.

"How about playing quarterback?" I asked. As the words tumbled out of my mouth, I wondered why I had made that choice. My initial conclusion seemed to make sense: I had watched several hundred football games on TV, and figured that might be enough for me to qualify for a set of downs.

As I was envisioning myself barking out signals before taking a snap, that trance was interrupted by the voice on the other line.

"Quarterback? That sounds great," said Donahue.

I purchased a football to prepare for the audition. I began to toss it around in the street with my wife.

"I'm going to quarterback a semipro team during a practice," I told her.

"You're what?" she said, throwing a short wobbly pass that landed on my big toe. "Do you have life insurance?"

Now, I was standing in front of new teammates who had greeted me with handshakes, helmet bumps, and slaps on the shoulder.

Shawn Tortorici, the Generals' red-haired center, ambles over and hands me a football. Tortorici, who is 25 and a barrel-chested recent graduate of Salem State, politely explains how I should call a hike.

"Down, set, hut" always works, he tells me.

After a few hikes, my confidence soars. Soon, it's time for the scrimmage. Germaine Sattiewhite, who once coached for the NFL's Carolina Panthers, calls the offense into the huddle and motions for me to join. On the first play, I'll fake a handoff to a running back and then hand it off to the second back.

I lean into the huddle and growl, "Right-open, Red-22 sting on one."

I'm all business when I reach Tortorici, my center who sports a big tattoo, "In loving memory of Nana and Papa," on his right bicep.

"Ready, set, go!" I yell, fake the handoff to the first back, and stick the ball in the second back's hands. He runs for 7 yards.

For two or three seconds I stand in a state of euphoria. I want to celebrate but there's no time for that. A few players slap my hand and the coach calls for another handoff, this time to the first back.

"Right-open, Red-40 Tiger, on one!" I say, and we all clap and run toward the line. "Ready, set, go," I bark, and hand it off to a halfback who

runs for another 7 yards.

The next three plays go by in a blur. I fake a handoff, keep the ball, and run for the sidelines. A safety closes in on me but stops inches from my shoulders. Before I can thank him for not breaking my neck, he swivels and disappears.

Meanwhile, I've got two more plays. I throw a short pass to a halfback who runs for several yards, and then I pitch the ball to a back who is supposed to throw it to me. I get locked up by a defensive back and the pass falls incomplete.

There is nothing more to be accomplished. I begin a slow walk toward the locker room and ponder my performance. The men were kind; they did not hurt me. Behind me, the players keep on practicing; the coaches' whistles blow; another play is run. I hesitate before I step off the field. I am still ageless, so why hurry?

July 26, 2015
The Boston Globe

A Summer Game

When the first fat raindrop falls from the dark clouds at 10 a.m., I look up and shake my head.

"Not today, please not today," I say, making a silent agreement with the creator. I offer to somehow act appropriate (for an unspecified amount of time) if the rain will hold off.

There should be no rain, because today is reserved for outdoor recreation, for a game that will be meaningful even if, somehow, the results do not fall in my favor. The sport is softball, an odd cousin to the hallowed pastime of baseball. I have long ago forgiven the person that deemed the sport could be played with a zaftig sphere that weighs in at 198 grams, or two whole ounces more than the real thing, the baseball.

It's rare that positive thinking or even prayer negates a forecast of rain. But sometimes machines are wrong, and at 4 p.m., when I gather with a bunch of other writers for the annual game, we don't discuss the sun that's now baking the field that was soaked just a few hours earlier. No one wants to jinx anything.

Over the last 12 months, I've thought about last year's game, specifically one at-bat that continued to linger — long past the fall, into the snowy months and even during the spring. With the game tied in one of the later innings, I slammed the ball high in the air and trotted toward first with a sense of accomplishment. It was — no doubt — in baseball parlance, gone. As I reached first base, however, I noticed a long-haired, bearded man standing patiently in the farthest part of left field and watched the ball drop into his glove.

Since then, there's been a sense of mystery about how the man found his way to that spot deep in left. Had he suspected that I was a slugger? Was he simply an overly cautious outfielder? As for the hit, at-bats always lead to the runner reaching base or being called out. I began to challenge this rule, and lobbied the baseball purist within to make an exception. If a person makes contact with the ball, and sends it to a far-away meadow from where one stands, can't something positive come from it, such as a good feeling?

I also wondered how the bearded man was able to remain focused over the past year. Had the outfielder gone back to that moment on the field and cherished his act of agility, say during a snowstorm, or a down moment at work? Had he realized the importance of his achievement?

Late in this year's game, I stand at the plate again with a runner on third and one out. Jamie, the poets' catcher and an English teacher, smiles and tells me to do it for the team. I relax and swing at an easy lob right over the plate. I watch the white, spinning mass shoot out like a rope toward center field.

I round first base, head toward second, and notice that no one's caught up to the ball. As I cross second, my jog turns into a full gallop. As I near third, I see the ball thrown toward the infield, and continue. I am smiling, sweating, and seeking absolution. Nothing seems more important than going home. The ball never reaches the catcher, and I catch my breath as I cross home plate.

The game lasts 1 hour and 23 minutes, and prose beats the poets 19-3. Players sip beer and pose for team photos. When I leave the field, a raindrop splashes on my forehead.

August 15, 2010
The Boston Globe

Meeting the Monster

A couple of summers ago I heard that the North Shore Spirit, Lynn's minor league baseball team, had planned an instructional session for kids.

"How would you like to meet the Monster?" I asked my son, Aaron, who was 8 at the time.

"What Monster?" he replied.

The Monster was a real life person, Dick Radatz, who once played for the Red Sox, and struck out Mickey Mantle 47 times, I answered, repeating the legend that grew throughout New England over the years. (Only recently did the truth surface that Mantle struck out 12 times in 16 official at-bats against Radatz.)

"The guy who was one of the best relief pitchers to ever play for the Red Sox. He's the pitching coach for the Spirit," I said.

On the drive over to the park, I dutifully recited Dick "the Monster" Radatz's remarkable statistics from 1962 to 1965. During that time, Radatz was virtually unhittable while playing for very bad Red Sox teams. Over those four years, he pitched in 270 games, threw 538 innings, won 49, saved 100, struck out 608 batters, and posted a combined 2.60 earned run average.

I knew the numbers because of my father. For him, baseball was not just a game to be played or watched, it was worthy of a lifetime of study. His bible was the baseball encyclopedia, which he read nearly every day for the last 25 years of his life. Secrets to greatness could be found in a player's statistics, he told me. Radatz had a chance to be the greatest reliever if only he had been used more sparingly, my dad insisted. "If Radatz had been brought in to pitch one inning a game like today's relievers, then he would have made the Hall of Fame," he used to say.

The stress and toll of all those innings caught up to Radatz in 1966, and that year, he was sent to Cleveland. There would be other stops with the Cubs, Tigers and Expos, but by 1970 the Monster was through.

Old Fraser Field was hot the day Aaron ran out to the outfield. Rich Gedman, a former Red Sox catcher and current Spirit coach, was showing the kids how to catch a ball. I whispered to Aaron that Gedman had caught Roger Clemens and also played in the World Series. Then there was a look of awe that appeared on my son's face; the kind that is beautiful and unpredictable, and sometimes occurs when miracles happen. He moved closer to Gedman, soaking up every word the baseball instructor was saying. When Gedman was finished, Aaron asked me if he had caught Pedro, too.

"No, but he hit a home run in the 1986 World Series," I said.

There was more fielding, and advice from players on how to hit, and then the session was over. Gedman and Spirit manager John Kennedy happily signed autographs until it was time for the kids to go home.

But Aaron wanted one last autograph. "What about the Monster?" he asked.

Right. The Monster. We couldn't leave without at least trying to get his signature.

We found him in the corner of the outfield, sitting alone on a chair in a shaded section of the bullpen. The sun was baking, and Radatz held his hand on his forehead. At first glance, it appeared he had dozed off. He was awake though, and lifted his head and smiled.

Aaron presented him with a ball to sign, and told Radatz that he also planned to become a pitcher. The old reliever then returned the ball to my son's right hand, and formed Aaron's index and middle finger around the seams of the ball. "You have to grip the ball right to throw," he said.

Aaron wanted to know about him and Mickey Mantle.

"Yeah, I don't know what it was about Mantle," he told Aaron. "He got some hits off of me though."

He shrugged when I asked if he would have had a longer career if he had pitched just an inning or two at a time. I sensed that it was not a new question, and that he had made peace with his managers' decisions a long time ago.

It was time to go, and he politely shook our hands, and wished us well.

When I told Aaron that Radatz had died in a fall last week at the age of 67, he was silent for a while, and shed a few tears. Death even comes to great ballplayers, we realized. Next month, during our annual pilgrimage to the Hall of Fame in Cooperstown, we're going to find a way to honor the Monster. Aaron's going to bring his picture; I'll have his stats in my pocket.

March 24, 2005
The Boston Globe

High Henry, and
Celtic Pride

With the NBA season set to begin next week, I've been thinking about how the game has gone from setting plays, playing defense, and grabbing rebounds to a 48-minute race.

Three-point shots, speed, and one-on-one drives now dominate each contest.

As sports evolve, change is inevitable, but I've wondered what an old-time Celtic — one who played on a team with future NBA coaches, general managers, and Hall of Famers — thought of the current game. I also wanted to know if Celtic pride, a mantra that sums up the intangibles that result from hard work, still existed.

On a recent afternoon, I met Hank Finkel and his wife, Kathy, at Brothers Deli in Danvers, where they are regulars. The two look like other older couples in the deli, until the 7-foot former center stands up.

"I'll probably take this home and have it later," he said, putting his fork down while staring at the turkey dinner. His big hands — the same hands that pushed away NBA giants like Wilt Chamberlain, Kareem Abdul-Jabbar, and Willis Reed — rested a few inches away from the dish, dwarfing much of the table.

Finkel, now 73, has lived in the same house in Lynnfield for the last 42 years. He retired last December after running an office business for 32 years.

As for basketball, he's hardly nostalgic about his NBA tenure: He hasn't played the game in 38 years, and the hoop he put up for his grandchildren in front of his house was crushed by a plow 10 years ago. Meanwhile, he's had hip replacement surgery, and these days suffers from numbness in his left leg.

He still watches parts of some games but doesn't find them very enjoyable. "There's no defense. We used to talk all of the time and told people on defense where to move. On offense we had plays to run — very few teams now have plays to run," he told me.

Finkel's life has always been about working hard and taking advantage of opportunities. After his father died when he was in high school, he attended St. Peter's College before dropping out and working for a year as a sandblaster in a Jersey City shipyard.

He might have made a career out of it if not for a chance meeting with a college recruiter, who spotted him in front of a Dairy Queen. He went on to star at the University of Dayton, was drafted by the Lakers, played for San Diego, and was traded to the Celtics in 1969, where he stayed until 1975.

After a rough start when fans expected him to replace Bill Russell — "the fans were merciless that first year," he said — he became a folk hero in a city that has always loved the underdog. Gangly, sometimes awkward, and admittedly slow — "I could never jump or rebound" — he found a bit role among hoop royalty that included Hall of Famers John Havlicek, Jo Jo White, Dave Cowens, coach Tom Heinsohn, and Finkel's basketball mentor, general manager Red Auerbach.

"What I did well was setting picks and blocking out. I figured it out because that's what I had to do to keep this job," said Finkel, who won a championship with the Celtics in 1974.

Although he hasn't been to a game in years, Finkel still considers himself a Celtic, and he says the lessons he learned in Boston helped him stay in business after he retired.

As for Celtic pride, Finkel says it's no myth and it continues to this day: "It had to do with business; it had to do with family. You give it 110 percent no matter what you do in life, especially bringing up children these days and your work ethic."

He said there is no succinct definition of Celtic pride because it encompasses so many attributes to deal with life. "It's an intangible; you can't define it," he said. "It's something that you want to do. It's the effort that you put forward."

Kathy said Celtic pride continued in the Finkel family long after he left the Celtics. "About 14 years ago, my doctors discovered breast cancer. Hank decided that he would handle my care and proceeded to take me to 42 different appointments. I counted them on a calendar because I was losing confidence to carry on. He just hung in there and said, 'What time? Where?' "

When Finkel stood he was, once again, the tallest person in the room. He clutched his leftovers and made his way to the exit. A man came over and shook his hand and Hank didn't have to say anything. The man had met a Celtic, and he felt the pride.

October 18, 2015
The Boston Globe

Champions of the Greasy Pole

T he 52-foot telephone pole that sticks out from a platform 200 feet from the shore of Pavilion Beach can be a blur to passing motorists, but for locals, the wooden beam is a cultural Mecca where honor, tradition, and emotion merge in a passionate contest three days a year.

Residents have welcomed the five-day festival of St. Peter's Fiesta for 76 years. The celebration kicks off this week, and will culminate Sunday with the procession of St. Peter through the streets of Gloucester and the annual blessing of the fleet.

But on Pavilion Beach, on Friday, Saturday, and Sunday, up to 10,000 people will line the boulevard and observe a unique Gloucester ritual — the greasy pole contest. All eyes will focus on the pole, which will be covered with 60 gallons of grease. On these days, dozens of men will huddle on the platform, and then, one by one, begin walking along the pole toward a 5-foot red flag nailed into the end. Some run, others sidestep, looking for balance in the six inches of grease that coats the pole. Nearly all fall into the water, and most are happy to escape breaking a nose or a rib if they strike the pole, until one lucky soul traverses the goo, grabs the flag, and is declared the winner.

"That's the whole pride of the fiesta — winning that. That's top honors," said Salvi Benson, the all-time greasy pole champion who has won 11 or 15 contests, depending on who you talk to.

Benson, who is 54 and a welder, is part of a cadre of pole walkers who speak about the contest with reverence, awe, and joy. Past winners refer to one another as "champ," and are celebrities — at least for a month or two — wherever they go in town.

"The first time is always the greatest," stated Anthony Saputo, who "runs" the pole, and decides who will walk or will not. Saputo, who is the only intercontinental winner — he won in 1983 in Terrasini, Italy, and in 1988 in Gloucester — has greasy pole-walking in his blood. His 90-year-old grandfather, Gasper Orlando, was the "Salvi Benson of Terrasini," winning 17 contests in Sicily, he said.

According to Saputo, walkers must have connections to get on the pole. To be eligible you must be the son or daughter of a fisherman, or be married into an Italian family. "If you're Joe Shmo, forget it," said the 36-year-old glazier.

Saputo, Benson, and Anthony "Matza" Giambanco have worked together for the last several months to coordinate the three-day event. Fridays are reserved for newcomers, Saturdays are for more experienced walkers, and Sundays are for past champions. Saputo fields phone calls from applicants, and on occasion will conduct informal interviews to size up potential walkers; Benson applies the 60 gallons of biodegradable grease on the morning of each contest; and Giambanco — known as "the sheriff" — runs the platform and makes sure all the rules are followed.

"The rules are simple," said Giambanco, a 46-year-old painter who has grabbed the flag five times. "You watch the guy in front of you and if he falls in and gets hurt you have to dive in after him. Also, you can't win it the first time you walk out on the pole. That's for practice."

With the exception of World War II and bad weather, they have walked the pole since 1931, when Sicilian immigrant fishermen stuck out a greased wooden pole over the old Birds Eye plant dock, and included it in the fiesta celebration. "I was there on the boardwalk watching and I said, 'What the hell, I'll try it,' " recalled Nat Misuraca, 85, who won the first contest, and repeated in 1935. "They all clapped to see a 14-year-old kid try it, and I ran and I got the flag."

After World War II, a new pole and a wooden platform was deemed necessary, and the structure was erected off the shore of Pavilion Beach.

Sebastian "Busty" Palazzola took custody of the care of the pole in 1949, greasing it, and creating the coveted red flag. Along with the late Sammy Balbo, Palazzola threw a new wrinkle into the contest — the two were the first contestants to dress up in costume. Dressed as clowns they were escorted to the beach by a marching band. "A couple of times they put us in a cage like two geeks, and they carried us down," said the retired fisherman, who is now 75. "And then there were kids dressed up like Batman and Robin, the Penguin, the Joker [or] the Riddler. I tell you them guys looked good. And they had the kids down there all over them."

After the old platform and pole blew down in the Blizzard of '78, Arizona Linquata helped oversee the construction of the current structure. "They got a barge and they stationed the pole straight out and they walked the pole in '78," said Linquata, "and they built a new stand in '79."

Gloucester attorney Wesley Prevost, who shimmied out on the pole as a teenager but never officially entered the contest, likened the champions to Super Bowl or World Series winners. "It's probably one of the earliest forms of an extreme sport. You get that rush of doing something dangerous, and you do it because it's there," he said.

Benson, Saputo, and Giambanco will sit down and have a meal later this week, which, they say, will begin quietly but will probably end in a loud debate about the lore of the pole. On Sunday, the men and other champions will sit down for a meal of Italian sausages, beef cutlets, lobsters, and clams at Giambanco's house, and then visit a number of other homes in the neighborhood to accept a traditional offering of food or drink. "It's a greasy pole family," explained Benson, who is unsure if he will walk the pole this year. "During the day we go house to house. We have our duty and that's it."

On a recent evening the three men gathered to consult and make last minute preparations for the walk. Benson agreed to Giambanco's request that the same artist recreate the greasy pole scene tattooed on his back. The men watched a video from the 1978 contest, and for a moment all agreed that if one lost interest in the pole, they would pass the responsibility of organizing the contest to new blood.

"But I'm going to be out there for 20 years," said Saputo. He then challenged Benson to an impromptu walk. "I've got three barrels of grease in the back of my truck," said Saputo.

"I've got two barrels in the back of my truck," replied Benson.

June 22, 2003
The Boston Globe

Slump Doctor On Call

To find Victor Gell you have to walk through Mike's Gym and negotiate the labyrinth of stairways and passages below Union Street. Past the last row of exercise bikes and Stairmasters the sound of a batted ball can be heard. This is the domain of one of the best-kept baseball secrets on the North Shore.

Inside the narrow, concrete room a dozen kids sit patiently, gripping their bats and squeezing their gloves. Within the net that forms a rectangular batting cage, Gell sits on an inverted plastic bucket, tossing underhand pitches to his students.

"Hitting a baseball is the hardest thing to do," said Gell, who runs the JRG baseball school in Lynn. "I get a tremendous amount of satisfaction teaching the game, and knowing that I'm doing something constructive for the children."

Spanish is the language of choice here, and Gell's classes are a mix of raw rookies and seasoned players. His youngest student, Jansiel Rivera, is 3 and is already hitting line drives. The kids listen as Gell analyzes their swings. After every hit he adds words of encouragement. Sometimes he'll jump up and show a student how to follow through on his extension.

"It's all in the hips," he says time and time again to his students.

Some, like Marcos Garcia, a 17-year-old shortstop from Chelsea, have been coming six days a week for several years to work on the fundamentals of hitting, fielding, and throwing.

"I don't think there's a better instructor than Victor," said Garcia, who plans to enter a baseball academy in his native Dominican Republic later this month. "He has great hitting techniques and teaches us the proper way of throwing and how to turn a double play. He knows the game better than anyone I ever met."

It's not just the city kids who think Gell is one of the best instructors in the business. Over the years he's been a personal hitting coach to several major leaguers. Manny Ramirez, Ivan Rodriguez, Fernando Tatis, David Ortiz, Sandy Alomar Jr., and former Red Sox starters Mo Vaughn, John Valentin, Troy O'Leary, Darren Bragg, Reggie Jefferson, and Darren Lewis have all worked on their hitting with Gell.

Gell has been playing baseball for 50 of his 52 years. He was born in the Dominican Republic and was only 2 when he fashioned a guava branch into a bat and grabbed an old paper bag to catch limes from his friends.

"I played with and without shoes the whole year round. It was a way of life. There was nothing else but baseball," Gell said.

Forty years ago he was considered one of the best shortstops in the Dominican Republic, and at the age of 12 he was already playing for the semi-professional Farmacia Baez team in Santa Domingo. Occasionally, he'd let one of his teacher's sons, Tony Pena, play in a pickup game with his team.

The scouts thought the 5-foot-4-inch shortstop was too short to play in the majors and suggested he become a jockey. Gell took their advice and spent 20 years riding horses, but he never forgot the game that was closest to his heart.

In 1990, he got a call from his old friend, Tony Pena, who had signed as a free agent with the Red Sox. "When Tony came to play for the Red Sox, we reunited and I was his right-hand man here," he said.

Soon Gell was back around the baseball diamond, this time at Fenway Park, casually dispensing tips to Red Sox stars.

The tips eventually turned into private instructional sessions and by 1997, he was the personal hitting instructor for eight Red Sox players.

Gell, who worked as a minor league instructor for the World Series champion Arizona Diamondbacks this spring, recently received a call from Valentin and Vaughn, both of whom now play for the New York Mets, asking him to come to Shea Stadium to help them shake their slumps. Gell hopped on a flight to New York and stood behind Vaughn and Valentin during batting practice, critiquing their swings.

Gell's tutorial seemed to work wonders for Vaughn. The first baseman has slugged five home runs since Gell's trip.

"Nothing was wrong with Mo, he just needed some adjustments," said Gell. "His hips weren't working because he was standing up too straight; there was no extension."

The walls above Gell's desk are decorated with pictures of the hitting coach with Valentin, Ramirez, and other major leaguers. Gell's students are impressed by the teacher's resume but are more focused on the task at hand. As 8-year-old Roberto Martinez waited in line, he reflected on his first complete week as a student of Gell's. "I've learned more in a week here than in the last five years," he said.

July 14, 2002
The Boston Globe

Thanksgiving Football

The field is frozen, the band is playing the team fight song, and the cheerleaders are whipping the crowd into a frenzy as old friends greet each other with bear hugs. It's 10 a.m. in northern Massachusetts on Thanksgiving Day, and thousands of families take a deep breath as the kicker approaches the ball and sends it into the air.

In two hours it will all be over — this moment where football, friendships, and nostalgia merge into a sphere of emotion and innocence. Here, in this cathedral of green where past meets present, and generations meld seamlessly, there is talk and teasing, sweat and sorrow, and, ultimately, victory and defeat.

Benjamin Colomycki of Newburyport will climb to the top of the bleachers at Landry Stadium in Amesbury once again this morning, and take his place at the 35-yard line just as he's done every year since 1935. The 88-year-old never played the game, but that hasn't stopped him from attending nearly every Newburyport football game, home and away, since 1940. "I haven't missed a game since Amesbury beat Newburyport, 99 to 6, in 1951," said Colomycki, who worked for 39 years at the former Merrimac Hat factory in Amesbury.

Colomycki believes that there is no great mystery as to why people attend high school football games on Thanksgiving. "It's a rivalry; things like that happen."

Down in Peabody, the Murdoch family also understands the importance of rivalry. Luke Murdoch, a guard and linebacker, will play his heart out today against Saugus, and will try to keep his legs warm, just in case he needs to kick a long field goal. The Peabody High junior set a team record with a 48-yard field goal earlier this year against Cambridge Rindge & Latin.

Murdoch's father, Kevin, will watch from the stands, and his mother, Gail, who is president of the team's booster club, will take photographs of the team from the sidelines. "Peabody High School football has been a great life-building experience for all of us," said Kevin, 50, who scored a touchdown in the 1969 Peabody-Saugus game.

Gail Murdoch, who oversees the fund-raising, concessions, and season-ending banquet for the boosters, said football has brought her family closer. "There's something about football that transcends everything," said Gail, who did not learn the rules of the game until she was an adult. "It's kind of like when women get together and have babies and talk about their war stories in labor. I love it when my sons come home and talk to Kevin about plays. It's a great camaraderie."

In Swampscott, men will gather in the Dunkin' Donuts in Vinnin Square long before the Swampscott-Marblehead kickoff and talk about former players and coaching decisions that might have taken place a half-century ago. Former Big Blue and NFL players such as Dick Jauron, Bill Adams, and the late Tom Toner will be mentioned, along with Stan Bondelevitch, the former Swampscott coach who died this year.

Somewhere in the crowd at Blocksidge Field, Dick Lynch will be standing and rooting for Swampscott. The former Big Blue assistant coach and former athletic director at Danvers High School has attended thousands of sporting events, but to him, the Thanksgiving game is still special. "When they run out on the field, and the band is playing, I always get a little chill up my back," said Lynch, who lists the 1969 Swampscott-Marblehead game as his favorite. In that game, with seconds remaining and Marblehead leading, 14-12, Lynch suggested that Bondelevitch go for a field goal. Lynch's son, Mike, kicked the field goal, lifting Swampscott to a 15-14 victory. The stunned home crowd stood in the stands as the Swampscott fans jumped out of their seats and swarmed the Marblehead field.

Jim Cornacchio, athletic director and school psychologist at Hamilton-Wenham Regional High School, will have one foot in Hamilton and another in Salem this morning. Cornacchio is one of five brothers who starred for Salem High School. His father, Joseph "Pep" Cornacchio, played at Salem in the 1930s, and recalls watching NFL Hall of Famer Wayne Milner play for Salem.

"The Thanksgiving game is an inexpensive way for people to connect to their past," said Cornacchio. "I think it grounds them. I think people occasionally need to come back to their roots and touch home plate, and to reconnect with what's important: family and friends and your old school."

James Stehlin, who coached Newburyport High School for 20 years, and won 38 games in a row in the 1970s, said the Thanksgiving game is unique because most other states have eliminated season-ending rivalries and gone to a playoff system by the end of November. The game works better than a formal homecoming event, said Stehlin. "It's sometimes even more successful than high school reunions are. It means so much," said Stehlin, who retired in 1983.

The rivalry between Salem and Beverly has changed markedly in the last 20 years. Gone are the days when residents threw rocks at each other on the Beverly-Salem Bridge on the eve of the Thanksgiving game. Since 1983, the teams' captains and cheerleaders, as well as elected officials from both cities, have met on the bridge and exchanged team jerseys during the week of the game. The two squads also meet during game week and eat dinner together. "It has really gotten the two communities together," said Frank Forti, 79, a former president of the Beverly boosters who has been going to Thanksgiving games since he was "able to walk."

"We have some people who have had the same seats for decades," said John Lyons, athletic director at Beverly.

Nate Finklestein, who played end on the 1944 Chelsea High School championship team that beat Everett, will be rooting on his old alma mater, which now plays Pope John. He remembers another era, when thousands of people lined the streets, and teams played for more than bragging rights. "There were big celebrations and banners and you'd march through the center of town," said the 75-year-old retired elementary school principal. "It meant a great deal of pride for the city."

No one knows if today's games will outdo past Thanksgiving performances. In Ipswich, Jo Jo Robishaw is still a near-deity, 64 years after he was the best quarterback in the state. In Lynn, there has never been an equal to the great Harry Agganis. In Gloucester, they remember coach Nate Ross's strategy and lucky brown hat. In Beverly, they wonder if there has ever been a greater Thanksgiving game than the snow-covered 3-0 victory over Salem in 1940.

For many players, it will be the last organized football game they will participate in. And, for that reason, said Dick Lynch, anything can happen. "More upsets take place on Thanksgiving Day because it's so meaningful," Lynch said. "They go all out, and get on a tremendous emotional high, and a lot of kids play beyond their means, and that's how upsets come about."

November 28, 2002
The Boston Globe

Kickball

Arthur Beane is not sure if kickball can solve the world's problems, but says anything is possible.

Beane, an assistant principal at the Fuller Elementary School, has relied on an old schoolyard sport to bring order and responsibility to his school's playground. Since 2002, Beane has organized a year-round kickball league for Gloucester children in grades 2 through 5. About half of the 350 children in those grades participate, while the others choose to play tag, climb on the monkey bars, or improvise their own game.

Beane, who is the administrator that students meet when they are sent out of class for disciplinary issues, said since he started kickball as a daily coed sport, problems at recess have been all but eliminated.

In 2001, when he arrived at his post, recess was dominated by older students. They played football, and excluded girls and less-athletic boys. "It was a Darwinian model of survival of the fittest," he said. Insults, fights, and harassment were not uncommon, pushing Beane to introduce kickball — his favorite childhood sport — as a regular activity.

The results have brought a sense of peace to the playing fields.

"We have fewer students showing up in the nurse's office after recess. We have fewer disciplinary issues with some of the children who have issues outside of school that make life a challenge for them," he said.

At the school, about 100 kickball games are played during the school year, broken up into six monthly seasons. The contests are held during recess, are 22 minutes long, and take place every day it's not raining, snowing, or less than 20 degrees. The game is similar to baseball, but instead of a batter there is a kicker. Kickers have two strikes allotted instead of three, and the offensive team is allowed two outs. Each offensive team is limited to scoring six runs per inning, and players can be forced or tagged out. They also can be called out if a defensive player strikes them below their shoulders after a ball has been kicked.

Each season, teams are broken into two leagues, with grades 2 and 3 grouped in one and grades 4 and 5 in the other. Teams are given a number instead of a nickname, and captains are not chosen. Instead, players take on the responsibility of creating their own batting order, and choose their own positions in the field. The increased responsibility, and the ability to run their own sport, has brought a sense of independence, as well as happiness, Beane said.

"It's fair play built upon several concepts of modesty, compassion, gratitude, enthusiasm, and self-control," he said.

The second kickball season recently ended. After the championships, certificates are awarded to children who play on the top three teams in the two leagues.

On a recent day, Beane gathered the classes, and walked outside of the two-story brick and concrete school. Answering questions from the students as he walked, he carried a paper box filled with four brown infield bases, a green rubber kickball, and clipboards to record game statistics.

When they reached the field, the teams quickly assembled a batting order, and took their defensive positions. Soon, a student rolled a ball off of the pitcher's mound toward an eager kicker. The ball sailed into left field over a student's head; players on the offensive team clapped, screamed, and encouraged the next kicker, while the defensive team regrouped.

"Batter up," Beane yelled from his spot at third base. When a ball is caught or a batter is tagged out, he yells "out," and then, to keep the game moving, he'll motion to home base with "batter up." He constantly encourages children, telling them "good catch" or "good play."

"It's a sport to keep you fun," said Eddy Rivera, a 10-year-old fourth-grader. With his arms draped around two teammates, he listed other benefits of his participation. "I didn't know some of the kids on my team, and I just met them and now I'm friends with them. There's a lot of teamwork in the game. We'll tell someone and they'll listen and they know how to do it again, and it's good."

Eleven-year-old Hannah Verga rooted on her classmates as she prepared to kick the ball. When asked about the game, she talked about kickball strategy and how it helps her think more clearly outside of the classroom. "It helps me build sportsmanship and to work with other people. It helps people follow the rules," said the fifth-grader.

November 25, 2004
The Boston Globe

CHAPTER 7

Homeless

Morning in Tent City, USA

The American Dream rolled over and died again on a recent morning. This time the setting was a spit of oceanfront land tucked behind the Lynnway, with views of Boston.

They call this patch of coastal woods Tent City, and it's the end of the line for those who have burned just about every connection to the outside world. Here, souls leave traces of their demons along the paths that circle a few small hills and trees. Used hypodermic needles, empty liquor bottles, and old crack pipes lead a trail to tents and sleeping bags alongside rusted cooking grills, clotheslines, and piles of moldy trash.

At the base of the hill, Stacey Woodruff pulled hard on a cigarillo outside of the lean-to she recently inherited from a few strangers.

Woodruff, a 38-year-old Sissy Spacek look-alike, wore a smudged yellow sweatshirt and jeans. She sat on an overturned shopping cart, rubbed her hands together to try to get warm, and stared at the Atlantic. When she saw Pat Byrne, she jumped up, threw her arms around a man with one of the biggest hearts in the city, and began to sob.

"If you see my children, please tell them I've looked everywhere for them," she said, as fat tears rolled down her cheeks.

She held onto Pat for almost a minute, and the former postman turned street worker for the homeless did not interrupt her.

If there's anyone who understands the homeless in this area, it's Pat. He's worked as a street advocate for the Lynn Shelter Association for nine years, and every year he gets to know as many as 400 people who pass through the city and sleep on the beach, cemeteries, in abandoned buildings, and in Tent City.

He also knows what addiction can do to a family. Last year, his son, Jamie — who held a master's degree from Boston University — died of a heroin overdose after a long stretch of sobriety.

In his son's obituary, Pat and his wife wrote about their son's battle with the disease of addiction. "The family asks that readers take the time to tell their children that they love them," the obituary concluded.

After Jamie's death, Pat somehow was able to find the strength to continue counseling to people like Stacey, who have lost everything. He'll try to find a person health insurance, food stamps, and a bed in the homeless shelter, and he even gives out his address so people can receive mail.

Many face addiction, criminal involvement, mental health issues, and childhood trauma. Many became victims — and some later, perpetrators — of sexual abuse. Pat is realistic about how he can influence their future. He smiles, listens, and acts as cheerleader to the cheerless.

"This is a job where victories are counted on one hand. We have dozens and dozens of failures or disappointments for each positive result," Pat said.

Pat has known Stacey for years, and in the past he has helped her get food stamps and arranged for doctor's appointments. She grew up in Salem and Beverly, married and had kids, and took a liking to heroin. In recent years she has lived down South, but last summer she returned to the North Shore to attend a funeral and stayed, working at carnivals and living in the woods.

Stacey lit another butt, tucked her red strands of hair inside the yellow hoodie, and wanted people to know that even though she once was a heroin addict and lost custody of her children, she still had a will to live and craved a sense of dignity. She asked that people not be quick to judge the homeless.

"It's hard and it's sad and it's heart-wrenching," she said, outside of the blue tarp strung between a couple of trees that's filled with clothes and a dirty mattress, where she has been sleeping since the snow melted. She spent much of the winter in a small tent in the woods behind Walmart in Salem, sleeping just above a bed of snow with her boyfriend and nearly freezing to death because she had no money.

She does not blame anyone for her troubles, and has modest hopes — to see her children again, to work for a paycheck, and somehow to find a way to sleep inside in a warm room again, on a clean bed.

"If you can't work, there's no way to get up," she told me, mustering a sad smile. "It's almost like death. You feel like dying, just killing yourself. I've felt it almost every day for a long time."

May 3, 2015
The Boston Globe

Tonight, My Roomies
Will Not Freeze to Death

The yellow room has the feel of an Army barracks and is the size of a large bedroom. Men arrive after dark and must leave as the sun rises 12 hours later. Here they are called guests; to the public they are homeless.

They eat dinner and sleep at River House, a Beverly shelter, because at some point in their past, something went wrong. Their focus now is on the future and the challenge of finding a respectable job.

I am here because I convinced my editor that it would be a good thing to write a column about what it's like to spend a night in a homeless shelter.

"I've got applications all over the place. I want a [demolition] job and then I'll move to Florida," Ray Jacobsen tells the dozen men as they finish their meatball sub and wild rice dinner.

Jacobsen, 47, hauled rubbish for 22 years, but now has a bad knee and a sore ankle. That kind of work, he says, is "a young kid's job." Last month, he moved out of his apartment because he couldn't pay the bills anymore.

His audience is quick to offer job-hunting advice.

"Whatever you do, don't put down that you live in a shelter. You won't get hired," says Steve Roberts, 40, who is a part-time sheetrock worker and plasterer in Lynn. "When people find out you're from a shelter, they back up like you're a disease."

At the end of the table, Chris Hall begins to talk.

"When you're a homeless person, it doesn't matter your skill set. Nobody wants to hire you," says the 54-year-old, formerly of Danvers, who works outside several hours a week holding going-out-of-business sale signs. Hall, who is 6 foot 2 inches and 240 pounds, lost his job as a liquor store clerk in July. "I've got 14 years retail experience, and I can't even get a job at CVS. I have to ask a friend to use his name and address when I apply for a job."

Hall's words resonate with the men. The room falls quiet.

Five feet away, shelter director Farris Ajalat, and his coworker Dee Pollard, sit at an L-shaped Formica counter supported by three file cabinets. Pollard, a 62-year-old grandmother, has worked nights at the shelter for almost five years. She makes sure the men eat dinner, take showers, and do their chores, which include cleaning the two bathrooms, and taking out the garbage. The two workers also monitor if someone's been drinking or taking drugs. Violators are allowed to remain in the shelter the night they are caught, but can be barred for up to a week.

"I think a lot of people here feel like they're part of a community. Everyone treats it as such," says Ajalat, who helped start the shelter five years ago.

The shelter is open from November through April but will become year-round next fall, Ajalat says. Five single-room occupancy units will be built on the second floor for additional guests.

For the last three weeks, the average census at the shelter has been 16, but Ajalat says it will rise as high as 24 on frigid nights. Seventeen men will sleep in the room on this particular night.

By 9 p.m., most of the men have showered, and the two dinner tables are folded up and stowed between a couple of bunk beds. Regulars have already staked a claim to most of the 12 bunk beds; the rest begin unfolding cots, and gathering sheets, blankets, and pillows.

Near the door, Roberts kneels on the floor and slides a plastic rectangular container under his bed. The box contains everything he owns.

Roberts dropped out of Salem schools, and began working when he was 13. He says he had a tough upbringing but hard work always gave him enough for an apartment and food. Two years ago, after he left his girlfriend and son in Maine, he returned to Salem, but couldn't find work, and ended up living in a train tunnel near Bridge Street for almost three months. "You get sick. You periodically sleep when you're not shivering," he says about the experience. "That, in itself, is an eye-opener."

A tape of the "The Royal Tenenbaums" movie is playing on the black-and-white TV, but only Hall seems to be watching. After a few minutes, Hall lies on his bed and wraps himself in a red blanket. He falls asleep on top of another quilt, leaving the hospital corners on the sheets immaculate.

Ray Jacobsen rolls a cigarette with Zig-Zag papers and walks outside onto the back stairway. He stands in stocking feet and smokes and chats about meteorites.

At the top of the stairway, a man who calls himself Lenny the Laborer looks out at the gravel driveway and into the cold night. The son of Holocaust survivors, he holds down a union job in Boston but says the work is unsteady. He declined to provide his last name. "This is a good place, they do a lot of good here," he says, pulling on a cigarette. He excuses himself and says he has to be up at 5 a.m. to take the train to work in Boston.

At 11 p.m., the lights and television are shut off, and the small room darkens. The air is choked with the smell of old clothes, cigarettes, and work boots. A little after 1 a.m., the last guest arrives from his late night shift in Boston and slips into bed. Throughout the night some men snore, cough, and get up to use the bathroom.

At 4 a.m., Johnny Bonacci, who works the overnight shift at the shelter, gets up from his post and walks around the room. At 5 a.m., Lenny the Laborer opens his eyes, quickly dresses and leaves. At 6 a.m., Bonacci turns on the lights and television. The men leave by 7 a.m.

It is 33 degrees outside and most have nowhere to go.

December 19, 2004
The Boston Globe

The Motel Kids

The motel kids don't know all the details that led their families to turn to the state for a roof over their heads. They just know that a motel room does not feel like home.

"I know we move a lot," said Emma Precourt, 9, who has lived with her mother and sister in a room with two beds for 18 months at the Super 8 in Weymouth.

"I have a tough life here; I want to go home," said Jaliyah Rogers, who is 6 and moved to the Home Suites Inn in Waltham seven months ago with her father.

"I just want to go back home and play with my toys again," said Pauly O'Brien, 7, who has spent the last 13 months living with his parents in a small room that has a window looking out at the Econo

Lodge parking lot in Danvers.

Each day, more than 3,600 children across the state who wake up in motel beds that they sometimes share with a brother, sister, or parent slip into a compartmentalized world of contradiction: mornings are often chaotic, where family members form a line to take showers, race to microwave food, and get the children dressed for school. Some kids go to nearby schools, while others are bused as far as an hour away. In the classroom, some find structure. At recess, they embrace open air.

At the end of the day, they leave their friends behind and return to the motels, where guests are not allowed in rooms, there are few places to play outside save for the parking lots, and early-evening curfews are enforced.

"We see homelessness as a trauma itself, and living with the burden of that and growing up with that, there's financial insecurity, food insecurity, and constant stress over the housing situation," said Dr. Aura Obando, who works for the Boston Health Care for the Homeless Program and treats kids and parents every week at a makeshift clinic set up in a hotel room at the Home Suites Inn in Waltham.

With a lack of affordable housing, the state turned to motels in the 1980s to provide temporary housing for homeless families. It costs about $84 a night for each room, and $58 million a year. The motel housing program was supposed to end this year, but its 2,700 affordable housing units statewide have not kept pace with the demand, forcing nearly 1,900 families into motels, according to the state.

While communities have worked hard to integrate the motel kids into their schools, some have had to dig deep into their budgets to pay for transportation costs. Under federal law, cities and towns have to provide transportation for students who want to stay in their home-town schools.

The parents still in motels spend their days meeting with case managers to find permanent housing. Kids return to motel rooms after school, to an environment some parents liken to a prison.

"I feel like I'm the warden, and that's not a good feeling," said Katrina Precourt, 34, the mother of Emma and Summa, 10. Precourt has lived with her daughters and boyfriend at the Super 8 in Weymouth for 18 months and hopes to move soon.

She knows living in a one-room motel has affected her children, but she's unclear how deep a psychological toll it's taken.

"I don't think they can even find the space to collect their thoughts because they're so scattered. It's hard for them because they aren't allowed to have a life here. They can't be with children their own age and play and get their energy out," said Precourt, who lost her job in Florida a couple of years ago and moved back to Weymouth to be close to family.

Jennifer Gearhart, who oversees therapists at South Bay Mental Health — which sends counselors to the motels to work with the kids — believes the earlier kids start expressing their feelings about motel life, the better they'll feel. Still, the combination of poverty, hunger, and witnessing everything from domestic violence to substance abuse can be a lot for a child to overcome, she said.

"You're going to see a lot of symptomology around depression, anxiety, and PTSD, because there's a lot of trauma that they're suffering from, and the fact that they're living in awful circumstances. They're really looking at their basic needs survival, so you see them focusing a lot on just being able to eat and sleep," said Gearhart.

At the Home Suites Inn in Waltham, about 100 rooms are filled by families. A few years ago, the hotel's management filled in the pool and put in basketball courts and picnic tables; conference rooms were turned over to nonprofits for early childhood classes; and a medical clinic was set up in a converted hotel room. In addition, the hotel helped bring in tutors from Bentley University to work with kids after school.

On a recent afternoon, Jaliyah Rogers, 6, played a board game in the Home Suites breakfast area, and yawned. "I worry a lot here," said Jaliyah, who lives with her dad and thinks constantly about returning to Braintree, where she remembers living in a white house a year ago.

Around that time, Josh Rogers, 38, quit his restaurant job in order to take care of Jaliyah full time. That's when he ran out of money and was given a motel room by the state.

Rogers wants to move out, but like the other families in the motel, is waiting for an affordable unit, a process that could take over a year. In the meantime, he takes Jaliyah on hikes in nearby woods to help clear her mind of the lack of privacy that comes with motel living, and the stigma he says that kids deal with in school.

"The kids lack confidence and self-esteem. They feel different from other kids in their class," said Rogers. "They see kids getting picked up and hear kids talking about their homes and rooms. My daughter told them she shares a room in a hotel with her dad, and kids don't understand that."

At the Econo Lodge in Danvers, Holly Brauner works out of a converted motel room, meeting with some of the 77 families that live in the two-floor motel behind a Denny's parking lot across from the Liberty Tree Mall. Brauner, who runs a nonprofit, assists parents who apply for affordable housing, medical insurance, and food stamps, and helps kids receive counseling.

"Any hotel would be a horrible place to raise your kids," said Brauner. "We're expecting people to live here, be at their best behavior, get over the stress that got them here to begin with in a very stressful environment."

With his mother in one bed and his two sisters in the other, Michael Pimentel, 13, sleeps on the floor near the door in Danvers, never getting a full night's rest.

"This is not a safe place for kids," he said. "It makes me very frustrated."

November 16, 2014
The Boston Globe

The Outsiders

"You want to know why I'm homeless?" Billy Hamilton asks. "It's simple. I'm an alcoholic."

He's standing on the corner of a lost part of Waltham, where machine shops grind metal all day and men and women like Hamilton approach strangers, seeking a buck or two for a nip of vodka.

Hamilton is 51 and a long way from Somerville, which he once called home. Now, he's almost a couple of miles from his bush behind McDonald's on Main Street, where he returns every midnight, wraps a couple of dank blankets around his body, drops to the ground, and sleeps sitting up.

Hamilton is one of more than 500 homeless adults in the state who have chosen to live outside during the winter. Some want to drink or do drugs whenever they want. Others have long struggled with mental health issues and experience too much anxiety to sleep in a shelter.

Marilyn Lee-Tom, who runs the Community Day Center of Waltham, which offers meals and counseling to those on the street, says a majority of the chronically homeless suffer from both mental health and alcohol or drug issues.

"They don't like the regimentation of being inside a shelter and being told what to do," says Lee-Tom, who estimates that at least 35 people have chosen to sleep outside in Waltham this winter.

While the Department of Housing and Urban Development estimates the number of chronically homeless adults in the state has dropped nearly 60 percent since 2010, adult shelters like MainSpring in Brockton and the Lynn Adult Emergency Shelter have stepped up their outreach in recent years. Street workers find the homeless in the woods, near abandoned buildings, along railroad tracks, in cars, and huddled in ATM lobbies.

Most depend on the workers to bring blankets, gloves, hats, socks, and other clothing and toiletries.

"I worry all the time about them freezing to death," says Margie St. Paul, executive director of the Lynn Shelter Association.

St. Paul has run the shelter for 12 years and estimates there are more than 40 people living outside in Lynn this winter, an unusually high number because of the mild weather. She says most are men, who in addition to dealing with mental health and/or substance abuse issues have experienced trauma such as physical or emotional abuse. Women who live outside suffer from similar problems, she says. In addition, St. Paul says, a majority of the women who live outside have been raped.

Inside the Lynn shelter, where as many as 90 men and women sleep nightly on mattresses and mats in nearly every corner of the building,

Richard McMahon sits on a bed and wheezes.

From June until December, he spent his days walking around down-town Lynn, drinking coffee to stay warm in the morning before heading to the library to read. At night, he'd walk back to a park bench by the Lynnway that he called his bed. Now 61, the former printer, who grew up in Woburn, says he's tired of sleeping on benches, in back alleys, or under a bridge. He says he stopped drinking about seven years ago and once was addicted to Percocet, but still struggles with depression.

The December cold and rain pushed him to make the half-mile walk from his park bench to the shelter, where he was given a bed.

"I was stubborn about going into a shelter. I have a lot of anxiety. My biggest fear was being down on the bench and not waking up one morning and somebody finding me dead," he says, placing his hand on the gray comforter that covers his shelter bed.

Even though he's been homeless for nearly 20 years, McMahon hopes to find an apartment and says he'll be able to manage his finances with the funds he receives from his monthly disability check.

In Brockton, the MainSpring homeless shelter's director, Sharon Williams, places almost 200 people a night in beds and on mats. She says there are another 60 or so who choose to sleep in the woods or near abandoned buildings, but sometimes come in for counseling or a hot meal.

In a stairway that leads to the building's second-floor dormitory, Rynnard Thomas says he wants to begin his life again. Thomas, 29, went to Brockton High School and hoped to become a construction worker. But about five years ago he got hooked on opiates and drifted over to Brockton's Tent City, a downtown wooded area where home-less people have lived for decades.

"I'm coming in now because I want to change my life. I want to be healthy," he says, his soft voice echoing through the empty hallway. He explains that he's been off of Percocet for a week, and he credits part of his recovery to a shelter caseworker whom he has known for three years.

"When someone else believes in you, you start believing in yourself again," he says.

Tent City is a five-minute ride from the shelter, and the wooded area borders an auto-repair shop, a scrap metal company, a cellphone tower, and the MBTA commuter rail.

In these woods, you'll encounter people like James "The Ratman" Bush, who says he's been homeless since his mother died four years ago. A stout man who wears several layers of fleece jackets, he explains the origins of his nickname.

"They call me the Ratman because I bought some rats at the pet store and used to feed them, and they didn't bother anyone," he says, adding that he usually sleeps in a downtown storefront and gets by on a disability check.

Deeper into Tent City, Charles Towers and Randy Detoma share a cigarette and a laugh. Towers says he's been on disability for 18 years and once had a cocaine habit. He showed up in the woods a year ago and sleeps alone under two sleeping bags, three blankets, and handwarmers that he's turned into footwarmers. He spends his days downtown, milling around the parks and at the Brockton Area Transit Authority terminal.

"I like it down here because I don't have to deal with nobody," Towers says.

A few feet away, Detoma hoists a large water container and begins his short walk back to his tent. He says he's been homeless since 1982 and declines to talk much about his past, except to say he's financially solvent and could live in an apartment if he desired. "I collect SSI — I got some mental health problems, enough to keep me from working," he says.

After nine years in the woods, Detoma is considered the dean of Tent City. If he has to, he'll mediate a dispute between neighbors. Otherwise, he spends most of his time with his wife at the campsite.

"It's a small community; we all get along. It's peaceful and quiet. With the drugs and alcohol there tends to be some problems sometimes, but other than that, it's nice down here," he says.

He stands outside his neatly kept tent and explains that if the water freezes and the temperature gets close to zero, he'll head to the Main-Spring shelter and stay until the spring thaw.

Detoma looks up at the trees and sky when he speaks. "I love the peace and quiet here, and I wake up to the birds in the morning. There's no regulations out here. In the shelter there are rules."

His wife, Maggie, emerges from the tent and the two embrace.

"We've got to go," Detoma says, taking her hand.

"God bless you," Maggie says, before the two walk into the woods and disappear into the deep brush.

January 3, 2016
The Boston Globe

Baghdad Blues

W hen the sun sets over the Colonial Traveler Inn, Ahmed and Abeer al Rubaye gather their seven children in a dimly lit room and form a small circle on the floor.

The memories of Baghdad's bombings, shootings, and violent crime — including the street execution of Ahmed al Rubaye's brother in 2012 — are not discussed. During dinner of chicken and rice cooked on a hot plate, the children joke and the parents offer advice. It is a far cry from Iraq, where they once owned a home and didn't need a handout from the state.

"I thought America was going to be paradise," Rubaye said.

Instead, since coming to Massachusetts nearly two years ago, the family has bounced from Lowell to Leominster to this motel room in Saugus, which has made it difficult for Rubaye to find steady work and forced the children to shuttle from one new school to another.

The family is among the 4,576 Iraqi refugees who have settled in Massachusetts since the 2003 US invasion, and many are foundering in their quest to assimilate, specialists say.

Like refugees from other countries, they receive limited federal and state financial assistance and are expected to find housing and work, and learn English almost immediately. But a combination of traumas many Iraqis have suffered and are still processing — witnessing atrocities or being victims of violence themselves — has made it particularly trying for them. And very large families like the Rubayes may face additional challenges finding suitable housing.

Dr. Sondra Crosby, director of Boston Medical Center's Immigrant & Refugee Health Program, said a combination of such factors has caused some Iraqi refugees to struggle.

"I find it appalling that this family is living in a motel. And they're not the first," Crosby said. "The Iraqis are a group that also come with a huge burden of trauma, post-traumatic stress disorder, depression, and they really need to be resettled in a safe environment, with access to medical and mental health care and to be embraced by the community."

At 42, Rubaye is square-shouldered, fit, and used to working with his hands. In Iraq he was a welder and a taxi driver, and he believes that an understanding of the street saved his life many times.

Back in Baghdad, he drove with three different ID cards, and, depending on the militia checkpoint, he would present himself as a Sunni Muslim, Shi'ite Muslim, or Christian.

Rubaye described the dark side of refugee life — a journey that began in 2013 when his family slipped over the Turkish border and waited to hear about their US refugee application.

In 2014, they arrived in Lowell and were allotted around $10,000 from the government to begin their new lives. For a few months, things looked bright: They settled into an apartment, and Rubaye found work in plastic and clothing factories. They bought a minivan, and the children enrolled in school and started to learn English.

"Then, more problems," Rubaye said in Arabic on a recent day, as a friend translated.

In Lowell, his son Abdul Wahab, who is now 11, began having epileptic seizures. Another son, Taha, 13, was diagnosed with diabetes, he said. And his wife, Abeer, who also suffers from epilepsy, became increasingly isolated in a new country.

Rubaye shuttled his sick boys to doctor's appointments and lost his job. And, after a year, the family ran out of money and lost their apartment, he said.

The state, which pays for homeless families with school-aged children to live in motels, found them a place at a Days Inn in Leominster. The family was split into two rooms, and the kids went off to a new school district.

But six months later, in February 2016, Rubaye said, he learned that his family had to uproot again.

His children returned from school that afternoon to find their belongings in a dozen trash bags next to their minivan. They were told to drive to a new motel in a place they had never heard of: Saugus.

There, just yards away from the constant hum of Route 1 traffic, the nine were assigned two small, yellow-paneled rooms. In the parents' room, 7-year-old twins Abdullah and Fatimah sleep with their mother, Abeer; Abdul Wahab is in another bed, while, Rubaye finds a place on the floor. In the other room, the oldest boys, Mohammed, 17, Mustafa, 16, and the twins Taha and Yaseen sleep in two beds.

The stresses have mounted. Two weeks after moving to Saugus, a member of the family attempted suicide, Rubaye said. There was a prolonged hospitalization that brought further despair, and a realization that the family was far from settled in their new country.

"We all get very sad," Rubaye said in a soft voice, as tears slid from his eyes.

Refugee families depend on the federal government to help once they arrive. To assist them, the State Department contracts with nonprofits to help families find an apartment, sign up for health care, enroll in ESL classes, obtain food stamps, and look for employment opportunities. But the organizations are only required to provide guidance for three months, and refugees who need more help must turn to state programs and case managers for other benefits such as welfare.

Samantha Kaufman, a spokeswoman for the Executive Office of Housing and Economic Development, declined to comment on the Rubayes' plight. "We can't release any personal information about individuals and families," she wrote in an e-mail.

Dr. Richard Mollica, director of the Harvard Program in Refugee Trauma, called for increased refugee benefits from the government.

"If you have a medical problem or a mental health problem or you're a survivor of torture, the probability that you're going to make it to independent living after eight or nine months is probably nil," Mollica said.

Currently, the biggest allotment of financial aid for refugees is a one-time federal payment of $2,025 for each family member. Some families pool those funds for rent and clothing, but at least $900 of each allowance goes to pay administrative costs to such resettlement agencies as the International Institute of New England, which was assigned to the family originally for three months, according to Rubaye. The International Institute did not respond to queries about resettling refugees.

Mohammed, 17, and Mustafa, 16, the family's oldest sons, enrolled at Saugus High School in February. They have made some friends but still haven't been able to master English.

"These are two great, great kids facing a very difficult situation," said Seth Minkoff, a teacher, who called the boys "amazingly resilient."

Mustafa wants to attend college but doesn't dwell too much on the future. Despite living in a motel for the last eight months and attending three different school districts, he prefers America to the war zone he grew up in.

"I like that there is law and order, because there is none in Iraq," he said.

Recently the family received a rent voucher from the state that would pay $2,200 a month to subsidize a market-rate apartment for nine people. Obtaining a subsidized public housing unit is not an option, since the waiting list is long and the process typically takes years.

Last Saturday, Rubaye drove over to Chelsea to see a five-bedroom apartment. "I waited and waited," Rubaye said.

An hour later, no one had showed up, so Rubaye drove back to his motel room and broke the news to his wife. Later that night, they did not discuss the apartment, as the family sat in their cramped dinner circle on the motel room floor.

April 23, 2016
The Boston Globe

Gang Love

By the time he was 6, Jonathan Bruno had lost part of his vision to a hit-and-run driver, witnessed his parents' drug binges, and learned to steal a car in less than a minute. By age 12, Kristin Hiett says she had grown weary of the beatings from her mother and father and decided to raise her own fists.

The couple, now older and in love, say they found the family they had always wanted when they joined a gang.

"I know that I'll have friends for the rest of my life," says Bruno, who, at 19, has been homeless for at least two years. Each night he sleeps at a different friend's house. "It's unconditional, like, you show love to other people, people show love back."

Bruno has been a member of the Avenue King Crips for several years. Hiett, who is 18, joined the Lady Avenue Crips last summer. Both were "jumped in," an initiation that lasts about 60 seconds and allows veteran gang members to pummel recruits.

Bruno wants to marry Hiett but the soft-spoken woman is unsure. She dreams of getting her GED, moving south, and going to college. Bruno wants to be a tattoo artist or own a sub shop.

But their dreams may have to be put on hold while they sort out their legal problems. Bruno is facing charges that he received a stolen car, resisted arrest, and violated a city ordinance by carrying a large buck knife. Hiett has been charged with stabbing a man and woman during a gang fight and assaulting a responding police officer. She also faces three other assault and battery charges from another incident.

"We're innocent, though," says Bruno, placing his hands on Hiett's arms during lunch at a Lynn roast beef shop.

Bruno walks several miles every day, up and down the streets of Lynn, in search of friends, food, and a place to warm his body. Speaking in a slow baritone drawl, the 6-foot-3-inch, 230-pound man describes his gang as a religion that's misunderstood by the public. He declines to speak of the gang's activities, but says he respects all who show him courtesy.

His arm reveals a scar that came from a Mexican man who demanded money with a knife. His neck bears a dark line that he says was caused by a guy named Steve, who had a machete. He says he has been victorious in most of his fights, because he has known violence since he was an infant.

But violence is only a part of what life in a gang entails, Bruno says, and it only occurs when rival gang members show disrespect toward one another. That could be as simple as calling one another a name or staring at someone the wrong way. Shootings and attacks by rival gang members happen nearly every day in Lynn, he says. Over time, Bruno has learned to meet violence with violence.

"That's how you have to be," he says. "You have to make your point. Because if you don't, they're going to come back and they're going to come with 50 people and they're going to do that to you."

In between those tense moments, Bruno spends time with other gang members smoking, drinking alcohol, watching TV, or competing at PlayStation. Hiett spends most of her weekends with the five other Lady Avenue Crip members. She relaxes by wrestling her friends, watching TV, and drinking vodka.

"We don't look for trouble," he says.

The Lynn police disagree. They say that people like Bruno and many of the 1,600 other identified Lynn gang members regularly break the law by dealing drugs, stealing cars, invading homes, and fighting.

Bruno's Avenue King Crips began as an Asian gang in Lynn in the early '90s, but now — like nearly every other gang in Lynn — allows all races to join. Their biggest rivals, say police, are members of the Blood gangs.

Inside her tidy studio apartment in downtown Lynn, Toni Bruno worries about her son. At 44, she has been off drugs for almost five years, and spends most of her hours working at a supermarket. The pills, alcohol, cocaine, and heroin, which she once loved even more than her family, are no longer in her system.

She says the adrenaline her son feels with his gang is similar to what she experienced with her addiction. That addiction separated her and Jonathan for nearly 10 years, as he moved in and out of foster homes, group homes, and Department of Youth Services programs in Saugus, Middleton, Lynn, and Framingham.

"He's either going to go to jail, he's going to hurt somebody, or somebody's really going to hurt him," says Bruno, with tears in her brown eyes.

Behind her couch are several framed pictures, including a shot of Jonathan Bruno at age 1. The boy is standing and smiling. Around that time, Toni Bruno and Jonathan were homeless and living in a motel paid for by the state on Route 1 in Peabody.

When he was 18 months old, a car ran over Jonathan when he was riding on his Big Wheel in the motel parking lot, crushing his body. The hit-and-run accident left him blind in his left eye and deaf in his left ear.

"He's had it rough. I'm not going to say his life has been easy," says his mother, who feels her advice is being ignored. Her hope is that he finds a job and leaves his gang.

Scott Carpenter also wants Jonathan Bruno to quit the gang and find a job. Carpenter met Bruno when he was a youth counselor at Bruno's group home in Middleton six years ago.

"I found a very caring person, really articulate, empathetic with other people's problems," Carpenter says. "Just a good kid to hang with, you know, a smart kid, but frustrating at the same time, because he could never seem to really get his act together, and it's still that way today, you know, all of these years later."

Now a tattoo artist, Carpenter offered Bruno a chance to apprentice last summer. But Bruno stopped training in the fall because he felt he needed to spend more time with gang members after a flurry of fights.

Bruno and Hiett know that finding a job is important. The two have never held full-time jobs, and currently receive money from friends. Bruno loves his gang, but acknowledges that even his "street credibility" will not bring him a job. Hiett appreciates her gang friends, but now sees her decision to join as a mistake.

"It's kind of stupid because it's causing me a bunch of problems," she says.

In the roast beef shop the teenagers smile, hold hands, and look into each other's eyes. Thoughts of jobs, gangs, and everything else will have to wait. They are young and free, at least for the moment.

February 10, 2005
The Boston Globe

Down by the River

As the sun sets, Lee Doucette flips over a plastic bucket and slides it to the edge of a wall that overlooks the Merrimack River. Shadows of tall weeds, and a tent — where she's lived since March — fall on the woman, who sits on the pail and methodically tears slices of bread into smaller and smaller pieces before tossing them to the waiting geese below.

"These are some of my friends," she says, nodding to the birds. "I got no family. All the people I know are homeless."

Alcohol has played a large role in Doucette's road to a sliver of land above the river. She is 49, grew up in North Andover, had six children — now ranging from 10 to 26 — and has spent most of her years working day jobs such as landscaping and for moving companies.

She first became homeless around a decade ago and has had some relatively minor run-ins with the law. Early last winter, she lost her ride to her landscaping job, and then her apartment, and showed up under the Central Bridge in downtown Lawrence. But she prefers to live alone, and within weeks she drifted to a spot above the Merrimack, where she set up a tent, complete with a mattress, battery-powered lights, and Nora Roberts paperback novels.

Doucette says she's no angel but she never figured she'd be looking at spending the winter outside. "I've made a lot of bad choices," says Doucette, who has a quick smile and a raspy voice. Like most of Lawrence's homeless, she eats breakfast and dinner at food kitchens in the city. She has declined to apply for state or federal aid because she wants to work, and she sees steady employment as a way back to a life that would include a room with a bed.

Most days she walks over to Labor Ready, where she sometimes finds day jobs as a landscaper and a mover. But those jobs are becoming harder to land, and when there's no work she walks over to Pemberton Park and meets up with her other homeless friends.

"She's a smart lady, and a hard worker," says a homeless middle-aged man, whom everyone calls Tall Mike. He points toward some brush near the river and says he's lived in a cubbyhole by the Central Bridge for three years. The two have a 10-year-old son they gave up for adoption years ago. "We wanted him to have a chance," says Doucette.

These days, the river is a lifeline for her. When there's no money for her to take her clothes to the laundromat, she washes them in the river. She also bathes in the Merrimack. At night, after the ducks move on and the sun goes down — leaving reflections of the old factories that line the shore — the river carries away the memories, and lulls her to sleep.

September 30, 2012
The Boston Globe

Wondering How This Can Be

David Rosario is a gracious host. He stands behind a fence he cobbled together from old wood pallets, next to his outdoor shack festooned with American flags. Under a maple tree, and just a few yards away from a set of rarely used railroad tracks, he offers coffee to visitors, insists that they pull up a chair, and asks if they're hungry.

Rosario is 60 but looks much younger. He squats, and lifts a coffee pot from his campfire. He pours the coffee into an old thermos, and leans back in a weathered sea captain's chair that he found a few streets away. For most of the last 16 months, he has lived in a wooded section of Lawrence's downtown.

At first he says he's not homeless, and explains he's only "camping out." But slowly, in between long articulate critiques of what's wrong with the country and how it can be fixed, he comes to a sobering admission: "You know why I'm homeless? I can't work."

Rosario once worked construction and did security details, but that was long before his injury. He'd rather not discuss the details, he says, but it happened decades ago when he says someone shot him in the stomach and leg.

He shows his scars, explains that he can barely walk because his leg is constantly swollen, and fishes around in his tiny bedroom for the high blood pressure pills he takes. He opens his bedroom door: It is simply adorned, with a foam mattress, and a blanket that once belonged to a moving company. Nearly every day, a visiting nurse comes to check his pulse and listen to his heart.

When asked about Rosario's health, she declines to speak.

There are dark periods of his life that he'd prefer not to share, including some arrests, and he says he could sleep on a friend's couch for a few nights if necessary. Although he says he doesn't mind spending the winter huddled in a frozen shack, he does wonder how long all of this can go on. He sees the tiny strip of land that he meticulously maintains as his way of staying independent.

He says he receives around $700 a month in disability, but that goes toward a family he doesn't like to discuss, and to pay for a storage facility where he's keeping his things.

"Anyway," he says, "I don't have enough money to put down for a deposit and the first month's rent."

He says he does not drink and smokes an occasional cigarette, and says if someone comes around with a bag of weed he'll take a couple of puffs to relieve his stomach pain. His mornings are spent dragging pails of water from an auto body shop back to his shack, where he heats the water and uses it for bathing.

He says he's not angry, but he does wonder why so many Americans are homeless.

"How can a great nation have people sleeping outside and under bridges?" he asks.

"We are part of the forgotten. They put us inside a drawer, and shut the drawer and forgot about us."

September 30, 2012
The Boston Globe

CHAPTER 8

Work

Nana Putt

The kids call her Nana Putt; everyone else in Marblehead calls her Putt. At this point, Marjorie Mace doesn't care what people call her, as long as she's still able to sip her cocoa at sunrise, then head over to the crosswalk at Lincoln Avenue.

The 95-year-old Putt became a crossing guard 10 years ago, after her brother Bud couldn't do the job anymore. She inherited his gear:

a worn yellow vest and a banged-up stop sign that had been nailed to an old rake. This winter, despite all the snow, Putt did not miss a school morning at her post by the sidewalk, and she can't remember ever not showing up for duty to cross the kids.

Putt taught Sunday school at Old North Church in Marblehead for 15 years and never missed a class. For years, she took it upon herself to beautify the landing at the end of State Street, planting flowers and even cleaning the public bathrooms. For another decade, she volunteered as a sewing teacher at the Gerry school, where her daughter taught for 45 years.

"The kids didn't know what to call me. I was old, and they figured they'd called me Nana Putt, and it stuck," she said.

There aren't many youngsters who walk to school anymore on her block. A handful saunter within the white crosswalk between 7:30 and 8:30 a.m., and when she returns after school, another 10 might need her assistance between 2 and 3 p.m.

No matter. Putt takes her job seriously, just like everything else she's ever done, like raising five children or playing the kazoo in a traveling band around town. And while she's paid around $20 an hour, the children's voices and smiles bring her a sense of joy that helps her stay connected to life.

"You don't know anyone when you get older. All of your friends are dead, so it's nice to communicate with little kids," said Putt, who learns the name of each kid she meets, and schools them in common courtesy, such as teaching them to say "thank you" and "you're welcome."

There are long pauses between groups of kids, and from her perch on the sidewalk she straddles two worlds. For her, every inch of this neighborhood and downtown is filled with memories. She blinks her eyes and it's the 1920s, when the roads were still dirt, and horse and buggy teams brought people around town; a trolley ran to Salem, a train to Boston.

"My mother didn't believe in hospitals and I was born at home," said Putt, who had eight siblings and is part of one of Marblehead's oldest families, the Ornes. She explained that after she was born near Fort Sewall, her father ran over to Dr. Sanborn's place, and the men took a horse and buggy back to the house, where the doctor cut the umbilical cord.

The fee? "Two chickens," said Putt. "We bartered in those days."

Her father, Fred Orne, was a photographer and a printer, and started to call her Putt after she announced she disliked the name Marjorie. "There used to be a song 'My Little Margie,' and every time they'd play it, I'd cry. When it was time for school, my father said, 'We'll call you Putt,' " she explained.

Cars and trucks rumbled along this gray morning, and soon, excited voices could be heard. Putt gripped her stop sign and slowly moved into traffic, smiling at Noah Feingold. He smiled back, and his mom, Leah Feingold, paused to schmooze with Putt.

"She's our little local hero. She brings cheer and a smile and joy and is always just happy to see us," said Feingold, waving to Putt as she continued on with her son to school.

Putt has never sat in front of a computer. She has heard about the Internet but can't understand why anyone would use it, and she has no need for a cellphone. "I don't want everyone to know where I am every minute," she said.

Besides, she's too busy for the virtual world. She tends to her garden, cuts her own grass, and brings the clippings to the town dump. This winter, she shoveled her own walk and driveway.

"Excuse me," she said, stepping into the street to allow Suleb and

Anouk Noir to cross, along with their mom, Talitha Reynolds.

The three walked toward the Coffin school, and when she returned, she grew silent.

Asked how she felt after the kids cross the street, Putt closed her eyes and took a few seconds to answer. "They're safe when they're with me," she said, keeping her eyes on the street.

April 5, 2015
The Boston Globe

The Last Gloucester Fisherman?

Mark Carroll can't explain why he's still fishing. He can't put into words how he fell in love with a profession that has put his life in danger too many times at sea, claimed a lot of his bank account, and his marriage.

But, at 40, Carroll says that even if he wanted to do something else, it's too late in life to learn another profession. And, despite the strict government regulations that prevent him from fishing much of the year, he hopes to fish forever.

"The reason I got into fishing in the first place was to be my own boss and to be outside," says Carroll, who has fished these waters for more than 17 years and remembers the glory days when fishermen could work as many days of the year that they wanted.

But, with government regulations limiting him to 48 days a year at sea on his boat Harvest Moon, he's now working on other vessels in order to pay his bills. Tonight, he'll captain the Explorer II, a 50-foot boat that a friend has hired him to run. His goal: catch 800 pounds of cod, the maximum federal daily allowance for North Shore fishermen.

It's after 8, and the sun has set over Rocky Neck. The sky's gray, and there's silence on a lone pier save for an occasional seagull's cry or the creaking sounds that come from the fishing boats that rock back and forth in the harbor.

Carroll emerges from his pickup truck, revealing a picture of the modern Gloucester fisherman. Wearing a Red Sox visor, a blue T-shirt, shorts, and open-toed sandals, he could blend in seamlessly with the locals who have packed a gallery this night to sip wine and reflect on a new collection of paintings.

But Carroll, who is 5 feet 9 inches, muscular, with thinning light hair, has fishing on his mind. He hops on the boat, fires up the engine, and chats briefly with his crewman Mark Favaloro. Just a few years ago, Favaloro served almost a year in Iraq as an Army welder. At 24, he's worked as a fisherman for almost 12 months, and likes the freedom of working in the open ocean.

At 8:15, Carroll steers the boat past the harbor's Paint Factory. Going 9 miles per hour, it will take about 90 minutes to reach the Middle Bank, a section of the fertile Stellwagen Bank about 15 miles off the coast.

By 9 p.m., a major thunderstorm with heavy rains is drumming against the boat. Lightning shoots from the sky, momentarily turning the black night into a hazy white aura. Carroll seems undisturbed and says the squall will pass. "This is about the 20th time I've seen lightning this summer," he says.

The sky again shoots down a jagged bolt, but this time toward the back of the boat. Carroll laughs. About four hours later, he wants to talk about that lightning bolt. "That was something, how the lightning hit the boat," he says.

The rains slow and then cease and by 10:30, the two fishermen don rain slickers. Carroll pushes a button to electronically lower the boat's net into the water. When it reaches the ocean floor, Carroll begins trawling, with the mesh scooping up fish. At 11, Carroll slows the boat and the fishermen raise the net.

"It's a small bag, that's OK," says Carroll, who guides the net toward a rectangular box. The net opens and about 100 fish fill the box. Most are 10-pound codfish, nestled along with some haddock and flounder.

The men quickly drop the net back into the water. Often fishermen catch thousands of extra cod that die in the net and have to be discarded because of the 800-pound catch limit.

By 12:15, the men have raised the net again and dropped another load onto the boat. Carroll discards about 30 flounder, mostly alive, and seems pleased with the trip.

"Any sane person wouldn't be doing this," Carroll says. He talks about the loss of close fishing friends, and how the industry has all but collapsed. "Who is going to get into this business after me? I don't want my kids doing it. It's a bad investment."

At 2:30 a.m., Carroll guides the boat back into Gloucester Harbor. It is silent as the men leave the vessel and the fish and return to their cars in the dark parking lot.

August 10, 2008
The Boston Globe

Story Men

It's the first Friday of the month and 12 men are sitting in the back of a Chinese restaurant in a strip mall in Danvers. Some have cameras around their necks as they head toward the buffet table. For nearby diners it looks like another group, but the assembled men have documented and become part of history: They are some of the best-known news photographers north of Boston.

On one side sits Don Young, who was the first on the scene to photograph Michael McDermott after he was arrested on charges of killing seven coworkers at the Edgewater Technology office in Wakefield in 2000.

Walter Hoey, a former Lynn Item photo editor, whose photos of the Lynn fire of 1981 were published in a book, sits opposite Young. A few feet away is Steven Alexander, who captured the shooting of Lee Harvey Oswald for NBC-TV with a 16mm film camera. And at the end of the table is Ray Wallman, a former Boston Herald and Record American photographer who took photos of presidents and prime ministers and is known in his hometown of Peabody as "the legend."

"You never realize it at the time, but after you take the picture, you understand that you were there when history was being made," said Wallman, 79, who started taking pictures with film seven decades ago and in recent years made the transition to digital.

For more than 15 years, the photographers have met at a handful of eateries in Danvers and Lynnfield; they have always been Chinese restaurants, and the group has always gathered at 1 p.m. on the first Friday of each month. Young, who helped initiate the monthly assembly, said the reason the group has met for so long is because photographers like to be around other photographers.

"It all started because we loved each other's company," said Young, 72, a retired Boston Herald-Traveler photographer. Young said they chose early Friday afternoon because it gave the photographers a chance to eat before shooting sports and news events later in the day. The group is composed mostly of retired and working news photographers, but in recent years others have come regularly — portrait photographers and retired firefighters.

At different points over the years, the group has included as many as 30 people — photographers who worked for publications including the Globe, Herald, Newsweek, National Geographic, Lynn Item, Salem News, and Wakefield Daily Item. Several have died in recent years, including Al Mellett, who shot for National Geographic, and Pete Zaharis, who worked for the Salem News and owned a camera shop where members of the group would buy supplies and congregate.

While several have switched from film to digital cameras, all worked in an era when the art of news photography was evolving, driving around in cars equipped with as many as a dozen police and fire scanners looking for news. With TV news in its infancy, newspapers were the main source of news in the country, and the photographers lugged around Graflex Speed Graphic cameras, which were bulky and required photographers to manually focus and cock the shutter before taking a picture. Then photographers had to rush back to their newspapers and develop the pictures in darkrooms — a lengthy process that required meticulous attention.

These days, few of the men still shoot film, and many say if they had been able to use digital cameras, which can transfer pictures from remote locations to computers at newspapers in seconds, their jobs would have been much easier. Still, even with the digital cameras, the photographers say the key to a good picture is telling a story.

"I don't care how good your technique is or how artistic you are. If the photograph doesn't communicate, it's just a snapshot," explained Alexander, 68, of Woburn, who started his career as a news photographer for the Fort Worth Star-Telegram. Besides telling a story, Alexander said it's important for photographers to be aware of his or her surroundings and to anticipate what might happen next.

Following your instincts is also critical, say the photographers. After the assassination of John F. Kennedy in Dallas in 1963, Alexander spent two days at the Dallas police station waiting for Oswald to be transferred to the county jail. As Oswald was being led to an armored car, Alexander was rolling his movie camera, standing in the front row of photographers covering the event — just 5 feet from Oswald when he was shot by Jack Ruby.

"I kept rolling, and I saw the back of Ruby and then I saw them wrestling with Ruby to get the gun away from him," Alexander said.

Wallman, who started taking pictures in the 1940s, also said it is best to scope out a room or outdoor area where the photos are being taken and not to have a preconceived idea of what type of picture you'll come away with. "The key is to observe what's going on," said Wallman, a longtime Record American photographer who took candids of President Kennedy and Prime Minister Winston Churchill and won Boston press awards for his spot-news coverage.

Hoey also said a photographer's instincts help create the best picture. Hoey covered many tragedies in his 30 years at the Lynn Item, including fires, crashes, and murders. "It doesn't bother you until you're in the darkroom and printing the pictures — that's when you think about it," he said.

After about an hour, just a few people are left at the table. The conversation shifts from digital cameras to film and then to stories about the old days and making deadlines and darkroom developing. When it's time to leave, there are no long goodbyes and soon the table is empty — until next month.

January 20, 2008
The Boston Globe

Hollywood Over the Tobin

On an overcast morning last week, Marianne Murray stood behind a waist-high yellow tape at the Topsfield Fair and could barely control her excitement.

Several yards away, actors Larry David and Kate Hudson were shooting a scene for "Clear History," an upcoming HBO film.

Murray, who is from Winthrop, once went to Hollywood in search of fame. But on this day, just the sight of Hudson — her favorite star — seemed enough.

"I've always wanted to be a movie star, so seeing Kate Hudson is almost like having my dream come true," she said, standing on her toes to get a better look at Goldie Hawn's daughter, best known for her performance in "Almost Famous."

Until a few years ago, Hollywood seldom set up cameras north of Boston. But that changed after the state began offering a tax credit that allows producers to recoup millions in rebates, a move that has lured major stars such as Michael Douglas and Sandra Bullock to shoot in the region.

"Clear History" is the second film that has set down roots on the North Shore this summer, following Adam Sandler's "Grown Ups 2." Sandler's film was shot in Lowell, Lynn, Marblehead, Saugus, Swampscott, and Tyngsborough, and provided a substantial revenue boost to local businesses.

David, who co-created "Seinfeld" and also created and stars in HBO's "Curb Your Enthusiasm," chose areas to replicate Martha's Vineyard, where the film — about a fallen marketing whiz — is set.

Monica Levinson, the film's producer, said there are now almost 300 full-time workers on the set, with at least 275 of them local residents. They include film technicians, art and wardrobe consultants, carpenters, and about 50 local actors who serve as extras.

"I'd say we're spending at least $10 million on the film during production," she said, and added that most of the Hollywood stars are staying in a local hotel.

The crew also spent two days shooting scenes at the North Shore Music Theatre in Beverly.

One afternoon last week, more than 300 volunteers were sitting in the theater in the round, along with dozens of paid extras.

Chris Carr, who processes computer parts, had the day off, and made the short drive from Danvers to volunteer. Carr once met Bruce Springsteen after a 1978 concert, and was hoping to meet David, whom he called "the funniest guy going."

By late afternoon, Carr and about 100 extras had sidled over to an aisle where David was filming a scene with Jon Hamm and Kate Hudson. David appeared aloof and occasionally practiced his lines aloud. He wore a denim shirt over a striped, buttoned-down shirt and T-shirt, brown slacks, and tan work boots. When a fan tried to engage him in a conversation, he took notice and addressed a small group of people.

"You volunteered? Oh, my God!" he said, breaking into a smile. "I had no idea. Does that mean I have to meet every one of you?"

The volunteers laughed and seemed satisfied that they had been noticed.

Meanwhile, in the next few hours, David did more than a dozen takes, occasionally going off the script and ad-libbing, as he is known to do in "Curb Your Enthusiasm." This seemed to please the volunteer extras, who gauged the filming and applauded when they deemed that a scene had been successful.

During one of the last scenes, Kati Enscoe walked into the theater as the cameras rolled and took a seat a few rows behind David, Hudson, and Hamm. Enscoe, who lost her full-time marketing job in September, said working a few days as a paid extra occurred at the right time. The Marblehead native has little acting experience but hopes to do more extra work, which pays around $150 a day.

Enscoe said part of the perk is schmoozing with the stars. "Larry David is just hilarious. He was super cool during the filming and telling us that we did a great job, and he gave us feedback," she said. She also stood next to Hudson for a couple of hours one day. "I said, 'I like your jacket,' and she said, 'I like your boots.' "

Carr, who was given a beer bottle (filled with water) that he pretended to drink during the filming, briefly met David and Hamm following the final scene.

After some small talk, he followed an exit sign and was descending a wide stairway when he heard voices behind him. When he turned around, he saw that it was David, Hudson, and Hamm discussing Japanese food. Carr kept on walking, content that he had done something different that day.

"It was fulfilling and kind of surreal," he said. "I never felt overwhelmed or intimidated. I felt like they were regular people, just like me."

October 11, 2012
The Boston Globe

Bottle Fishing

I t's 30 degrees and windy, and Angel Morales is tired. For more than four hours he's been wheeling his shopping basket through the back streets of Salem and Peabody, looking for redeemable cans and bottles. After walking about 10 miles, he counts out 300 containers and places them on a counter in a chilly bottle-and-can redemption center in Peabody.

"I do this just to put food on the table," says Morales, 64, who worked as a fisherman for 37 years on the North Shore but can't work on boats anymore because of a bad back. For more than a year he's followed this canning route three days a week, collecting enough empties to earn about $35 a day.

"I only get $700 a month from Social Security and I can't live on it. With the economy the way it is what can you do with $700?" says Morales, who lives in a small apartment in Salem.

Can collecting, or "bottle fishing" — in order to redeem 5 cents an empty — has long been seen as a cultural divide between upper and lower class. But with the economy in a nose dive and unemployment in the state climbing, more and more people are returning their empty cans and bottles, while others have taken to the streets in search of empties.

"It's just the consumer being more frugal. Why throw something away that will give you some cash?" said professor Dorothy Siden, chairwoman of the department of economics at Salem State College.

Every year since 1998, consumers have purchased about 2 billion redeemable cans and bottles in the state. But retailers who own liquor stores and redemption centers say they're seeing new faces and increased returns. Also, more organizations have found that returning empties brings revenue.

"I've seen an increase of 10 percent over the last year. People don't have the money they used to have," said Chris Palazola, who owns Chrispy's Liquors in Beverly. "I see all walks of life — professionals right down to the homeless. Now, the working class are the new people who are bringing them in."

Just a few blocks away, Mike Kessel sorted through a mountain of cans at Beverly Bottle & Can Return. "Business is up at least 10 percent," said Kessel. "The economy is the number one reason why people are coming in. People are watching their nickels. I'm seeing more retirees, and unemployed, and young families coming in with their children."

Kessel's warehouse smells like beer, and people carry in large plastic bags and place their empties on a counter as workers sort cans and bottles in large bins according to manufacturer. For hours every day, the echo of aluminum clashing creates a monotonous thwacking sound.

Meanwhile, people like Michael Howard and Vicki O'Brien, both of Beverly, stood in line waiting to exchange their empties for dollars.

Howard said he's new to recycling, and usually gets about $6 from his collection — just enough to put a few gallons of gas into his car. "I lost my job a couple of years ago and the job I have now pays one-half of what I used to make, so this helps out," he explained.

O'Brien, who works as a sales clerk at a mall department store, said the few dollars she collects will go toward feeding her children. "I was never really into it but I've got four kids," she said.

Outside, Eli DiPaolo toted a bag with 150 cans. "It's lunch money for my grandchildren," said DiPaolo, 82, a retired welder from Beverly who remembers eating at soup kitchens as a child during the Depression.

In Lynn, Thy Vorn, manager of J & K Redemption, said the downturn in the economy has brought fewer returns from restaurants and more new customers — like retirees and blue-collar workers. "There's a lot of new people bringing in less amounts," said Vorn.

A year ago Cheryl DiVecchia would throw out her plastic soda bottles. But everything from high gas prices and electric bills to increased food costs made her change her mind about saving bottles.

"In the past I wouldn't save them, but times are really tight," said DiVecchia, who brings her bottles to J & K twice a month. She said the money she gets, about $16 a month, goes toward food. "I'm working two jobs to pay bills. I'm almost on a third job."

December 4, 2008
The Boston Globe

Court Is Adjourned

They have been prosecuting cases in this town since 1636, when Ipswich joined Boston, Salem, and Newton as the centers of justice for the Massachusetts Bay Colony. John Adams argued cases here before becoming president. Daniel Webster also made impassioned pleas here, as did native son Rufus Choate, who succeeded Webster as US senator from Massachusetts.

But come summer, the Ipswich court will end its 368-year residency. The Ipswich District Court will retain its name, and its 11 employees, as cases from the district which serves Ipswich, Topsfield, Hamilton, and Wenham will shift from Ipswich to the Newburyport District Courthouse.

According to Bruce Brock, a spokesman for the Trial Court of Massachusetts, the state has decided to end its rental agreement at the former Ipswich Town Hall, where the court has been since 1843.

The court's days have been numbered since last year, when Governor Mitt Romney proposed consolidating the Ipswich court with the Gloucester District Court. That consolidation was rejected by the Legislature.

Judge Allen Swan, who has served as the presiding justice of the Ipswich court for the last five years, will continue to sit on the bench when the court shifts to Newburyport. Swan presides over the small courtroom every Thursday. The court is also open two Tuesdays a month.

Swan, who has researched the history of the court, says the cases he hears are similar to those in the 17th century: landlord/tenant disputes, domestic assaults, substance abuse. "The basic underlying conflicts that we have in society are still with us 350 years later," he said.

In one of the earliest records of the Ipswich Quarterly Court, the court heard dozens of civil and criminal cases in December of 1641. Some cases were similar to that of Joseph Lee, who was accused of lying and stealing a Bible; others like Joseph Pemerton and the wife of John Robinson faced civil charges of "obscene and filthy speeches."

Swan said justice has come a long way from the 17th century, when "things were done with perhaps a lot more dispatch but with a lot less due process."

The courthouse, on South Main Street, once shared space with the town's police station and Town Hall offices. Today the top floor is deserted, and the downstairs is a narrow labyrinth of brown paneled offices stuffed with furniture, computers, copying machines, and telephones. There is no bell that announces visitors to the building. Instead, workers can tell when someone arrives by the loud slam of the front door.

There's also not much elbow room in Swan's 980-square-foot courtroom, where visitors have to walk slowly between the wooden benches and two steel columns as they approach the witness box, and desks for attorneys and court officials.

Even with the upgrade to the more modern Newburyport court, several court employees would rather not leave.

Michael Bulgaris, who was the Rowley police chief before becoming chief probation officer of the court 20 years ago, will still spend much of his time visiting parolees in Ipswich, Hamilton, Wenham, and Topsfield. "Thank God we're all going together," he said of the court's employees. Bulgaris takes pride in his staff, and also in the men and women he once supervised. Through his ties to the local Greek church, Bulgaris has been able to find work for paroled residents who want employment.

Bulgaris, who started as a one-man department with a small desk, still walks though the courtroom with a sense of awe and deep respect for justice. Pointing to a mural of former judge Joseph Furnari, Bulgaris said, "He was the greatest judge of all time." He then paused and stood silently for several seconds, looking at the judge's desk and the law books.

"It's like Mayberry RFD here," said Julie Gilligan, the court's probation operations supervisor. "Yesterday, somebody brought us some cookies."

"We also had someone bring us a pizza," said Tiffany Ray, a probation officer.

Ray and Gilligan stood next to each other and wondered about how things would change in Newburyport. The two have become good friends and help plan birthday celebrations and the office Christmas party. The women believe the small office they help run allows them to communicate better and be more efficient. "We're afraid we're going to lose what we have — the closeness, the birthdays everything," said Ray.

March 25, 2004
The Boston Globe

A Writer Presses
the Reset Button

K OH PHANGAN, Thailand — I do not understand all of the psychological implications of escapism. But after spending the last six weeks on an island in Thailand, I must conclude that there is plenty of merit to stepping out of your routine and pondering life's meaning, while, in the process, getting to know yourself a whole lot better.

I contemplate this in a bungalow some 8,500 miles from my home, just days before I am set to return to the North Shore. In our parlance, this can only be understood as an island that exists over the rainbow, where the water is so warm and nourishing that even the most skeptical Bostonian can look up at the sky and offer thanks, where people smile and make eye contact when saying hello.

While the average worker earns $300 a month here, complaining, criticizing, blaming, and judging others is not part of the culture — rather, there's a sense of optimism and acceptance. I have observed no public confrontations, arguments, or loud voices — and, if you can believe it — little public cellphone use. In short, the dictum used in journalism and other American professions of "more, better, faster" does not apply here. Rather, one can look to Hemingway's minimalistic style for definition: Less is more.

And so, now comes the challenge of returning to America with new lessons about myself and society and how to live with a sense of respect for others in a divided country.

For clues I look to the immediate past. For decades, a typical day focused on getting things accomplished almost as fast as possible, and began with a coffee routine at Dunkin' Donuts. Since the growth of the check-out window, it has been a largely solitary experience, and now feels no more than a transaction. I hand the person a couple of bucks and am handed back a coffee. I say thanks and drive off.

I then head back to my desk and begin a story. To some, a journalist's job may seem glamorous. We rub shoulders with the famous, but most of our hours are spent on the phone, trying to track down a person for a quote or waiting for a call back. In between, we might knock on the doors of others who have something to do with the piece and write down their words, or go to a courthouse, a library, or a city hall to obtain a document. Then it's back to the computer, where there's hours more research to be done as we try to become experts on subjects we often know little about. Everything revolves around making deadline and getting people to go on the record, and filing the story — ideally by 5 p.m.

There's not a lot of time for chitchat in between, and by dinner time I'm usually drained. As with so many other Americans, there's no lunchtime walk or moments of contemplation on a park bench, and strikingly few spontaneous conversations with strangers. Dinner is usually after 7, and my wife is also wiped out after a long work day. We talk, try to inspire one another, and then I usually turn on the wide-screen TV and watch a movie or a game.

I'm not suggesting it's boring or that I dislike my profession. But here, I'm getting a sense that a new routine can be established. It focuses on interacting with others with no specific agenda. The early results are promising.

This culture encourages interaction, and mornings I saunter over to La Dolce Vita, the Italian restaurant just a few yards away from my room, for my coffee. I order an Americano and usually talk with Fausto, the bistro's manager, who happens to be one of the most hard-core Celtic fans I've met. He's from Milan, a yacht designer by trade, and he waxes nostalgic about Celtic pride, declaring that our basketball team embodies the way society is meant to function. He traces it back to the partnership of Bill Russell and Red Auerbach.

"Auerbach played the best players, and it didn't matter what color their skin was," Fausto told me. "He showed that team effort can also help build community."

Afternoons are spent on the beach, where I alternately swim, read, and talk to people who greet me with a smile. Sunsets are the highlight of the day, and it seems like everybody stops to stare at the sky and pause in gratitude. The other day I was watching the sunset when Paulina, a Swedish woman on a yoga retreat, asked me my line of work. I told her I was a writer and she nodded, as if she knew something about me.

"Your creative energy is a little blocked," she said.

Sometimes it takes a fresh set of eyes to cut to the truth. She was right. But had it been that obvious? I felt I had no real motivation to write as I processed who I had become and how I might return to my authentic self. At that moment, though, I remembered that writers must write or lose their passion.

The sun went down, and we said goodbye and went on our way. I started writing again that night and casually typed the word Paulina into a Google search. A close match came up. In Greek mythology, nine goddesses who symbolized the arts, literature, and sciences were known as muses. One of the nine, it turns out, was named Polyhymnia. She protected sacred poetry and is credited with bringing distinction to writers whose words won them immortal fame.

I suppose when I return I can take a lesson from the people I've met here, and have more unplanned conversations. They have a way of building community, right?

December 11, 2016
Boston Globe

CHAPTER 9

Weather

A Time to Look into the Sun

On these early August evenings I go down to the ocean, where I seek refuge from the noise of life.

I sit on hard brown sand that is underwater at least 20 hours a day. It's only accessible during low tide, and when I finally reach my spot, I surrender. There are no dings or chimes from texts and e-mails out here. I'm alone on a 30-foot stretch of coast where gentle 3-inch waves turn into white foam and sparkle before disappearing.

I'm a few feet from a large crab that may or may not be alive. And I'm just 20 yards or so from two small boulders I once climbed as a child with a group of schoolmates. I am always surprised that few people take the time to trek out past the delicate tide pools and seaweed-covered rocks to reach this place.

I swim here because I am a North Shore guy, and natives are supposed to get to know these waters. I swim here because it's August and all the warmth that accompanies these days will be gone soon. I swim here because there are answers in this mystical cove that seem to be accessible only if I wade out into the green, clear shoreline and slip beneath the waves.

Each step from the shore allows for a new jolt of numbness. My body adjusts, and I sense that I am letting go of thoughts that are not facts, worries that I have no control of. The current laps over my arms and shoulders. A few seagulls stand guard over the rocks. One faces toward Boston, the others look to the north.

I allow the cool water to reach my chest. This form of ablution seems necessary, and for a moment I feel this massive mikveh washing away all of the burdens that I've carried here, and even some that I'm not even aware of. Lulled by the otherworldly trickle and rhythm of the soft waves, the numbness gives way to a gentle trance.

Each wave seems to carry off a different part of my identity. In 5 feet of cold water, I am immersed in an unexpected, yet welcome prayer. But I am aware that in a matter of minutes, much of what I had deemed important has become irrelevant. Out here, I have no career, no pressing appointments, no money in my pocket. My name even seems irrelevant. And yet I feel as connected as one can become with the earth.

When I open my eyes, I understand that the waves have delivered a simple dose of gratitude. I am warmed by the sun, and then hum along to the Jethro Tull song, "Look Into the Sun," which is about finding hope during the summer:

"So when you look into the sun
And see the words you could have sung:
It's not too late, only begun,
We can still make summer.
Yes, summer always comes anyway."

I stand on my toes, lean forward, and push as my shoulders and head slide under the waves. After all the anticipation, my body doesn't protest and I begin to swim. The seagulls continue to call. The rocks look the same, the seaweed meanders on the ocean floor, and I float around until the tide carries me toward the sand.

On my way back toward the main beach, much of the area that had been dry is now underwater. Along the way, I walk over barnacle-covered rocks, slippery patches of seaweed, and through warm tide pools.

I reach out to touch the reflection of the sun along the surf as I walk. Soon, I come upon two excited girls on kickboards.

"Let's go out deeper, that's where the mermaids are," one tells her friend.

I nod and smile, and look back to the cove. The girls meander and splash one another. And then, I resume my walk, raise my head, and look into the sun.

August 21, 2016
The Boston Globe

Chasing Down Summer

T he old Volvo steers into the driveway, and for a moment I rest. But, inside the garage, the trusty brown three-speed beckons. More than 20 years ago, a friend insisted that I accept her former boyfriend's bike as a gift; we compromised and I gave her $15 for the barely used cycle.

Now there is rust on the handlebars, and the wheels wobble and squeak. I hop on the stodgy brown seat and pedal downhill toward King's Beach and the Nahant circle. There's a hot wind blowing in my face and ears, and the low tide's waves crash on a few people still holding on to summer.

I glide along the bike path at Nahant Beach, and see faces I have learned to recognize over the summer. There is the Russian woman and her small son, who sit in silence on a bench looking out at the Atlantic; there is the Arabic-speaking woman, who smiles and adjusts her hijab as she walks hand and hand with her son; there is the jogger who looks like Ted Turner and runs with a big key around his neck.

My bike creaks over the asphalt, and I weave in between the walkers and joggers. The sun has a red tint as it begins to set over the Resco plant in Saugus. The wind is still hot, and lifts blades of the beach grass into the air. The grass is turning white and wilting; I wonder if this happens every September.

A woman with sunglasses smiles as she walks by. I pass two Asian women who are collecting soda cans and bottles from garbage bins. A Haitian man sits on one of the numerous concrete picnic tables on the edge of the path and writes. He looks up at me but our eyes do not meet. A few seconds later, I notice a college-aged woman at another table, writing left-handed. She wears her blond hair in a ponytail, and scribbles fast. I pass an elderly man who walks briskly, carrying a stick that appears to have been fashioned from a broom. The number 103 is on his baseball hat.

I reach the end of the beach, and rest for a minute in the parking lot. Three bikers laugh, and smoke, and their motorcycles make my three-speed look like a toy. A man stands in the ocean with both of his arms raised above his head. He is waving to someone near me.

I circle around the lot, and begin my ride home. It is still warm, and the wind hums. I look out at the island of Egg Rock, where they say a child was once born. Then my eyes focus on the waves, and I remember the story of the sea serpent that was said to have been spotted by lots of people right along this beach.

Now the sun is an exquisite pink, and the color falls on the sand, and the skyline is filled with pastels. The wind tosses the beach grass; the jogger with the big key around his neck sweats as he runs past the man with the 103 on his hat.

I return to speed, and shift into third gear. The wheels click, the wind hums, the sun has almost set, and I know that I am chasing the warmth that will not be here in a few weeks. I look down at the beach grass, and over at the waves, and gulp in a hot breeze that will help provide sustenance until the spring.

September 24, 2006
The Boston Globe

Hurricane Comin'

How does one prepare for a storm? Besides hunkering down with groceries, flashlights, and plenty of water, we are advised to stay inside, listen to weather advisories, and not drive.

I planned to do the opposite on Monday morning. I would spend the day outside, seeking meaning from those who enjoy standing at the edge of seawalls during major storms, deep in thought. Perhaps they could explain what draws them to the edge of catastrophe. I also planned to speak with those whose lives would change during the day. Some who had power in the morning and would later be sitting in darkness. Or replaying the moment a tree crashed into their house.

There was nothing unusual about Monday's gray, dour sky. We live with it from late fall through the winter and into the spring. There were no torrential rains on the North Shore as Hurricane Sandy barreled toward the coast. But the sky sounded like a giant fan that suggested something bad was on its way.

The noise followed me to Nahant Beach just before high tide, around 11:30 a.m. There, Laura Taurasi and Herbie Robbins were standing at the edge of the Nahant Causeway, leaning into the wind and watching the waves pummel the shoreline.

The Saugus couple had just come from Revere, where a wind storm had turned America's oldest public beach into an aquatic miasma. The two planned to head to Lynn Beach after getting a good soaking from the curtain of waves in Nahant. When I asked them why they weren't inside, they said they were drawn to the waves.

"I live dangerously. I'm curious," said Taurasi.

Just north in Lynn, about 100 people had congregated at the seawall next to Red Rock at King's Beach. Most stood alone, staring at the whitecaps as they swirled from a distance before gathering steam and finally crashing against the seawall. Some waves looked harmless; others were ominous, rising like a chariot going full force into battle.

The wall seemed like an afterthought. We mostly took for granted that it would stay intact. I snapped hundreds of photos while dodging vertical sheets of salt water, and then focused on the wall again. Wasn't it built to hold back ferocious storms like this? But walls have collapsed before, and my mind shifted to Katrina before I started taking photos again. The 10-foot waves rose from the Atlantic and curled liked seahorses seeking to conquer land. The wall stood proudly and held firm; its culverts shot out streams of salt water after taking a hit.

Dozens of people lined the pavilion that sticks out over the beach. They gripped cellphone and pocket cameras, looking to interpret the surges, and did their best to get out of the way when the mist from the giant surf crashed as high as 20 feet above their heads.

Karen Cahill usually cooks on weekdays at Lynn Tech, but the school was closed and her apartment building across from King's Beach was shaking. She had a perfect view of the ocean from her eighth-floor unit, but she wanted more. She needed to be in the middle of the storm.

"I could sell tickets to this," she said, as she snapped photos of the waves and mist. "A lot of my friends wanted to come over, but they can't get here."

Around 2 p.m., I learned that around one-third of Swampscott had lost its electricity. The areas without power stretched from King's Beach all the way to Vinnin Square, the town's main shopping center.

Rabbi Yossi Lipsker, the leader of Chabad Lubavitch of the North Shore, spent most of the day at his synagogue, just a block from the beach. There, the power flickered on and off. He said he often goes to the beach during storms and could relate to those who were standing before the surf.

"When you see something that you don't normally see, oftentimes it allows you to feel something spiritually that you don't normally feel," he said.

In Marblehead, I stood on a cliff overlooking Preston Beach. Its pristine seawall seemed no match for the colossal waves. Meanwhile, people sauntered past me and squeezed along the narrow path on top of the seawall to get a better view. People behind me yelled out warnings to the storm watchers, but they kept on walking.

I wondered about their safety and then noticed Rich Messinger, a Marblehead photographer, who also had been driving from one beach to another all day.

"I'm looking for the perfect wave," he told me. The wave, he explained, would be a combination of two breakers. When they smash together

it's like a sandwich, he said. "I like the unpredictability of storms. You don't know what's going to happen," he said.

"The ocean fascinates me, and it fascinates everybody."

Back on dry land, I came upon a house where a large tree crashed onto a roof.

"The wind was blowing heavy and all of sudden I heard a crashing sound," Glover Preble explained, looking up at his roof. Preble is named after two famous relatives: Revolutionary War General John Glover was his great-great-great-great-great-great-grandfather, and Edward Preble was once the commodore of the USS Constitution.

"We just count our blessings that we didn't get hit any harder," said the retired Marblehead police sergeant.

Back in Swampscott, Vinnin Square was dark even before sundown. Parts of the shopping center were under water last October, when a storm dumped 6 inches of rain on the town during high tide. During Sandy, it was mostly dry but silent.

On a nearby street, Gregg Hamel, a Swampscott native who still lives in town, was wondering when his power would come back on.

He had gone to the beaches and seen the waves, played guitar at a friend's house, and was ready to eat dinner. "When you lose all your electrical power and Internet connectivity to the world, you feel isolated," he told me.

I headed home, turned on the computer, and looked for lost clues of the day in my photos. I have lived next to the ocean nearly all of my life, and on different days the waves have seemed mostly green, blue, aqua, and white. On this day the waves just seemed to be gasping for something we could never understand.

They appeared to be drowning in their own fury, while begging to be released from an ocean that edged closer and closer to us.

November 4, 2012
The Boston Globe

Gotta Shovel

It snowed all night again and I gotta shovel.

I grab a shovel. It's a really bad design but it was the cheapest one I could buy at the downtown hardware store. "It's 14 bucks," the hardware guy said. "It works."

It's about the eighth shovel I've owned since I moved into the house. The first one I used was a flat aluminum shovel that had belonged to the previous owner. It had a large crack in it and barely lasted the winter. I bought a big blue shovel the next year that made it through exactly one snowstorm. Content with my work, I gently placed it next to the front door at the top of the steps and went inside to relax. A few hours later, I noticed the shovel was missing. I looked for the thief but he was gone. "Ah, welcome to the city," I thought.

Another time, a person who talked his way into shoveling my walk asked whether he could use our shovel since his had broken. "Sure," I said. My wife paid him $10 and a few minutes later, I went out to check his work. At the top of the steps, I found his shovel, with the broken handle. "The old shovel switch," I thought. "Now that's chutzpah." I laughed and cursed and then picked up his shovel — which was my new shovel. The broken handle dug into my palms and, after another season, I had to get rid of it.

The snow is about 2 feet deep by the edge of the driveway. It's soggy and heavy and I wonder if I should be shoveling at all. I start thinking about the middle-aged men whom you read about in the obituary section who were in the best of health and were found in snowbanks

— done in by the shoveling.

I keep pushing the snow around anyway, and I'm brought back to Orchard Road in the 1960s, where it seemed like it snowed like this every week in the winter and it wasn't a big deal. Back then, I insisted on shoveling and got up really early so my dad could get his car out of the driveway.

I was a horrible beginner, and my father instructed me not to just push the snow. "You've got to pick it up, Stevie," he told me. He'd grab another shovel and we'd stand there talking about sports for an hour while we cleared the driveway, and I'd announce how many more days there were until pitchers and catchers reported to spring training.

Inevitably he'd start talking about the old Red Sox-Yankees teams from the 1940s, and didn't Joe DiMaggio and Ted Williams have the sweetest swings in baseball?

I look up and a man who walks by my house twice a day with his dog looks at my shoveling work, and says, "At least it's white snow."

I don't know what to say so I just smile, and then I notice a thin, short guy with a beard and glasses who I see all the time in the neighborhood walking toward me.

He looks like someone I went to UMass with in the 1970s, or somebody I'd see at a Grateful Dead concert. "Not too heavy, is it?" he asks, and I tell him, no, it's not bad.

I look down the hill at the Atlantic. The sun is already high and hits the waves and the water is gold, blue, and green. I wonder who's out fishing today.

I want to walk down to the ocean and look at the waves and stare out as far as I can.

I keep pushing the shovel, though, and the snow is just as heavy as ever.

March 2, 2008
The Boston Globe

The Winter Hat

I have never liked wearing a winter hat. When I was a child, the only options were stiff woolen hats and long stocking offerings. I hated both, especially the drab woolen hats that made my ears and neck itch.

By the time I realized I was allergic to wool it was too late — even on the most frigid winter days I would go hatless. I didn't care for gloves either, and as a high school student in the mid-1970s I would spend hours trekking through the snow-filled woods of Swampscott clad in a snorkel jacket. All of that walking and laughing with my friends made me feel good about life, but did not keep me warm.

The first hat I wore in college was a mauve ski nylon weave that looked fine in the store, but bulbous when it stretched over my head. I was breaking with custom; it was time to conform and stay warm. When I reached the center of campus my hat drew no attention, and I was comforted by the anonymity that comes with attending a large state university.

Since then, I have worn several types of hats, but none consistently throughout an entire winter. And for a couple of winters I've gone without a hat or gloves.

In 1984, I didn't plan to not wear gloves or a hat — I just didn't get around to it. In 1994, however, I decided at the beginning of the winter to go with just a warm jacket. I felt like I had to prove something; I would greet the winter the same way I embraced other seasons. So what if the wind and rain and snow would cover my hands and head at times? I could handle it.

I was wrong. I had entered the season hoping to be enriched by the changing temperature, but by late March, I was nearly a broken man. I had spent most of the winter working outside, leaving my hands stiff and my back creaky. I had succeeded in whatever I had set out to accomplish, and swore that I would never do something that stupid again.

But I've done a lot of stupid things since then, including wearing silly winter hats. Once, while interviewing Bill Weld, the former Massachusetts governor, I wore an Indiana Jones-style hat. Weld later put the hat on his head and asked if he could keep it. I should have given it to him because I lost it a few days later.

In 1999, I wore a trapper's hat with swaths of imitation mink that I mercifully left behind one Friday on a Blue Line train at Wonderland. In 2001, I wore a hat made of nutria — "a wonderfully warm hat," my wife said, as she presented it to me. It had golden fur like the rat-like animal it came from, earmuffs, and a chin strap, and made me feel like a hunting dog.

In recent years, I have worn Red Sox hats, fedoras, and simple ski caps.

This winter, the weather has been mild and there has been no real need to wear a hat. In January, I bought a blue ski hat and promptly lost it. In February, I wore my son's Washington Nationals hat and misplaced that, too (I have not told my son about it yet); this month I have worn hats with emblems representing the Cleveland Indians, Baltimore Orioles, and Dunkin' Donuts.

Also this month, I decided it was time to buy gloves. I went to three stores before finding any in stock. In Swampscott, at TJ Maxx, I settled on a pair of oversized red gloves that no one with any style would purchase. I paid $4 and eased my hands into the red fabric. The woman behind the counter smiled politely.

"These are really ugly," I said.

"They're warm, and who cares what other people think?" she said.

I guess I do.

March 29, 2007
The Boston Globe

Dear Rain

Dear Rain:

There's an adage in the newspaper business that if you write a story about a prolonged change in the weather, then by the time the story comes out the drought, snow, heat, or in this case rain will disappear, thus making the story irrelevant.

So to test this theory I write these words: It's been raining for weeks and it's the summer and that's unusual.

There, I did it, and that's a good start. But more detail is needed.

It's a late afternoon and from my window, I can see the Atlantic. Usually at this hour during the summer, there's still plenty of people walking and hanging out on the beach.

But the waves are choppy, and even though I stare at the water for a minute I see no one. Not a swimmer, not a runner, not a biker.

It's August and it's still raining. It rained in the middle of the July 3 barbecue, the night of the fireworks. It rained the night I saw Bruce Springsteen in concert. It rained the day I drove my son to overnight camp. It rained on my birthday. It even rained the one day I went to the beach when it was virtually cloudless.

There's been lightning and thunderstorms so many nights over the last two months I've lost count. One night a couple of weeks ago, the heavy rains and winds seeped into my dreams, and suddenly I was a native in the rain forest, living in a thatched hut.

For the last few weeks we've said goodbye to the outdoor grills, pondered the locals who have been hit by lightning, seen their cars swept away by flash floods. Even the drives into the country for ice cream and meditation have been put off. Worst of all, I've avoided the beach, and with the clouds massing each night, missed the stars.

In June, when the rains usually stop and the days grow long, there is a feeling of release. The emphasis is on getting outside, and fast. We know all of this warmth doesn't last long and we want it now.

And so, with just two more weeks left in the month it continues to rain. Still, I am confident that the sun will return soon, and a lot of us will forget about these waterlogged weeks.

We'll forget because we know what's coming. In less than a month it will turn surprisingly cold for at least a day, and then we will think about heavy clothes, and another winter.

But we still have at least two weeks of potential goofing off if the sun comes back. Sun, we know you're out there and we appreciate you. We want to return to beaches, barbecues, late-night walks in the neighborhood.

We want to get out of the car and office and breathe fresh air. We want to go on family vacations and not be cooped up in stuffy hotel rooms or camp cabins.

We want it because we deserve it. After all, we're from New England and we know weather, right?

August 14, 2008
The Boston Globe

CHAPTER 10

Jewish

Goodbye to What Could Not Be Saved

Selling a house can sometimes be a simple process. A bunch of papers are signed, you hand over the keys, and you move somewhere else.

But what happens when someone else sells a place you never owned but still feel a part of?

The sledgehammer came to my old temple last month in Swampscott, Massachusetts. It was not unexpected: It had sat idle for almost a decade after its former congregation, Temple Israel, merged with another synagogue. Soon, 14 homes will be built on the site.

The temple was once one of the grandest, most elegant open-domed Conservative sanctuaries in America — built by the estimable Italian architect Pietro Belluschi in 1953.

It represented the hopes and dreams of a new Jewish working class.

Most were American-born Jews who had fled the congestion in places like Chelsea, Revere, and Lynn. Some had gone to college and were lawyers, doctors, and accountants. Others ran scrap metal yards, owned real estate, drove trucks and cabs, or had family businesses, such as my father, who was a deli man. Some were wealthy, but most just made a living and wanted something better for their children.

Inside the building, there were traditional Jewish services every day, and a few pious men could be seen in the sanctuary. But Temple Israel functioned as much more than a house of prayer. It was part of a new era of the American Jewish experience: Ushering in a new society, brimming with great ambition, where people who had grown up in cold-water flats could find a home outside of the urban ring hard by the Mystic River.

Save for Hebrew School, it was largely empty most of the week. No matter. People drove by it, noticed its Star of David and took note that the Jews had a home and planned to stay. It also helped diffuse the not-so-subtle hints that we didn't belong everywhere: As late as the 1990s, there was a nearby golf course and a beach club where Jews did not feel welcome.

There was no grand religious or spiritual plan at the temple. We learned the Hebrew alphabet and practiced reading the foreign language. At the time, those in charge probably thought it would be unfair to burden American children with Jewish history. After all, what would be gained in describing our largely tumultuous existence? Instead we were assigned two goals: Complete your bar or bat mitzvah and graduate from college.

If anything, it was a building that belonged to our parents. Most were hardly religious, and only a few kept kosher. But there were weddings and bar mitzvahs and brotherhood breakfasts to organize, attend, and to later reminisce about. It became a community, built on some common social values, such as giving to charity, supporting Israel, and performing good deeds. These days, modern Jewish professionals have created a whole subset of Judaism around that concept and call it Tikkun Olam, or repairing the world.

But no one ever said Tikkun Olam was a path to sustain dues-paying members, and these days there is no repairing of the temple. Its honey brick courtyards have been toppled; its burnished redwood halls where plaques once honored the founding temple members gleamed in the open-aired wreckage. Its maples have been uprooted, sawed into blocks and carted away.

In its heyday in the 1970s, when more than 2,000 people crowded into services on Yom Kippur, or raised tens of thousands of dollars for Israel during the 1973 Arab-Israeli War, the temple seemed like it would go on forever. But things were changing. America was opening its doors to Jews, and with intermarriage, Jews began the process of entering the majority religion.

When I drive by the temple, my car slows to a crawl and I realize a little piece of me is somewhere in that wreckage. Was it the 13-year-old, surrounded by Old World relatives after my bar mitzvah? Or the college student who wiped away a tear alongside my sister's wedding canopy? Or, perhaps, it was the teen who found solace sitting alone in the vast sanctuary, filled with abundant natural light that streamed through the stained glass windows and made everything seem golden and perfect.

I pull into the temple parking lot, and begin to snap photos of the debris. A construction worker shrugs when I ask if it's OK to go inside. I move quickly through the lower level, choking on dust as I pass by

the remnants of the old Hebrew School classrooms. One floor above, a bulldozer rumbles in the open air where the ornate reception hall had stood just a week earlier. I step up my pace and wander, all the way walking toward the rear entrance of the sanctuary.

And then, up a back staircase, and past a darkened hallway, I press against a heavy wooden door and stand in the balcony of the basilica. The bulldozer continues its thwacking; I hear nothing though. Above me, the six stained glass windows glisten. When I think about saying a prayer, I realize that my appeal has already begun. In 48 hours, this will all be rubble.

But today, it is still a structure. Nothing suggests it is preparing to die. An other-world luminosity streams from above and touches the edges of the balcony; it falls on the old sanctuary floor and splashes on the area where the ark once stood, and held old Torahs.

As I snap more photos, I acknowledge that I will be the last Jew to stand in this sanctuary. I look down from the balcony and wonder about all the prayer that took place here. Were people's wishes fulfilled? Were the sick healed? Did lives really change after people spoke to

God? And what of the prayers that still lingered; that, to date, had gone unanswered? Was there still time in this world, or in the world to come, to have them granted? And where would they go once the building was demolished?

I want to stay; to tell the old shul that it brought a lot of people together and made so many of them happy. I want to cry, if not for American Judaism, then for the lost community that includes my family. And I want to close my eyes and remember the light. There is hope that comes from this kind of stillness, I decide.

January 2, 2014
The Boston Globe

The Freedom Box

T he man and woman saw Hitler's evil early in their lives and then went on to start families and careers.

Sixty years removed from the crematoriums and mass graves of Europe, they met in a nursing home in Rowley last week, so John Meagher could give Sonia Weitz a box that represents freedom.

Meagher, 82, sat in a wheelchair cradling a brown container that once held cigarettes.

As a medic in General George Patton's Third Army in 1945, the Gloucester native helped liberate the Buchenwald Concentration Camp in Germany and treat camp survivors. Meagher spoke English with one survivor, who said he was from Poland and had a cousin in Brooklyn. Meagher gave the man some chocolate from his K rations and the man gave Meagher the box.

With glue and rice, the prisoner had formed two striking images on the box, reflecting reality and fantasy. On one side was the imposing multileveled entrance to the death camp; the other side showed the sun shining on a star at the top of a steeple. Inside the box, the prisoner had inscribed in Russian, "To Buchenwald."

"You could smell that place the minute you got close to it," Meagher said, as Weitz nodded in agreement.

Weitz, of Peabody, survived several concentration camps, including Auschwitz. For the last 22 years she has helped run the Holocaust Center in Peabody. Meagher, who lived in Lynn and Rowley after the war and became a well-known massage therapist for professional athletes and horses, handed Weitz the box and told her it was for her library.

He does not remember the name of the man, and can't describe the artist's face. Since 1945, he kept the box in a drawer with his personal possessions and on occasion would examine the gift.

"I did think about it," said Meagher. "I thought how much freedom meant to him."

Meagher, who has fought cancer and is undergoing kidney dialysis, wanted to place the box in secure hands. He smiled as he was hugged by Weitz. The Peabody woman has spent much of her life educating children and adults about the Holocaust, and is a member of the US Holocaust Memorial Council.

Sixty years ago, stricken with typhus, she was saved by an American soldier who helped open the doors of the Mauthausen death camp in Austria.

The box has been photographed, and documented at the US Holocaust Memorial Museum in Washington, D.C. It will be placed on exhibit at the Holocaust Center in Peabody soon.

"I know having this incredible piece at the center will really mean an awful lot to people who come. I think something like this makes it more real. You know, you can hear about it, but if you meet a survivor, or a liberator, it becomes not just history but real," she said.

After a final embrace, the brief meeting ended. Meagher smiled, and wheeled away. Weitz held the box. A piece of history was safe.

February 24, 2005
The Boston Globe

Prison Seder

Some would call it a glorified storage closet. To these inmates, it's a sanctuary.

Inside a worn, brick structure last week at MCI-Norfolk, 10 inmates were singing Hebrew songs, just as they've done for the last several years in the days following Passover. As at any Seder, the men sat down to tell the story of the Jewish exodus from slavery in Egypt. The group munched on matzo and ate kosher pot roast and chicken.

They looked like a typical temple brotherhood.

"This is the Yeshiva Gedolah of Norfolk," said inmate Paul Sheehy, referring to the traditional intensive style of Jewish learning that he participates in several days a week with other inmates in a cramped concrete room in Building 36, which serves as their synagogue.

The men learn the Talmud and the Torah, and study the works of Hasidic luminaries such as Rabbi Nachman of Breslov; the Lubavitcher Rebbe, Menachem M. Schneerson; and Rabbi Shlomo Carlebach.

In a perfect world, Sheehy and fellow inmates Richard Shuman and Bobby Jenner would not have found God only after committing murder. In this world, however, they spend much of their day contemplating what they have done, dealing with the dichotomy presented in the Talmud: He who takes a life destroys the world; he who saves a single life saves the entire world.

Their inspiration and teacher is Rabbi Natan Schafer, a soft-spoken man with a gentle smile who serves as the Jewish chaplain for seven

Massachusetts prisons. Schafer, who is 58, was a student and friend of the late Rabbi Carlebach, the prolific Jewish songwriter and storyteller.

Schafer works at the prisons 20 hours a week, and holds classes at the Norfolk jail on Wednesdays and Sundays. His message focuses on prayer, study, friendship, and following God's commandments.

"If you fix yourself, then you'll have the power to fix others as well. The brokenness of your life can lead to the greatest wholeness," he tells his students. "The most important thing isn't the knowledge that they're accumulating about Torah and Judaism. It's how they're treating each other. They should treat each other and everyone in their lives with dignity and respect."

Before last week's Seder, the graying, middle-aged men approached Schafer and hugged him. The Hasidic rabbi then sat down alongside his wife, Channah, who has taught the men how to meditate. The gray light from the outside was fading, and as the rabbi began to talk, the room fell silent.

"Being in prison is a form of exile, and the purpose of exile is to give a person an atonement, to cleanse the person's soul when a person has done wrong," he said. "I bless you that the exile that you're living in should give you the vessels to hold the light which will shine in your life during times of darkness, so that no matter how dark your world appears on the outside . . . you'll know that God is watching over you and caring about you every moment. And that even this painful exile is a gift that God has given you in this life."

This seemed to resonate with the men, who nodded their heads and sipped grape juice from white Styrofoam cups. Soon Shuman was preparing to ask the Four Questions of Passover for the first time in more than half a century.

Shuman's recitation is like a blues dirge. His Hebrew is perfect. He moves his head in a semicircle during his lamentation, seamlessly shifting from baritone to tenor. The rabbi hums along and most of the men close their eyes. On the last verse, Shuman is overcome with emotion and hesitates for a moment, then wipes away his tears. Sheehy places his hand on his friend's shoulder as Shuman finishes the song.

As the main course is served, the men remove the plastic from the hot kosher dinners. Sheehy offers seconds to Leonard Fruchtman, who says he's finishing a 15-year sentence. Fruchtman smiles when he remembers a previous Norfolk Seder when he ate too much maror, or bitter herbs.

Before the Seder, Shuman and Sheehy sat at a small table and talked about the Torah, Passover, and "taking a life." The men proudly showed their Hebrew books, and freely quoted verses from the Torah, Carlebach sayings, and the Talmud.

Sheehy, who is 37, became observant seven years ago and is now known by his Hebrew name, Shlomo. He has been in jail for 18 years, and is serving a sentence of 15 years to life for second-degree murder.

When asked about Passover, he discussed the four sons mentioned in the Seder prayer book known as the Haggadah — the wise, wicked, simple, and the one who does not know enough to ask. Sheehy once identified with the wicked son, but now sees himself as the simple son.

"I was the one who was meshuga, crazy," said Sheehy, who became a certified heating, ventilation, and air-conditioning technician while incarcerated and will go before the parole board in two years. "I feel great sadness for the harm and pain that I caused. I no longer need to be confrontational. I want to bring healing. Rabbi Schafer brought me to the point where I am now."

Shuman, who once had a home in Sharon and employed more than 100 people at his printing company in Stoughton, killed two men in

August 1997. He is 56, serving two life sentences, and also is filled with remorse.

"Right now I consider myself in galut [exile]. I'm at the lowest form of existence," he said. "The darkness is caused by what we did."

Exile is the subject later during Passover dinner, and Bobby Jenner, a 48-year-old former South Boston resident, wanted to talk.

"They can keep my body in exile, but not my mind," he said, to the approval of the men around the table.

"I just started coming here a few years ago," Jenner continued. "I look forward to it. I take that personally. I didn't have many friends."

"Being Bobby's friend is a real privilege," replied Schafer.

The men recited the Hebrew blessing after the meal. The Haggadah calls for the door to be opened for the prophet Elijah who, according to Jewish tradition, will herald the coming of the messiah. But there is no open door policy in prison — even on Passover — and the door remained closed, as a guard stood in the hallway. No one seemed to mind, though, and in a matter of 30 minutes the Seder was finished. There was one last song, "Next Year in Jerusalem," and it was time for the men to say goodnight to their rabbi with one final hug.

The room emptied, and there was silence again. The inmates were escorted back to their cells. Their smiles suggested that they were free men, at least for one night.

April 22, 2004
The Boston Globe

Soul Doctor On Call

For the last 17 years, Rabbi Shmuel Posner has been singing Hebrew and Yiddish melodies every Friday night in the basement of Chabad House, his educational center that sits between a funeral home and a tanning parlor in the heart of Kenmore Square.

Step out of the streets and into the warmth of the room, and you'll find up to 75 people sitting at long row tables, welcoming the Jewish Sabbath with Hasidic songs as they eat challah, sip wine, and pass along trays of gefilte fish, chicken, noodle pudding, and sweet cake.

The people at the table represent a microcosm of the Jewish diaspora, with emigrants from the former Soviet Union, South Africa, Iraq, and South America mixing with students, professionals, and seniors from the Boston area. Few are strictly observant of Jewish laws or customs, and for many, their initial appearance is motivated by curiosity rather than spiritual hunger.

Down in the Commonwealth Avenue cellar, where Old World meets the 21st century, Posner sits surrounded by his wife, Chani, and their ten children. "My dear friends," he says, and within seconds the conversations in English, Russian, Hebrew, and Spanish cease. Part Billy Crystal, part drummer Max Weinberg, and part Baal Shem Tov, he draws people into the conversation with a combination of one-liners, music, and Torah. At the end of his talk, the rabbi will invariably raise his cup of wine and offer a toast to a time when people will recognize the world as a place where God dwells. Then he will start a song, leading to clapping and singing.

"It's much more than just coming here once to experience Shabbes [Sabbath]," Posner says. "People are looking for meaning, and there's something inherent in the Jewish soul that drives them to connect with who they really are."

A fast-talking former New Yorker, Posner descends from the branch of Lubavitch Hasidism, one of the only sects dedicated to outreach among secular Jews.

Posner fields dozens of calls each day, balancing his cell phone on his shoulder while replying to e-mails from the thousands who have proclaimed him their rabbi. When former congregants return to visit, they take their place along with students and neighborhood residents who file into his second-floor office, presenting their personal dilemmas before Posner offers up his own remedies.

"He's an in-your-face guy in a nice way," explains Alan Wilensky, who first met Posner 15 years ago. "He shoots out questions to students and older people like a Las Vegas emcee or a group therapist, but when he senses that someone's getting uncomfortable he breaks the tension with a piquant anecdote."

This week, 150 of Posner's congregants will gather for a Megillah reading to mark the beginning of Purim, which documents a Persian king's last-minute revocation of a death decree for all Jews. Down in the basement, a Hasidic jazz group will perform, and Posner and his Hasidim will dance and offer up a L'Chaim (usually a Crown Royal) to celebrate the miracle.

"It's a time to get real," he says, before excusing himself to take another call.

February 24, 2002
The Boston Globe

Finding God in a Moshpit

Rosh Hashana begins this week, and on a recent day, Rabbi Darby Leigh needed to practice blowing the shofar — the ram's horn that is tooted on the Jewish new year and other high holidays.

After hitting a few high notes inside his synagogue's sanctuary, he gripped the 3-foot-long instrument, threw a corner of his prayer shawl over his shoulder, and stepped into a courtyard of Congregation Kerem Shalom, just a few miles away from Walden Pond in Concord.

"It's all about nature. Peace and love and nature," he said, before planting his feet in front a tree and blowing the shofar toward an open field. The sound pierced the quiet. After some more practice, in which he was able to find a lower key, Leigh seemed satisfied. "I prefer the lower bassy sound — I can feel it better," he said when he returned to the sanctuary.

There, he noticed a cricket jumping under a row of seats, and soon he was on his hands and knees cupping the insect before returning it to the courtyard. When he returned, he broke into a big smile.

Leigh, who is 40 and was born deaf, always seems to be smiling, and he exudes enthusiasm as he goes about the simple tasks of the day. He is just the second deaf rabbi to lead a congregation in the United States.

"My tagline is, 'my ears are broken but I make a great listener,' " said Leigh, who has developed his own way to listen to people. He wears two hearing aids that amplify sounds. He also lip reads, and observes body language. And, on the phone, Leigh shuts off a hearing aid and clicks on a switch that changes over to an electromagnetic frequency.

"I concentrate really hard and I don't get everything. But I puzzle it together and get enough," said Leigh, who recenty joined Kerem Shalom, a congregation of about 250 members.

"He has a way of electrifying people so that they want to listen and they want to learn, and he does it not with bells and whistles but with a true depth of knowledge and character," said Miriam Zarchan, a co-president of Kerem Shalom.

As a youth, Leigh liked performing — whether it was as a fire juggler, street magician, or off on a mountain snowboarding. But he was walled off from many things that people take for granted — such as watching a movie, going to the theater, or even watching TV (closed captioning had yet to be implemented when he was a child).

Growing up as a Jewish teen in Manhattan, he was drawn to listening to heavy metal bands. Leigh's body found joy in the chords and musical vibration that emanated from the emphasis on bass and percussion. He also found community and faith when he attended concerts.

"I found God in a mosh pit," said Leigh, who attended his first concert, a Twisted Sister performance in New York, when he was 14. "Heavy metal saved my life. The experience of growing up deaf in the hearing world means that you grow up as a minority. So many of us have the experience growing up where we feel like we don't fit in, or we don't fully belong.

"I found in heavy metal a music and a culture that supported individuality and rejection of the social norm. I found a culture that said, 'you don't have to be like that. You're not. It's OK to be different, it's OK to be you. And guess what? There's a whole army of metal heads out here like you, that are "freaks" and don't fit into normal society.' And the celebration of that and the outlet for anger and frustration as a teenage adolescent male just totally resonated with me."

After studying religion in college, Leigh — who alternately colored his hair blue, green, and red and also fashioned a Mohawk at one point — began to grow dreadlocks. He kept them for about 10 years, including a four-year stint when he toured as an actor for the National Theatre of the Deaf.

While he had studied religions in college, including Christianity, Islam, and Buddhism, he knew little about Judaism, and didn't set foot in a synagogue during most of his 20s. His return to Judaism started when he began to research dreadlocks, which led him to the revelation that Rastafarians, in part, grow dreadlocks to fulfill a Nazirite oath of not cutting one's hair, cited as one of the 613 commandments in the Torah.

A trip to Poland, where he accompanied teens on the March of the Living — a silent walk from Auschwitz to Birkenau — served as an epiphany. There, where Nazis killed about 1 million Jews, he remembers crouching over a puddle of water and feeling a connection to his grandparents, who had survived the Holocaust.

"I got called," he explained. "And the call was this really strong, really clear voice inside me that said it's time to go home."

Since his ordination as a Reconstructionist rabbi in 2008, he has led a congregation in Montclair, N.J. and served as rabbi of the New Shul, a progressive synagogue in Manhattan.

In between his rabbinical duties, he still found time to listen to heavy metal music, and in recent years he has appeared on stage alongside his heroes, Twisted Sister and Jane's Addiction, to sign their songs to their fans.

Not surprisingly, Leigh has been known to write his sermons while listening to heavy metal. His Rosh Hashana message this year will focus on Psalm 27 and the desire to dwell in the house of the Lord forever.

For Leigh, the interpretation is simple: "It's the ability to cultivate the expressions of appreciation, gratitude, awe, and wonder for your life, and to be able to remember that every day."

September 1, 2013
The Boston Globe

Men on the Moon
at Camp Simcha

The vision of the little black-and-white television on a card table usually returns in the summer.

The TV sat in the shade of a cinderblock bathhouse at a day camp, and flickered in the heat of the woods of Middleton on a Sunday in July. I stood and looked at the grainy image of the Apollo 11 capsule sitting on the moon. It was 1969, and I was 10 and sensed that a lot would change from that day forward. Others were watching the little TV, but I was the only person younger than 30 there. Everybody else was old.

The other day, I had a hankering to return to that spot. I couldn't figure out why the image of the men on the moon in that spot in the woods was still in my head. I wanted to find out.

In the late 1960s, the camp had been carved out of a forest of evergreens, birch trees, and wetlands. There were mosquitoes everywhere, and flies would arrive when bees and other insects had finished with us. There were no bunks, and little organized activity. We played a form of baseball that required a volleyball and a bat, and if you hit the old barn on the fly, it was a home run.

The only thing that brought relief from the heat was swimming in the camp's Z-shaped pool. Three times a day, we would trudge the half-mile on the rocky main road from the barn to the pool.

The pool was the saving grace of the camp. This was not a group of campers willing to embrace Outward Bound challenges in the woods. We did not demand that counselors take us on rope climbs or long hikes. We were children of mostly middle-class Jews who had moved from places like Chelsea, Lynn, Malden, Revere, and Salem to the suburbs of Marblehead, Peabody, and Swampscott. There were some Boy Scouts, but most of us just wanted to swim and cool off.

As if five days a week was not enough at the camp, the facility also was open on Sundays so parents could get some fresh air on their day off. So, on Sundays my parents would load up the beach wagon with beach chairs and enough food to feed two or three families. There was no air conditioning in the car, and we were lucky if we were able to pull in a signal from the Red Sox game.

During the week, all activity around the pool was carefully monitored, and only a limited number of kids would be in the water at any one time during swimming classes. On Sundays, the same rules did not exist, and hundreds of people would arrive, place their belongings on the crabgrass, and jump in the pool.

There was no organization, and when an activity — such as a group barbecue — was initiated, it met with limited success.

On one occasion, a severe thunderstorm ended the barbecue before it could even begin. People ran for their cars; my aunts from New York ran, too, but en route to the car, they scooped up a dozen whole chickens that had been abandoned on the grill.

This infuriated one of the organizers, who yelled at my aunts while they scampered down the hill with the bags of chickens. "If they wanted them so bad, they should have cooked them," said Aunt Fanny, who owned a dress shop in the Bronx.

On that Sunday, after several hours of playing in the pool, I wandered over to the little TV behind the bathrooms. That's when I saw the Apollo capsule.

On a recent Sunday, I found the camp again. New homes stood on half of the land; the same rocky path was there, along with the buggy athletic field. A new homeowner told me the old barn had been moved to another part of the property.

The pool still glistened, but fewer than a dozen people were there. In the four decades since I had been a camper, families had found other places to relax on Sundays.

I dipped into the Z-shaped pool, sat in a beach chair for a spell, and then walked toward my car and stood where I had watched the TV. There was nothing on the patch of blacktop, and behind it was an office building with the word "Adam" written on a wall. I stood for a few minutes and looked at the empty space. Lots of conversations had taken place here in the last four decades, I thought. Maybe, during that time, someone had even placed a little color TV on a rickety old card table.

August 30, 2007
The Boston Globe

Hall of Fame Linebacker Lights the Menorah

Andre Tippett is a towering man with a gentle voice. When he starts to speak about the meaning of Hanukkah, his voice grows even softer.

"Hanukkah means dedication and is about miracles," said Tippett, sounding more like a rabbi than a member of the Pro Football Hall of Fame. Throughout his life, though, he has acknowledged the miracles that led him from the tough streets of Newark to Foxborough, where he became a five-time all-pro linebacker for the New England Patriots. Tippet recorded 100 career sacks while earning a name as one of the game's most feared pass rushers.

On Tuesday evening, he will gather with his wife Rhonda and their son Coby (daughter Madison will be away at college) and sing Hebrew prayers as they light the first candle on their menorah to mark the beginning of Hanukkah.

"I'm probably more excited than most of the family because I look forward to any type of celebration when it comes to holidays," said Tippett, who will turn 55 later this month.

Tippett was raised in a Baptist family, and said he has always believed in a higher being. After he joined the Patriots, he started to date Rhonda Kenney, who grew up in a close-knit Jewish family in Framingham. He soon realized just how much Judaism meant to her.

"What was important to her was that we raise our kids in the Jewish faith and have a Jewish home," said Tippett, who still works for the Patriots, serving as the executive director of community affairs.

The couple married in 1993, and in 1996 Tippett began to take classes that led to his conversion a year later.

"I knew that it was important that I engulf myself in learning," said Tippett, who calls himself a proud Jew. "I did this for my family. It was probably one of the easiest things I had to do in my life. It was fun. It was an opportunity to learn about a new culture and history, and to study."

For Tippet, much of Judaism is about family and dedication. He attends synagogue in Sharon, observes the other Jewish holidays, and enjoys fasting on Yom Kippur.

"It's good for the body," he said.

Also since converting, he has spoken at numerous Jewish events, traveled to Israel with his family and watched Madison recite her bat mitzvah prayers in Jerusalem, and was inducted into the National Jewish Sports Hall of Fame.

Tippett does not ignore the Christmas season. After Thanksgiving, he loads up his iPod with favorite Christmas songs, performed by Sam Cooke, Otis Redding, and the Temptations. On Christmas, he calls and texts his mother and other relatives in New Jersey.

Like a lot of others, he has taken on the unofficial Jewish-American tradition on Christmas day: "We go out for Chinese food and then to a movie," he said.

Meanwhile, Tippet's family is gearing up for its annual Hanukkah party. Like many Jews, he gravitates toward latkes, the potato pancakes that are fried to commemorate the menorah's oil lasting eight days during the Maccabean revolt in the second century BC, which the holiday remembers.

Tippett is partial to his father-in-law's latkes.

"I love them," he said. "I put some applesauce on them and I can probably eat a plate by myself."

December 14, 2014
The Boston Globe

The iPad Does a Mitzvah

The 12-year-old boy sat in the synagogue, looked out at the congregation, and waved. On a day when Jewish tradition marks the transition from boy to man, Matthew Emmi smiled often and moved his hands to the music of the Hebrew songs. During prayers, he alternately slouched and sat erect.

And when it was time for him to say a prayer before the Torah, he touched the screen of an iPad.

Matthew is severely autistic and cannot read, write, or speak sentences. His family, friends, and educators never know exactly what he is thinking, but they know Matthew likes going to synagogue. He has been a regular at the Sunday service at Andover's Temple Emanuel, where he hums, claps and smiles when Cantor Idan Irelander plays traditional Hebrew prayers on his guitar.

Several months ago, Suzanne and Michael Emmi decided their son's autism would not prevent him from having a bar mitzvah.

"Because of the issues in his life, he's not going to have a wedding or a high school or college graduation," his mother said. "We wanted him to have that opportunity to have a special moment and shine."

After some discussion, one of Matthew's teachers came up with an idea. Jamie Hoover, who is also the executive director of the May Center for Child Development School, met with Mathew, his family, and the temple clergy.

During the meeting, she handed Matthew an iPad and after little prompting, got him to touch an icon on the screen. The iPad responded by reciting the name of his younger sister, Mia, and Matthew was delighted.

"It gave him a voice," said Hoover.

The structure of the bar mitzvah was set: Matthew could essentially lead the service by touching iPad icons. School staff recorded Matthew reciting "mama" and "dada" and the names of other relatives who would be called up to the Torah. Irelander recorded blessings and Torah readings that a boy being bar mitzvahed would ordinarily recite, and e-mailed them to Hoover — who matched the prayers to icons and photographs.

"It's quite amazing," said Rabbi Robert Goldstein, of Temple Emanuel, who has known Matthew for several years. "We're blending the most cutting-edge technology with tradition; with reading the ancient text of Torah. It's facilitating spirituality."

Early yesterday morning, Matthew and his family arrived at the synagogue. After posing for photographs, he began to race around the mostly empty building — something he does often around the house, in addition to his regular routine of bouncing balls, riding a scooter, and listening to Disney and Broadway show tunes. When guests arrived, Matthew greeted them with a high-five and an enthusiastic "ha" — his way for saying "hi."

Shortly before the service, he sat at a table in between his parents, and opposite the ark, which holds the Torahs.

His mother held the iPad and his father placed his hands on a laminated blue cardboard that had 30 large icons representing the parts of the service that Matthew would announce by pressing the iPad.

Shortly after Irelander began strumming the guitar with an opening blessing, Suzanne held the portable tablet in front of her son, who confidently touched the screen with his left index finger.

"Pappa," came forth from the sound system. It was Matthew's pre-recorded voice, and soon his grandfather, Harvey Glass of Peabody, was standing before him with a prayer shawl, or tallis.

"This is for you. It was given to me by my grandfather," said Glass, before placing it on Matthew's shoulders.

A few minutes later Matthew pressed on an icon that resembled an ear, and the cantor's recitation of one of Judaism's holiest prayers — the "Sh'ma" — reverberated.

After he had touched the IPad many more times — alternating between index and pinky fingers — calling his parents and other relatives to the Torah, it was time for his name to be recited. Soon, Irelander's pre-recorded voice was playing again — filling in for Matthew — as the Torah reading prayers were sung.

Matthew fidgeted, waved again to friends, and sat pensively during the chanting. Once he pushed his father's yarmulke from his head. Mike Emmi calmly reached for the skullcap and gently placed it back on his head.

Soon Matthew's parents were giving him their blessing.

"Matthew, you are a remarkable young man," they said, turning to their son. "Continue shining the special light of your love on the world and making it a better place. That is your gift to the world, and a mighty special gift it is. We love you."

After the family had walked through the synagogue with the rabbi and cantor and Torah, the service was over.

Matthew seemed relieved. He began to race throughout the room and seemed to find comfort in running up a long handicapped-access ramp. After most of the people had left, he ran in between the seats several times before pausing at a banister in front of the ark.

He looked back at the few remaining people in the temple, closed his eyes and sighed.

March 4, 2012
The Boston Globe

A Wiseguy Goes to Shul

Kevin Weeks looked like any other any suburban guy who had put in a long day at the office. Wearing a crew-neck shirt, blue jeans, and black work boots, he leaned against a sculptured menorah outside Swampscott's Congregation Shirat Hayam, trying to hold a conversation on his cell phone. "Can you hear me now?" he asked.

Weeks is a former associate of James "Whitey" Bulger, and spent more than five years in prison for murder. He doesn't know Swampscott from Stow, but was up on the North Shore for one reason: to sell books. Penned with Marblehead author Phyllis Karas, his memoir, "Brutal: The Untold Story of My Life Inside Whitey Bulger's Irish Mob," made this week's New York Times best-seller list.

Inside the temple's social hall, Karas moved gracefully on her home turf, exchanging hugs and smiles from friends as she accepted congratulations on her latest book. While Swampscott has had its share of mob residents over the years including former Angiulo consigliere Ilario Zannino, and Joe "The Animal" Barboza, many of those attending seemed satisfied just to glimpse a real-life wise guy.

Lauren Goldman grabbed a third row seat but not before she offered a gracious smile and welcome to Weeks, who was setting foot in his first synagogue in more than 30 years.

"I'm fascinated with the Mafia, with the Italian mob, with the Jewish mob," she gushed. "They do things that are so over the edge, they act out things that some of us might like to do but in our good conscience, being the people we are, we don't. Haven't you ever wanted to just whack somebody?"

Warren Sadow was similarly intrigued. "I guess you could say it's a bit of living vicariously," said Sadow, a former schoolteacher who lives in Lynn.

At the lectern, emcee Susan Steigman offered a hearty "mazel tov" to Karas, whom she called a "native daughter." She then announced that 40 percent of the proceeds from books sold that evening would be divided between the temple and the JCC. "We have a great crowd here today," she told the audience of 120.

To generous applause, Karas then took to the microphone, speaking slowly in a high-pitched voice. She grew up in Malden, and is married to Jack Karas, a Marblehead physician.

"Shalom," said Karas, offering a wide smile before returning to her prepared text.

" 'Brutal' is not for the weak of heart nor for the squeamish," she warned before introducing Weeks, whom she described as a man who wants "to settle down to anonymity and peace and quiet."

Weeks, who is 50 and broad-chested, stood straight and spoke softly, without notes. In his talk, Weeks glossed over the details of conducting brutal acts such as who killed whom, or why someone was murdered, robbed, or beaten. Instead, he focused on questions of morality, Whitey and Billy Bulger's relationship, and the adrenaline that comes from being a criminal.

Weeks said he was sorry about some of what he did, but doesn't have too much compassion for the people who were killed or maimed. "People that got hurt were basically in the life of crime. But I have remorse toward their families that didn't choose that life," he said.

After his 45-minute talk, Weeks and Karas sat at a long folding table, autographing copies of their book. On the opening page, above the title "Brutal," Weeks repeatedly signed "Best wishes, Kevin Weeks." Below her co-author's signature and the word "Brutal," Karas' dedications were more personable, often ending with "Love, Phyllis Karas."

With just a handful of books left to sign, Weeks looked up at a visitor, smiled, and extended his hand. The two men, and Bulger, had done business together in the old days, they said. Weeks signed the book, and wished his friend well. "I knew him as a stand-up guy when I did business with him," said the heavy-set man in the green raincoat who declined to give his name. "And it was the same with Jim [Bulger] too."

April 6, 2006
The Boston Globe

Elul

In the late summer I drive to the cemetery in Everett during the Hebrew month of Elul — a month of contemplation before the Jewish New Year of Rosh Hashana, when it's customary to visit the dead.

As a kid I watched my father place a stone on each of his relatives' graves, and now it's my turn. Sand still covers the modest gray rock I set down on his headstone. On the other side, I place a red-colored stone, also found at the beach, above my mother's name. When it touches the granite it makes no sound. I step backwards and stare at my parents' names etched in English and Hebrew: Samuel and Ruby Rosenberg.

The newly placed stones are surrounded by pebbles and larger rocks that rise up and resemble an altar from a few feet away. There is no great mystery or Jewish law attached to the stones: It's just a tradition that marks a person's visit and is a sign of respect. While the mound looks impressive I wonder why the stones have stayed in place for a few years. Over the winter, the wind usually blows them off the headstones and creates a proper stock of rocks so people don't have to look too long during Elul.

"Mom, Dad: Happy New Year," I say, my hands clasped, my eyes fixed on their names. "I'll be right back."

Every trip here is a family reunion, although I do all the talking. My father's mother, two aunts, sister, and two brothers and their wives are buried in the last four rows of the cemetery (another sister is buried in Lynn with her husband). For most of their lives they saw or spoke to one another every day; my father ran a deli with my two uncles in Chelsea;

on Sundays, we all gathered at my bubbe's (grandmother's) not far from the deli.

I place a stone on each grave and say a Hebrew prayer for each relative. Their stories help form my own narrative but I only know the basics. None went to college; only their spouses graduated from high school; all wanted better for the next generation. And so I visit.

There's my bubbe, who left Europe for Chelsea and lost her husband in her early 30s when she had five young children; her two sisters, who never married and helped raise my father and his siblings; my Uncle Murray, the oldest child who was a World War II hero; Uncle Eddy, who ran the deli slicer and seemed closest to my father; my Aunt Eileene, who raised three children without a husband and rarely judged others.

I return to my parents' graves, recite more prayers and begin to talk. I tell them they were more than just a deli man and a clothing store owner.

I thank them for teaching me right and wrong. They learn that I am still a writer at the Globe and my wife, Devorah, still has a health clinic. I report that my son, Aaron, is now a college sophomore. I mention that my sister Phyllis's daughters have moved to Israel, and that Sheri — their youngest — has two beautiful children in Los Angeles.

I pause and notice the wind rustling the slender branches that shade the graves.

It is awkward saying goodbye and when I turn to leave, I run my hand over the Hebrew inscriptions on their graves. At least I can take the letters of their names with me.

September 21, 2014
The Boston Globe

Yom Kippur Travels

Failure is often followed by clarity, and beginning Tuesday night, I'll have an opportunity to think about just how cathartic changing your routine can be.

Yom Kippur is not for rookies, and if you take the liturgy literally, it can be a major bummer. Observant Jews believe it is the day that God judges who will live and who will die. During five services — stretching over a 25-hour period — we will remember the dead in a memorial prayer, read about rabbis who were tortured because of their brilliant scholarship, and beg for our lives numerous times. All the while abstaining from eating and drinking and just about everything else that's part of our daily routine.

On the surface, there's little joy to the holiday, especially around breakfast time, some 12 hours after your last meal. Instead of coffee and the morning paper, there's prayer awaiting, hours and hours of it. I used to dread this, even as a child when I didn't fast. In recent years, though, I've decided that the fast is the most appealing part of the holiday.

Since I was in my late teens, I've been able to complete the fast almost every year, but I use common sense: If I feel faint or sick, the fast is over.

As the day progresses, the pageantry and mournful melodies form a portal for those who fast. Where do you go while abstaining from food and drink for a day? I travel to the past and future, holding a prayer book.

When the memorial prayer for the dead is chanted, I am a child again, walking with my father to shul on this holiday. We're dressed in suits; he carries his prayer shawl in a velvet bag and smokes a Salem as we stroll. Every other day, he is a deli man — headed off to work slicing meat and serving up huge corned beef and pastrami sandwiches to the working class of the 1960s and '70s.

Today, though, he is regal. His suit fits perfectly; his gait is that of a philosopher. His words are few and he smiles for the entire walk. When we reach the shul, it is packed with congregants, and our seats are on a stage at the end of the sanctuary. I ask him why we don't sit closer and he shrugs. "We're here. That's what matters," he tells me.

There are no assigned seats at the synagogue I now attend, and people are free to roam as they like. Sometimes, I stand next to the ark, which holds the Torahs. But now, I feel most comfortable in the balcony. There I can view the entire congregation and feel the wave of song, which grows more authentic as the day progresses.

I close my eyes, and I can see Ben, a friend whose presence and words unfold like a prayer. A trained rabbi, psychotherapist, and attorney, he seems to have the answer to every question. He has been dead for four years now, but when I find my way to our place up in the balcony, I open the window because I know he liked fresh air. I hear his raspy voice lost between the melodies. His seat is empty, but is he not with me?

Morning and early afternoon move slowly. With all of this talk of living and dying, I wonder how many more years I will live. A collage of happiness washes over me, and clips as from a filmstrip play: I am 20, swimming in the Red Sea by the Sinai and thinking about world peace; I am 33, it's the end of the Yom Kippur fast, and I propose to

Devorah; two years later, Aaron is born, and he joins me each holiday at the shul. This year he is in college in London. What is he doing today?

On this day of atonement, the rabbi usually talks about never giving up. I embrace this as a central theme to the holiday, that perfection can emerge from repeated failure; that action, not just thought, is required to complete something that you really want; that the process is just as important as the outcome.

As the fast nears its end, and the congregation joins in a final plea to be included in the book of life, I await the blast of the shofar, the ram's horn that is sounded at the end of the holiday. It pierces the air like no other instrument and I try to grab hold of the notes as they float toward the heavens.

Soon, I eat and talk about the same old things. Does the holiday have any lasting impact on my life, or is it just ritual? I may never know.

September 20, 2015
The Boston Globe

Shlomo's Lesson of Love

O ver the years I have wondered what had become of Shlomo, the mystical man I found one day resting on my front steps. He had a gentle face, kind blue eyes and a quick smile. Before I had a chance to introduce myself he spoke, and his voice and words were so comforting that I lowered myself onto a step, and listened.

His words were Yiddish, a language I had heard most of my childhood but had forgotten after my parents had passed. Shlomo talked non-stop and I eagerly soaked up his words, even though I only understood a fraction of what he was talking about.

I had met a new friend. All I knew was that he had come from the former Soviet Union, lived in downtown Lynn and walked to synagogue every morning. For the next few years, we'd meet on the front steps — albeit, he did most of the talking, and while I never really understood what he was saying I felt good sitting near him. I knew almost nothing about his life, and how he came to live in America, but he reminded me of my own relatives who had left Europe and sought a better life here.

After we moved, I would think about him and wonder why he had chosen to sit on my steps. Judaism holds that there are 36 holy people scattered throughout the globe who help sustain the world. Was Shlomo — the tender man with the raspy voice who appeared out of nowhere, and would seemingly disappear after our conversations, one of the 36?

And then, last week, I heard that Shlomo Masis was still alive and had recently turned 100. His granddaughter, Julie Masis, was working on a book about him and told him another writer wanted to meet with him.

I found Shlomo sitting by his bedroom window on the fourth floor of an assisted living facility in Peabody. He didn't seem to remember me, but offered up a big hug and what sounded like a blessing in Yiddish. He then reached into his top dresser drawer and pulled out an orange. "Take," he said in Yiddish, handing it to Julie to peel.

If you know anything about the Holocaust then his story will sound familiar. In 1941, in his mid-twenties, he was working in a factory in his shtetl in Moldova. That fall, Romanian fascists loyal to Nazi Germany rounded up thousands of Jews in his town and made them remove their clothes and shoes. Wearing just underwear, they were sent on a barefoot 72-mile death march out of their village to a work camp in Ukraine. Along the way, a brother, Issac, was singled out — along with 150 others — to dig a huge pit, and when they were finished the Romanian soldiers gunned them down and pushed them into a mass grave. Of the thousands who marched, half were killed or died of starvation before they reached Obodovka, a Ukraine ghetto.

Somehow, Shlomo managed to survive three years in that ghetto. Jews slept in windowless, unheated sheds — sometimes alongside corpses that couldn't be buried because the ground was frozen. He was sent to work on a farm, and befriended a Ukrainian family who fed him breakfast and gave him potatoes to bring back to the shed. His father, Srul, died in the ghetto, along with another brother, Chaim.

After the ghetto was liberated by the Russians, he was drafted into the Red Army as a radio operator. In 1945, he returned to his old street in Moldova, where he married, had two children, and worked in a tobacco factory. In 1994, he left for the US and arrived in Lynn.

Shlomo insisted that I eat a part of the orange, and smiled when I acquiesced.

I wanted to know how he summoned the strength to survive.

He explained that it was mostly curiosity about the future of mankind. "I wanted to keep living to see who would win the war. I wanted to know how it would end," he told me.

I asked him if he was angry with the Romanians or the Nazis. "I have forgiven them," he said.

There were so many questions I wanted to ask, but the sun was going down and he wanted to eat dinner and he explained that Yom Kippur was coming. He hummed a few bars of the seminal prayer "Avinu Malkeinu" — "Our Father, Our King" — which is recited at the end of the fast, and insisted that he would not be eating on the Jewish Day of Atonement.

He stood, leaned on his walker, and headed toward the dining room with Julie.

All these years later, Shlomo seemed the same: gentle, absent of judgment, delivering long sentences in a high raspy voice that soothed his guest and proved otherworldly. Instead of anger and blame, he had decided to begin again and rebuild a world that focused on family. For a person in his position, that's almost an impossible achievement.

Perhaps he really is one of 36 righteous who roam the world.

October 13, 2016
The Boston Globe

CHAPTER 11

Food and Drink

Old Sully's

T here was a time after World War II when you could walk into 77 places within this one-square-mile section of Boston and order a beer.

Bar owners would swing open their doors at 8 a.m. and welcome thirsty sailors and workers who had just finished their shifts.

Today, just one of those neighborhood bars remains in Charlestown. Old Sully's sits in the middle of what locals call "the valley," at the bottom of Union Street. There is no sign on the outside of the aging, brown-shingled building — it blew down during the 1938 hurricane, and was never replaced.

Its owner, Dan Sullivan, who began mixing drinks in the cellar during Prohibition and expanded upstairs in the 1930s, had declared that enough people knew where the bar was — and if they wanted a drink they knew where to find him.

Sullivan's son, Dan Jr., has run the bar and been a co-owner since his father died in 1959.

The younger Sullivan, now 75, immediately dismisses discussion regarding the demise of the neighborhood bar. Stocky and polite, he speaks in short, clipped sentences and says the key to success is "to not let things get out of hand. There's no trouble here because we don't allow any."

The bar is a long and narrow combination of wood paneling, red Formica, and checkered tile. The pay phone is still the main line, and in the back room, where barmaids such as Tuttie, Duckie, and Joanie once roamed, a jukebox offers up Chiffons and Kingsmen tunes.

Sullivan once poured a scotch and soda for Jack Kennedy when he was a congressman. Tip O'Neill and dozens of other Boston pols made Bunker Hill Day pilgrimages. But, for Sullivan, the heart and soul of the bar were the neighborhood families such as the McLaughlins, who had 16 children; the firefighters and policemen who pulled up a chair after a long day; and Charlestown characters such as Huck Finn, BLT, Whimpy, Suitcase Fidler, and Salty Allwood. Finn drove a Rolls Royce; BLT was a longshoreman; Allwood was a bartender. Their names are now engraved in an honor roll in the back.

From the outside, only two wreaths and a string of Christmas lights greet passersby. Ray Ehscheid, a designer for the Rockport Corp., lives a few blocks from Union Street and walks by Old Sully's every day. He's never ventured inside, and expressed surprise when told that it was a bar. Ehscheid, 33, said he's probably not an Old Sully's guy.

"If I'm going to have a drink somewhere," he offered, "I'll probably go to the bar at Olives or Figs."

These days the bar stools are left for Old Sully's regulars like Billy Smith, a 43-year-old former welterweight boxer who now delivers Budweiser. "This is a place to be with the boys," he explained. "If it was up to us, we'd solve the world's problems in a day."

December 16, 2001
The Boston Globe

Have a Latke

Latke is the Yiddish word for potato pancake, and at the Butcherie, the kosher market on Harvard Street, they are serious about latkes.

The Butcherie is the latke nerve center of New England. Over the last three weeks its kitchen has produced 168,000 latkes, peaking during Hanukkah, when Jews eat oil-based treats to commemorate the miracle of rekindling Jerusalem's ancient temple menorah with oil. This past week, production reached an astonishing 19,000 latkes per day.

Some are shipped to synagogues, hotels, rehabilitation centers and private parties, but most end up only a few yards away from the kitchen, on the latke shelf.

The operation begins every morning at 5 o'clock, when four women, under the direction of manager Joshua Ruboy and Maria Krzwicka, report for duty. Once the potatoes are pealed and shredded and the other ingredients mixed in, the batch sits for about five minutes until it forms a rich texture, then is transferred to smaller pots. The actual frying of the latkes is an art, taught over the last 14 years by Krzwicka.

"Every latke is perfect," she says. "I make sure of it." Her protege Stasha, a middle-aged Polish immigrant, scoops the batter onto one of the special latke spoons, and gently plops it onto one of the six omelet skillets she's working.

After being placed in the cooler, they are checked for quality control and packed. Not all make the cut.

"Sometimes they get squished, or they're just small," said Ruboy, who admits to eating many of the rejects. Once on the shelves, they are subject to close inspection by customers.

Ruboy made his first latke when he was five. He believes the magic of latkes lies in the holiday as seen through a child's eyes.

"It brings you back to your childhood, when you were a kid during Hanukkah, and you made them at home," he said wistfully.

December 16, 2001
The Boston Globe

Why We Need the Deli

There was a time when each big-city neighborhood had a deli. The owners knew your family, the countermen greeted you and quickly prepared your favorite dish, and soon you were rewarded with a mountain of pastrami on a bulkie or a wedge of corned beef on rye.

We loved the food, but knew that the accompanying schmoozefest — often with complete strangers — was also a reward. Deli patrons were part of a system that did not recognize class. Seats were always at a premium, and often you'd see bookies sitting with lawyers, mayors, drunks, cabbies, new moms, cops, and teachers.

As the son of a deli owner, I witnessed this during my short apprenticeship as a busboy/dishwasher during the '70s in Chelsea. The talk, which covered sports, politics, and local gossip, was often as good as the meal.

If you look hard enough, you can still find a deli that still has some character, and where the portions and people fulfill fundamental needs of the human condition: eating and communicating.

Walk into New Brothers Restaurant & Deli in Danvers, and it's like stepping back in time. It's self-serve, which patrons love because they get their food fast and save on the tip. They also get to chat with the guys behind the counter — Costa, Peter, Elias, and Anthony — who know exactly how you like your meal and show interest in your life.

Brothers started in 1986, when a couple of men from southern Greece, Kary Andrinopoulos and Ted Kougianos, purchased an existing restaurant in Peabody Square. In 1999, the men decided to buy a block of buildings in Danvers, and their customers followed.

On a recent afternoon, Kary sipped a coffee from his seat near the register. If anyone is the moral conscience of the deli, it's this former accountant from Greece. He came here for a job at the old Sylvania plant in Salem, where he rose from floor worker to supervisor before joining Ted, his brother-in-law, in the restaurant business.

People love him for the atmosphere he's helped create and the fact that he's concerned about his guests. There are 120 seats in the joint, and instead of people jabbing at their cellphone or phablets, you'll find a gabfest each breakfast, lunch, and dinner.

"How you doin; how was your food?" Kary asked, as he made his way from guest to guest, often carrying a tray of baklava or small slices of spinach pie, which he hands out to all. Kary is in the people business, and his customers are eager to share a story.

"Any fishing this year?" Kary asked Luis DaSilva of Rowley, who has been coming to Brothers sometimes five days a week — since 1986.

DaSilva flashed a quick smile and handed Kary his phone, where the screen displayed a photo of a huge tuna he caught last summer. "This one was 1,500 pounds," said DaSilva, who finished his leg of lamb dinner and pronounced it one of the best meals of his life. "This place is like family."

Cynthea Michaels of Beverly told Kary she knows about deli. "The words deli and comfort are synonymous. They create an ethnic diversity here. There's always a table here and we came at least two hours ago and did not feel rushed. I just love the atmosphere," she said, thanking Kary for her corned beef on rye before giving him a goodbye hug.

Paul Brumby of Hamilton, who works in sales, calls himself a regular and usually gets the beef stew or a Greek salad. He also has spent a lot of time in delis, including a chance luncheon with Richard Nixon at a place near Wall Street.

"It was just a crowded place, and he was looking for a place to sit, and I said, 'Over here, Mr. Nixon,' and he sat down," Brumby said. "This country has lost its tradition and this is one of the places left with tradition."

It took me about 10 minutes to say goodbye to everyone, and during my visit, I did not look at my cellphone once. I stood and watched the people engaged with their food and friends or newspaper and realized just how much we need these special places. Even if you're not old enough to remember the corner deli, the taste and the salt and the smells transport us to a time in America when families were closer and life moved slower.

Our routine and culture meant more than work and looking at an iPhone.

March 8, 2015
The Boston Globe

When Brand Loyalty Becomes an Addiction

Change is inevitable as we move through life, and as I grow older, I have embraced shedding patterns and trying new paths.

Lately, I have been thinking hard about whether I should continue to attend to my morning Dunkin' Donuts preference.

As I ponder change I present the facts: Almost every day for the past 25 years, I have purchased at least one coffee from Dunkin'; as I have aged I have become increasingly loyal to the brand.

Call it a preference, a predilection, a fondness for a French roast with cream. That's a lot less confrontational than saying it's an addiction. Part of me says it's time to move on and drink any old coffee that's available.

Back in the 1980s I was a coffee maven, and bragged to my friends about my bean grinder and different varieties I kept in the freezer. But, with the proliferation of Dunkin' Donuts huts, I have grown lazy and, in the process, dare I say, a loyal customer?

I write now because of the behavior modification I have undergone over the years. It's not a full-blown transformation, but I now am fully aware that I am part of a culture that is greater than my own existence. Along with the coffee, there's a familiarity of being in a place that's just like the coffee shop down the street from my house. There's the same smiling cashiers; the letters that adorn the familiar logo; the parking lot trash cans that provide a home for all of the junk that happens to be in my car.

All of this appeals to the mobile worker. But with this attraction, ultimately, comes change.

Consider the case of a close friend who requested anonymity while recently retelling how he risked — and ultimately broke up with — a woman partly over his allegiance to Dunkin' Donuts. About eight years ago, he walked into one in Westport, Conn., and ordered a coffee with his then-girlfriend. As a collector of baseball caps, he asked one of the employees about the possibility of purchasing a Dunkin' Donuts hat. A deal was quickly consummated. He handed the clerk $15, and the person handed him the hat.

His girlfriend immediately objected to the hat, which was tan and brown, and had an embroidered steaming cup of coffee and chocolate doughnut stitched above the lid. "I won't go anywhere with you and the hat," she said. And she didn't. The two broke up. "The way I see it," says my friend, "is the woman I'm going to marry has to be comfortable with me wearing a hat like this."

I, too, have made wardrobe sacrifices that have drawn stares from acquaintances and friends. In recent years, a recently retired Dunkin' Donuts manager happily gave me two hats that I wore on occasion.

Lately, my friends have been encouraging me to join them for their Sunday morning soiree at Starbucks. I will not use this occasion to knock Starbucks and I admire much about their operation, especially the Bob Dylan music they sell and the comfy chairs they offer. I do not drink their coffee simply because it is dark roasted.

To participate in the regular Sunday conversation, I improvised a scheme that makes me feel a lot like George Costanza and Jackie Mason. I still drive to my hometown Dunkin' Donuts, get my coffee, and then head over to the nearby Starbucks where my friends sit by the window. I walk in, shake hands with everyone, and then casually stride over to the cashier and ask for a large empty cup. My request is always fulfilled and I go back to my car, grab my coffee, and walk toward the side of the building.

It's at that location where asphalt runs up against a neat brick Starbucks retaining wall where I often wonder if I am losing it. I deftly transfer the coffee from the Styrofoam Dunkin' Donuts container to the white and green Starbucks paper cup. At that moment, I feel a sense of chutzpah and shame. Then I stride inside with a wide smile like I own the place.

Actions like these put the whole coffee routine into perspective. From now on, I resolve not to take note of every new Dunkin' Donuts that pops up on a local highway or inside a filling station. I will wean myself slowly so I can consider the options out there, such as a good cup of hot tea.

May 31, 2007
The Boston Globe

The Tao of Potato Salad

T he call from my cousin, Barry, was not unexpected.

There was a sense of relief and mellowness to his voice.

"I think I've found it," he said.

I knew right away what he was talking about. For years, I have been troubled by the disappearance of the family recipe for potato salad. For 25 years, our fathers, Sam and Eddy, had run a deli in Chelsea with another brother, Murray. Since Murray & Eddy's closed in 1979, nearly everything about the place had taken on a gilded resonance, and while the deli was known for its huge corned beef and hot pastrami sandwiches, it's the potato salad that people still talk about.

I discovered the potato salad — wonderfully tart, sweet, and filling — at age 11 when I worked there as a busboy.

At the round table by the entrance, I watched bookies, intellectuals, and luminaries argue and philosophize between plates of potato salad. There was Abe Sax, the 80-year-old, Yiddish-speaking bookie schmoozing with Boston Celtics general manager Red Auerbach and announcer Johnny Most. "Subway" Sam Silverman, the boxing promoter often was around that table. Former House speaker George Keverian frequently would order takeout. There were cops and firefighters, teachers, social workers, even mobsters like Joe "The Animal" Barboza.

I felt like I had stepped into a great American novel every time I was in the deli.

"I remember the potato salad," Keverian told me during a recent phone conversation. I wanted to know what he liked about it. "The potatoes," he replied.

In recent years, the search for the recipe had taken on a new urgency. My father and uncles had passed, and my sisters and I often lamented not having asked for the recipe. Also, in the past couple of months, the potato salad had come up frequently in conversations. All of a sudden, everybody seemed to be asking about it. One friend, Ben, had offered a ransom to either Barry or myself for the recipe. And there was also an e-mail to my Globe address from a former Chelsea guy who wanted to know if I was the son of the deli man with the famed potato salad. He pleaded for the recipe.

I gave up eating potato salad at least 15 years ago after an unsuccessful search for a suitable replacement for Murray & Eddy's version. While the exact formula was a guarded secret, there was no mystery about the process. Dad and his brothers would make the salad weekdays at 3 a.m., a couple of hours before they would open the restaurant to customers.

They would hand-cut dozens of pounds of potatoes, boil them in an enormous pot, and then add mayonnaise, salt, vinegar, sugar, onions, and parsley. Several large containers would be filled and then stored in the walk-in refrigerated chest, alongside racks of corned beef and hanging salamis.

After breakfast, people would start ordering potato salad, and the servings would continue until closing time. The deli was self-serve, and pols, working stiffs, and hustlers sat side-by-side regaling one another with stories as they ate those enormous corned beef and hot pastrami sandwiches, and potato salad.

I was a reluctant deli man, and more interested in the stories I overheard from customers than the workings of the operation. This never bothered my father, who made it clear to me that I would be something other than a deli man, and that I would choose college and a typewriter over a meat slicer and an apron.

I had no aspirations to work behind the counter and was happy with my busboy job. I'd spend hours standing next to the cart as I waited to pick up dishes when people finished a meal. I'd strain to eavesdrop on conversations I had no business hearing. I eagerly awaited punch lines that sometimes were said in Yiddish, Polish, or Italian.

I knew that Barry would be the only person capable of delivering the recipe. He had worked behind the counter and had lived in Chelsea; I was a pretender, and lived in Swampscott, which seemed like a different country.

All last month, we had talked about trying our hand at making the potato salad. And then the phone call came. Barry instructed me to go to Market Basket and to ask for the grocery store's home-style potato salad. "It's as close as we're going to get," he said.

My wife and I drove to Market Basket, and I jogged to the deli area and asked for a sample. In the corner of the supermarket, I tasted the same tart and sweet potato salad I remembered from the deli. I ordered 5 pounds, and gave two large containers to a neighbor.

I ate until there was no more, and then felt like I had cheated the past. It had tasted the same but it was just food, I concluded. What I had longed for was the same voices and faces that went along with the potato salad.

The chase was over. The potato salad belongs to another era, where the food is good, the conversation is lively, and nobody cares what your line of work is as long as you've got something to say.

June 17, 2007
The Boston Globe

CHAPTER 12

Death

If You Live to 110

Antonio "Tony" Pierro's smile is contagious, and his laugh seems to crackle with wisdom. If anyone could talk about the meaning of life, it would be Pierro. He was born before the Wright brothers flew at Kitty Hawk, was a teenager when the Model T was produced, married soon after returning from World War I, and retired 30 years before anyone had heard of the Internet.

Pierro, who was born 110 years ago yesterday, explains his longevity in one word: genetics. His parents lived to 90 and 91, and one of his grandfathers made it to 103. Three brothers lived past 80, and his youngest brother, Nicholas, turns 97 in April.

Besides good genes, Pierro said a strong will to live and common sense have kept him healthy all his life. Inside a two-story house on a wooded hillside in this seacoast town, Pierro spends much of his time thinking about the decisions he made, and he has concluded that life is a struggle between good and evil.

"It's all up to you to do what you want in life. There are pleasant things to do, and there are terrible things not to do, and that's the way I see it," said Pierro, who speaks slowly, and wears thick-framed glasses.

At 5 feet, 120 pounds, Pierro shuffles through the house he shares with his brother Nicholas and Nicholas's son, Rick. Although he sleeps at least 16 hours a day, Pierro also stays active. He shovels snow, rakes leaves, and washes the dishes after every meal. "If you don't have exercise, you get stiff, you're not worth anything," said Pierro, who often reads medical journals and the Bible.

Despite having eaten eggs, bacon, and red meat for at least 70 years and smoking until he was 60, Pierro has a normal cholesterol level and blood pressure. He takes no daily medication — just a multivitamin. As a young adult, he began the practice of covering every scratch or bruise with a swab of iodine. And instead of gargling with Listerine, he took to drinking it every morning in the belief that it would make him healthier.

"The most important fact is his family history, which tells us that he has inherited very important genes," said Dr. L. Stephen Coles, who heads the Gerontology Research Group in Los Angeles, which has identified 66 of the oldest people in the world. All of the 66 are 110 or older, and 20 live in the United States.

On Feb. 15, 1896, Pierro was born on his family's vineyard in Forenza, Italy, a mountaintop village southeast of Naples. With little income except for that derived from grapes from the vineyard, Pierro sought a better life and arrived in Boston in 1914. He soon found work in shoe shops and factories in Lynn, staying with cousins in Boston and

Swampscott. "You do things when you have to, and I had to," he said. "I was in a strange country, strange language, and I had to learn the way the other people lived."

He entered the Army on Oct. 4, 1917, and served in Battery E, 320 Field Artillery of the 82nd Division in France from May 1918 to May 1919. His enlistment papers record that he fought in the Meuse-Argonne offensive, in which more than 26,000 Americans died, and the battles of St. Mihiel and Ilse-Aisne.

As one of the last surviving World War I veterans, Pierro declined to talk about the battles. "You were there for a purpose," he said. According to the US Department of Veterans Affairs, there are fewer than 50 World War I veterans still alive.

Following the war, he returned to Lynn and married a distant cousin, Mary Pierre. In 1922, the two built a house in Swampscott, and Pierro found new work as an auto body repair manager in Boston. The couple did not have children and, in 1946, they sold all of their belongings and moved to start a new life in Pomona, Calif. Discouraged by the winter rain in Southern California, the two moved back to the North Shore a year later and, in 1950, built a four-room Cape in Marblehead. With his auto body background, Pierro took a job at the Lynn General Electric plant as a sheet-metal worker.

At GE, he was known for his ability to read blueprints and for his meticulous attention to his work, as well as his appearance. "At the GE, they used to call him the Duke because he always came in with a suit on, and then he'd change into his work outfit," said his nephew Rick.

Pierro retired in 1961 and expanded his backyard garden, growing romaine lettuce, tomatoes, and cucumbers. In 1984, 17 years after his wife died, he sold his house to another nephew, Robert Pierro, although he continued to live there until 1996. Nearing 100, Pierro kept up his regimen of chopping wood and doing yard work. When he hit the century mark, Rick invited him to move into his house.

Pierro has had some close calls over the years. He beat cancer more than 20 years ago and once broke a rib after falling from a ladder.

When he was 93, he saw a dangling branch at the top of an evergreen in his backyard. After ascending the tree by ladder, he found a sturdy branch to sit on, and began to trim the broken limb. Alone in the tree, he noticed that the ladder had fallen. Pierro sat patiently on a branch for the next eight hours before he was found by his brother Vito.

"Nothing bothers him," explained his brother Nicholas, who still drives every day and prepares meals for his older brother. Since moving in with his brother and nephew, Pierro has slightly modified his diet. He now eats eggs for breakfast once a week, has a turkey sandwich for lunch, and meat, chicken, or fish for dinner. Still, he eats chocolate and cupcakes regularly and can eat up to three muffins in one sitting.

"When he came here 10 years ago, I said he's going to live to be 110. I'm saying he's got another five years," Nicholas Pierro said. A few feet away, his older brother stood over the kitchen sink, eating a plum and drinking milk from a gallon container. He found the cap to the milk and opened the refrigerator. He then gripped the nearly full gallon of milk by its handle and with a swinging motion, thrust the container onto the top shelf and closed the door.

"Day in and day out we have this problem," said Nicholas, who prefers that his brother use a glass when he drinks milk. Nicholas, who, like his brother, has smooth skin and few wrinkles on his face, acknowledged that the two can get on each other's nerves, but said that comes with having a brother. "Whatever advice I try to give him, he doesn't listen to me. I'm his younger brother, remember."

When Pierro's nephews or nieces visit, he gives them the same advice that he said he tried to follow most of his life. "He always said, 'Don't steal with your hands, steal with your eyes,' " said Robert Pierro. "What he meant by that is if you see somebody doing something, if you watch what they do, you will learn. And that's a very good philosophy."

At his kitchen table, Pierro pondered the difficulties of a life spent trying to do the right thing. He believes in God, and said honesty and hard work could extend one's life. "You run up against life itself. It's hard to do, but still, you've got to do it. You've to got to put your foot forward so the other foot can drag next to it, and that's when you pay attention."

Pierro has not set a goal to live to a certain year. Nor does he have a set philosophy about death. As his 110th birthday approached, Pierro said, "Life goes on, on and on, until you kick the bucket."

February 16, 2006
The Boston Globe

Lenny Doesn't Live at
River House Anymore

W hy should the world care that Lenny Lublinski has died?

For most of his life, he was just another working stiff who found a way to get by. He was the guy you might have seen working a jackhammer during Boston's Big Dig or wiping his brow at some other roadside construction site. Maybe you sat next to him on a flight to Amsterdam once or had a laugh with him on a beach in Morocco. Perhaps you might have bummed a cigarette from him late one night at North Station.

People like Lenny are not destined to become wealthy or famous, but they are likely to make a lot of friends and leave plenty of kindness behind as they move from city to city. And a lot of the time, people like Lenny — complicated, imperfect, big-hearted souls who are sometimes drawn to a drug that will numb their pain just for a short while — don't live long lives or die surrounded by loving family members.

This month, they found his body in a studio apartment on the top floor of River House, a homeless shelter hard by the Bass River in Beverly, where he had lived for most of the past 15 years.

I met Lenny in 2004, after convincing an editor that I should spend a night in such a shelter and then write about the experience. Most of the guests were eager to tell their stories, and when I stepped outside to get some fresh air, I met a fast-talking, broad-shouldered guy with a New Jersey accent who was finishing a cigarette.

I wanted his take on life in the shelter, but he begged off. "I'm the black sheep of my family. Everyone else is successful," he told me. I asked him if I could quote him and wanted to use his name. "Call me Lenny the Laborer," he told me.

And then our small talk turned unexpectedly heavy and I realized that he had plenty of reasons to be angry at life, and with people. Lenny was born in Sweden, a Yiddish-speaking child in a country far from Eastern Europe, where his parents had lived. They somehow had survived Auschwitz, made a short stop in Sweden, then moved to the Bronx and New Jersey, where Lenny picked up English as a kid.

After high school, Lenny did some relocating of his own, finding solace in Europe and Morocco, where he lived for many years.

He worked odd jobs, did landscaping and construction work, and didn't mind sleeping on a sofa for months on end.

He offered up a handshake, scrawled his cellphone number in my notebook, and stamped out his cigarette butt. "This is a good place," he told me that night. "They do a lot of good here."

For years we talked about getting together for coffee, and then one fall I invited him for a Rosh Hashana dinner. He arrived with a smile, accompanied by Anne Strong, who helped run the Beverly shelter. "I gotta call my mom and tell her I'm here," he said excitedly, and stepped outside on my porch.

That night he told stories of Sweden, of picking grapes in southern France, of his travels through Morocco. He insisted on wearing a yarmulke, sipped wine, complimented my wife on her chicken soup, and smiled the entire evening — from the gefilte fish to the brisket and all the way to the pound cake.

I also smiled a lot that night. Was he not just like a member of my family? He looked like a cousin, ate like a brother, and talked and gestured like a long-lost relative.

After that, I'd find a bottle of wine at my doorstep before Passover every year, and it was a sign that Lenny had stopped by. Why didn't I invite him again for another meal? Hadn't I enjoyed his company?

I guess the best I could do was offer him some yard work. Once, I asked him about the Nazis and their impact on his family. "I don't know," he said. After a long silence, he told me he wasn't bitter or angry with anyone. "I don't judge people, and I'm no victim," he said.

After Lenny died at age 62, I learned that his heart had given out.

His friends, Nadine, Scotty, Kate, and Anne, told long stories about how generous he had been. Anyone who needed a ride, or a cup of coffee, or a couple of bucks could count on Lenny.

When the shelter needed a good-will ambassador to talk to politicians about homeless people, Lenny had stepped forward.

When a longtime homeless man was dying at the shelter, Lenny had helped organize a 24-hour hospice.

After the man died, Lenny helped push the gurney out into the fresh air.

"Give him a car, a cellphone, and a half-pack of smokes," his pal

Scotty told me last week, "and he would have gone anywhere he needed to be comfortable, and he would have made sure his friends were, too."

Our society suggests that it's best to present our idealized self when we meet someone new or post something on Facebook. But Lenny understood that it's best to be yourself.

It didn't always help him, but in this world where everyone seems a little broken, he seemed comfortable with his fate and his small community of friends.

Lenny the Laborer did not cure cancer or make a million bucks, but he made a connection with people, and really cared.

That's about all anyone could ask from a friend.

July 24, 2016
The Boston Globe

A Boy and a Bridge

The name of the 15-year-old, brown-eyed boy who loved tennis, got straight A's, and smiled wherever he went is written in blue ink on the upper right side of a loose-leaf notebook in neat letters.

Every morning, shortly after dawn, for the last 10 years, Don Ross has opened his eyes, moved toward his study, picked up a pen, and written three words: Stephen Blaine Ross. He had done this nearly 4,000 times. This is a way, he says, to keep the memory of his boy alive.

That boy was his son, Stephen, who died on a misty December night in 1993 after being hit by a drunk driver on a stone bridge in Annisquam that had no sidewalks. Recently, the state built a 500-foot footpath that runs parallel to the bridge, allowing pedestrians and bikers safe passage. It has been named the Stephen B. Ross Memorial Walkway.

On a recent afternoon, the wind was whipping hard off the Annisquam River, and Don Ross was slowly surveying the new walkway that separates the river and Goose Cove. He stopped and pointed to the middle of the stone bridge, just below the white cross that was nailed to a telephone pole the day after his son was killed. "This is the spot, and even before the accident it was an awful dangerous place to be," said Ross, who grew up in this quiet, isolated section of Gloucester.

Inside his house, Ross and his wife, Sandra, repeatedly thanked the state for building the walkway. "We're so grateful and thankful that no one else will be injured or killed," said Sandra Ross.

While the walkway will honor their son, they know that a memorial cannot bring healing or closure to their wound. They do not know why their son had to die so young. His actions and deeds, though, reveal proud parents. Several times a day they remember their son as a focused, hard-working teenager who excelled in school and tennis and nearly anything else that he put his mind to.

"He didn't waste his life that's for sure," said Sandra Ross, noting that her son would be 26 if he were alive today. "He lived it to its fullest, and did the best he could in everything he did. He was a smart guy, played hard, worked hard, studied hard."

"He was as friendly as can be," Don Ross said. "You always say something about your own children, but I have yet to see anyone really with a smile as friendly as Stevie's."

They revisit the scene of the accident every day, passing along the Goose Cove bridge, just a little over a mile from their house, where their son spent his last moments talking to his best friend, Robbie Gillis, as the two walked back from a Friday night party. The boys had never walked across the bridge at night before and decided to walk against the traffic when Stephen was struck from behind.

"The police knocked on the door, and I remember them saying your son needs you," Don Ross remembered. The couple rushed to Addison-Gilbert Hospital to find their son on a respirator, with the doctors preparing to send him to Massachusetts General Hospital. When they arrived at the Boston hospital they were told that Stephen had died in the ambulance.

In the weeks and months after the funeral, the grief in the community was channeled into dedications and memorials for Stephen. The Annisquam Yacht Club and the tennis courts at Gloucester High School were named after Stephen Ross. Three annual sports scholarships at the high school were also started in his name.

Also, in May 1994, a tougher state drunken driving bill was named after Stephen B. Ross, lowering the legal alcohol level for drivers from 0.1 to 0.08.

Sandra Ross believes a tragedy like this either pulls a family together or breaks it apart. She has found solace in preserving everything her son cherished. Two electric candles have brought light to his room since the day after his death. Inside, posters of Michael Jordan, Bo Jackson, and Cindy Crawford hang on the wall, above Little League pictures and photos of Stephen playing in a pile of leaves. His Angels baseball cap hangs in the closet, next to his track uniform and long-sleeve shirts.

Below his second floor bedroom is a memorial garden, where his ashes rest below a weeping cherry tree. Sandra often sits on a granite bench and looks at the garden.

Robbie Gillis, who remembers talking about girlfriends with his best friend right before the accident, recently returned to live in Gloucester. "Reality ceased to be there that night," he said, recalling the minutes after the accident when he sat on the road consoling his friend, waiting for the ambulance to arrive.

Stephen's sister, Dawn Ross, is 28, and hopes to name a child after her brother one day. She has already tested out the walkway several times and has found comfort during her walks.

"I like it, I just get a good feeling," said Dawn Ross, a special needs teacher at the Fuller Elementary School. "I don't know, it's an airy feeling. I just feel he might be there too."

May 16, 2004
The Boston Globe

The Night the Cops
Became Killers

"We are the police and we're going to kill you."

The voice came from the other side of the door to Room 209. Around 4:30 on a brisk summer morning in July 1982 inside a tiny motel room above a strip joint in Chelsea, 12 people prepared to die.

The men and women barricaded the door with a couch and waited. A group of Everett and Chelsea police officers banged on the door. Then they drilled a hole and injected mace. An Everett cop fired two shots into the door. Finally, one of the cops grabbed an ax and chopped through the door. Soon, an Everett man, Vincent Bordonaro, would be fatally injured, and dozens of other lives changed forever.

Long before Whitey Bulger's celebrated trial, Greater Boston was focused on the courtroom drama that grew out of that night at King Arthur's Motel. While Bulger was charged with 19 gang-related murders, King Arthur's was about police brutality and cops being accused of murdering a sleeping man.

"It was police brutality. There's no question about it," said Robert A. Barton, the since-retired Superior Court judge who presided over the King Arthur's trials.

During the trials, held in April, May, and June of 1983, people questioned just what happened at the drab, concrete strip club and motel tucked just over the Everett border in Chelsea. At the end of the first trial, Everett police officers John McLeod and Richard Aiello were found guilty of second-degree murder.

It marked the first time in state history that an on-duty cop — Aiello — had been found guilty of murder.

Another Everett cop, John Macauda, was found guilty of manslaughter. Everett police officer William McClusky was found not guilty of second-degree murder, and Michael Nadworny of the Chelsea police force was found not guilty of assault and battery.

In the second trial, which ended on June 20, four civilians who had been accused of assaulting McLeod were acquitted.

Finally, in February 1984, six Chelsea cops admitted they filed false police reports about the incident, and entered into a plea agreement for which they received discipline within the Police Department.

While Everett and Chelsea chiefs now point to that night as the beginning of reform in their departments, it took almost another decade before either department overhauled its policies and regulations, and added comprehensive training, along with additional layers of supervision, to prevent an event like King Arthur's from happening again.

In July 1982, Everett police had little or no training, and were operating under policies that had last been updated in 1951. In Chelsea, the depart-ment was in disarray: Its vice squad did not work weekends, and bars like King Arthur's regularly stayed open after hours, said Chelsea Patrolman John Gravallese, one of the officers who admitted to falsifying a police report about the incident.

"A lot changed after King Arthur's," said Gravallese, 63, who received a 22-month suspension without pay, and blames the dissolution of his marriage on that night. "It changed everybody's lives, the victims and the police."

Josh Resnek, a former editor of the Chelsea Record, described the King Arthur's incident as a metaphor for the way the city was run. By the time the state took control of Chelsea after it went bankrupt in 1991, four former mayors had been sent to jail or were under house arrest, and a Chelsea police captain also had been jailed.

"Police were called [to King Arthur's] repeatedly for beatings, stabbings, shootings over the years. The city condoned it; the police overlooked it," said Resnek.

On a curved strip where the rutted streets are filled with potholes capable of swallowing up tires, King Arthur's still sits. In the shadow of Everett's LNG tanks, and hard by the New England Produce Center, tractor-trailer drivers have long sought refuge in its windowless bar, seeking strong drink, a seat with a view of a naked dancer, and a room for the night.

The night that changed both cities started out like any other, said Beverly Farrairo Guttadauro, who later married Arthur Guttadauro, the late owner of King Arthur's. She headed over to the Village Pub, a bar that was owned by Bordonaro. There, she met several others who later found themselves in Room 209. One was McLeod, who was off duty and consumed four drinks at the pub, according to court records.

"That place was closing down, and I said 'I'm going over to my boyfriend's bar,' and I said, 'Anyone who wants to come is welcome,' " she said in a recent interview.

The group arrived at King Arthur's and met Bordonaro, who bought a couple of rounds before excusing himself and heading up to sleep in Room 209. McLeod also bought a round.

Nicholas Medugno, who is now 80, was sitting at the bar around 3:30 that morning. "There were just people drinking and a little argument broke out," said Medugno, who owned a pizza shop in downtown Everett and recalled frequenting King Arthur's.

Alfred "Da" Mattuchio, an Everett bar owner who died in 2003, had testified that McLeod confronted him and threw a punch.

The two had history: Years earlier, Mattuchio's son had been shot by Charles Carter, an Everett auxiliary police officer who had been McLeod's partner on the force. After the incident, Carter was shot and killed in Medford.

According to Mattuchio's testimony, McLeod was subdued by Charles Dimino, the son of Anthony Dimino, the bar manager. Mattuchio and others would testify that some punches were thrown, and a bruised and bloodied McLeod was told to leave the bar. McLeod would tell the juries that he had been beaten with a bat by Mattuchio, Charles Cella, and the Diminos.

Sometime after 4 a.m., McLeod stumbled to a nearby guard shack and told a security officer to call the Everett police to report that a cop had been attacked. The department's entire night watch of five officers sped across the city line into Chelsea and arrived at King Arthur's. McLeod greeted the police, and first reached for an officer's rifle in a cruiser before settling on a set of nunchaku, two hardwood sticks joined by a short length of chain.

Other officers would fortify themselves with nightsticks, clubs, bats, and tire irons in addition to their guns. They moved toward the bar, found it locked, shattered a window, and got in. Around 4:30, Chelsea police arrived and were told that an Everett officer had been beaten by a crowd with bats.

"That's when we went into Room 209," said Medugno. "And when we went into that room, they started breaking down the door. We said 'Call the police,' and they said, 'We are the police.'"

Over the next several minutes, two sets of beatings occurred. According to testimony, Aiello and Macauda made the first entry, and struck several people with blunt instruments. Helen Bozzi, who was also in the room, testified she saw Macauda hit Bordonaro — who was sleeping on a bed — with a tire iron.

"It was just a nightmare, a slaughter," said Medugno, who was hit over the head and later hospitalized. He said he thinks about the attack often, and 30 years later still suffers from dizziness from the beatings. In court, he testified: "It was like a stick hitting meat."

Back in the hallway, the policemen regrouped. An ambulance arrived to treat McLeod, who waved the paramedic away. After a brief respite, Aiello walked McLeod back into the room with a baseball bat. There, several of the people were already bloodied and unconscious. Inside the room, witnesses testified that the second set of beatings began when McLeod used the bat on Bordonaro and Mattuchio.

After every swing, witnesses reported him saying, "My name is John McLeod, and don't you forget it."

Bordonaro, 54, slipped into a coma and died seven days after the attack. McLeod and the other Everett officers continued to work until a month later, when they were formally charged with murder.

McLeod was released in 2000 after serving 17 years, and Aiello was set free in 1998 after 15 years in prison. Both still live in the area; Aiello declined to comment for this article, and McLeod did not respond to interview requests.

Macauda served six years for manslaughter; he could not be reached for comment.

After the beatings and the trials, the victims sued the cities of Chelsea and Everett and received millions of dollars in damages. Residents picketed outside the Everett police station, and sometimes heckled officers in public.

Meanwhile, both departments carried on for years with few changes. "Nothing happened. That was the big criticism that little had been done," said John McCarthy, who took over as Everett's mayor in 1986 and subsequently appointed a new police chief who instilled mandatory training and a formal chain of command. In Chelsea, the police began to implement new training and policies after the city entered into receivership in 1991.

"It became known pretty much as a watershed moment in what was deemed police misconduct," said Chelsea Police Chief Brian Kyes. He said his officers now write event narratives while compiling criminal reports, and those documents are reviewed by a supervisor and a crime reporting and analysis unit to make sure they are accurate.

Everett Police Chief Steven Mazzie believes the incident ultimately changed his department for the better. These days, no one likens Everett's law enforcement to the Wild West.

"I think we've learned a lot from King Arthur's," said Mazzie. "We've become a more professional agency. We've instituted rules and regulations, policies and procedures; values that reflect who we are now and how we're supposed to conduct ourselves in the community."

June 23, 2013
The Boston Globe

A Private Death

The sky was full of clouds, darkness was coming, and silence had returned to a rocky ledge the teenagers called SV, or Swampscott View. Soon it would rain hard, and all night. On the ledge, buried beneath a pile of leaves, lay Henry Bedard Jr. He was 15, and by 4 p.m. on Dec. 16, 1974, his skull had been crushed. Yards away lay the murder weapon, a baseball bat. His killer or killers were farther away.

Thirty years after his brutal death, no one knows who killed Bedard.

An investigation by the Swampscott police and the State Police never led to an arrest.

There were no suspects. No leads. No motive.

"We never got anything that was worthwhile. Nothing. Nothing at all," said James Hanley, the retired Swampscott police captain who oversaw the investigation. "There were all kinds of theories. Theories like some hobo came down the track and killed him. A nut from Lynn could have done it. I never got anything that would kind to seem to have any credence to it."

The pain, shock, and confusion that overtook the small North Shore town in 1974 has eased over the years. Bedard is no longer a household name. His parents divorced and moved away. Classmates grew up and married. And along the way, Swampscott matured from a working-class town filled with craftsmen and General Electric employees to a select destination for professionals with six-figure incomes.

Still, every Dec. 16, Bedard's father and a core group of the murdered boy's childhood friends wonder why no one could ever have been charged with the crime in this close knit town of 14,000 people where everyone seems to know everyone else.

"I was hoping that it would have been solved before I died," said Henry Bedard Sr., who is retired and living in Florida. "But it looks like it'll never be solved."

Childhood friends like Paul Zuchero have spent dozens of sleepless nights over the years going over scenarios that could have led to the murder and searching for any kind of motive. "It's unbelievable," said Zuchero, who remembers sitting next to Bedard at church the day before the teenager was killed. Zuchero, who is now 45, still has his dead friend's ninth-grade graduation picture hanging on his refrigerator door. "I want him in the middle of everything," he said, pointing to a montage of family photos surrounding Bedard. At this point, he hopes that the murderer — if he or she is still alive — leaves a deathbed confession someday.

Over the past two years, Swampscott police and State Police have taken a renewed interest in the case. Thirteen months ago, Bedard's clothing and the murder weapon — a 31-inch Louisville Slugger bat with cryptic markings on its handle — were sent out for DNA testing. Police hope to match two partial fingerprints that were found on the blood-splattered bat.

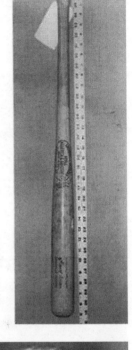

The wooded area where Bedard was killed looks the same as it did 30 years ago. A path ascends from a former Boston & Maine rail bed up a small hill to the rocky clearing. The area can be seen from Paradise Road — the second busiest street in town — and overlooks Swampscott's Department of Public Works yard. Fading brown leaves are piled deep and make walking slow.

Just why Bedard walked along that clearing 30 years ago is still a mystery. In the summer, he had played cards with friends at the site, but when winter set in, the rocky clearing was no longer a place where kids would meet. Nor was it considered a shortcut back to

his home, 1 mile away. "I just want to know why he was up there that day," his mother, Gloria Bedard, said in a short telephone interview.

At 15, the high school sophomore was on track to be a success. Street-smart and confident, he was less than a year away from buying his first car with the $900 he had saved from caddying and pumping

gas at his father's gas station in Danvers. At 5-foot-4 and 135 pounds, he had earned a spot on the junior varsity football team. Friends remember him as a scrappy kid with a good sense of humor who would never back down from a threat. With his quick smile and blond hair, he was not shy when it came to asking a girl out for a date.

"I'd give an arm, a leg to find out who did it," said Cindy Cavallaro, who took Bedard to her eighth-grade dance. She remembers the small ring Bedard gave her when she was 14. After his death she wore it every day for two years, until it disappeared down her bathroom sink. "I was devastated. It was the last thing I had from him."

Retracing his steps

Henry Bedard began his last day of life by walking his younger brother to school and then continuing on for another 2 miles to Swampscott

High School. Bedard attended all of his classes that day, but after school let out at 2:15 p.m. he altered his routine. Instead of walking home with friends, he took a bus from the school to the Vinnin Square shopping center. Between 2:30 and 3 p.m., he dropped off a roll of 8-millimeter film to be developed at CVS and purchased a bottle of perfume as a Christmas gift for his sister.

Around 3 p.m., two-fifths of a mile from the CVS, he was seen by then-lieutenant Peter Cassidy on Paradise Road. Cassidy waved to him and noticed that Bedard was walking fast. "He looked like he was in a hurry to get somewhere," Cassidy said. By 3:40, Bedard was almost a mile south of the CVS when several town workers spotted him walking across the DPW lot.

"He looked up and said, 'Merry Christmas,' " said Tom Scanlon, who remembers seeing Bedard walking toward the abandoned railroad tracks that sit next to the DPW yard. Scanlon said Bedard held up a bag and told the town workers he was going home to wrap Christmas presents. The men watched Bedard disappear into the woods, onto the path of the former rail line. Scanlon then went back to work inside the wooden building just 10 feet underneath the ledge. Within the next 15 minutes, Bedard would be attacked just above the workers' heads and left to die. "We never heard anything," said Scanlon.

Around that time, Cliff Goodman was getting ready for his 10th birthday party. Two of his friends arrived at about 4 p.m. They didn't tell anyone that they had just found — and then left — an empty brown wallet and a CVS bag with a bottle of perfume on the ledge behind Goodman's house.

As darkness fell on the town, an icy rain began. Meanwhile, Bedard's parents began to worry when their son didn't come home for supper. "We knew something was wrong right away, because Henry was always home by 5:30 p.m.," said Zuchero. By 7 p.m., Bedard's father had picked up Zuchero, and together with friends and family, they drove in the heavy rain, searching in parks, woods, and back paths for Henry. "We were hollering in the middle of the woods; we thought he had fallen and hurt himself and couldn't move," said Zuchero. "We never, ever thought he was dead."

By the next day, Swampscott police had arranged for a helicopter to help search the town. During school that day, one of Goodman's friends told the 10-year-old about the empty wallet and perfume by the ledge. Intrigued by the find, Goodman and his friend reached the spot after school, around 2:30 p.m., and scanned the leaves for the perfume and wallet. Then Goodman and his friend started to scream. They had found Bedard, covered in leaves and blood; his head was cracked open.

"After all these years I don't like anything scary, or to be in the dark," said Goodman, who is now 40. He remembers being overwhelmed by a wave of emotions that followed in the hours after discovering Bedard's body. That night he kept the light on in his room as he lay in his bed. As he tried to sort out his feelings, he could hear the hum of portable generators that lit up the hill as police searched for clues. Since that night he has visited Bedard's grave more than a dozen times. "I never knew him, but I felt like I had to go," Goodman said.

On Dec. 20, 1974, 1,500 people packed St. John's Church in Swampscott. Children and adults wept as the priest described Bedard as "a good man." Inside the coffin, Bedard wore a Swampscott football jersey with the number 30. It was the same number his older brother had once worn for the high school football team.

The seaside town known for its quaint beaches, storied football team, and quiet neighborhoods was in shock. People began to lock their doors. Kids walked in pairs. Residents expected an arrest right away. "It was like a little hamlet, really; you felt that you were living in a really special place," said Zuchero. "My feeling is that on Dec. 16, 1974, that Swampscott died, the day Henry died, never to be seen again."

Cavallaro, who still lives less than a half-mile from the murder site, has never walked near the murder scene, and she drives out of her way to bypass the site. "It changed everything," she said, describing a town gripped with fear. "I don't think I ever looked at anyone or trusted anybody the same way after that."

A failed investigation

Right away, police acknowledged they had few clues outside of the bat, which had the Roman numeral VI carved into the butt. Any footprints around Bedard's body had been washed away by the half-inch of rain that had fallen during the night of the murder. The autopsy was delayed a day, and when it was performed, Bedard was not fingerprinted. Six months after the murder, a partial fingerprint was found on the bat when it was examined at the State Police lab in Boston. Despite interviewing coaches, Little League players, sporting-goods store owners, and the bat's manufacturer, police were never able to identify the bat's owner.

In 1998 the bat was sent to the State Police lab again, and a second partial imprint was identified. Because Bedard was never fingerprinted, police still don't know whether the prints are Bedard's or the murderers.

Bedard's closest friends are hesitant to place any blame on the investigation, yet some wonder whether the Swampscott police were qualified to conduct a murder investigation. While some people were singled out 30 years ago for questioning by police, others were never contacted.

Mark Gambale is still waiting to talk to the police about his memories of Bedard, who lived two doors away. Gambale remembers spending family vacations at the Bedards' summer home in New Hampshire, and he first played with Bedard as an infant. The two boys walked home from school together often, and they never used the clearing where Bedard was found murdered as a shortcut home. "Nothing is going to fix it, but you thought there would be a resolution to what happened," said Gambale. "Thirty years later, we're still waiting."

With a force of 35 officers in a town of 13,500 people, crime was a rare occurrence in Swampscott in 1974. According to the town's 1974 annual report, there were two armed robberies and five drug-related arrests. Patrol officers spent most of their time that year responding to service calls, issuing 548 parking tickets, investigating 296 car accidents, and transporting 330 people to the hospital.

The Bedard murder was Hanley's first homicide investigation. He interviewed nearly 100 people. Nine teenagers took polygraph tests, and all passed. By the spring of 1975, four months after the murder, the case had turned cold and Hanley returned to other duties. With the hope of generating leads, a $10,000 reward was offered to help find the killer. There were no takers.

After several months, frustration, grief, and disbelief gave way to a numbness that settled on his close friends and his father. "I kept saying to myself that they were going to find out who, why, or what," said Bedard's father. "I just don't know what happened."

With time, the memory of the feisty boy who loved sports and was always home for dinner by 5:30 p.m. faded into the town's subconsciousness. A college scholarship was established in his name, and two high school yearbooks were dedicated to him in the first few years after his murder. But investigators who worked on the case have long retired, and now Bedard is usually referenced only when anybody

talks about the town's sole unsolved murder.

"It's like an urban legend now," Ron Madigan, the current police chief, said of the Bedard case.

While three generations have been born since Bedard was last seen slipping into the twilight by the railroad tracks, longtime residents have not tired of the mystery. At the recent Swampscott-Marblehead Thanksgiving football game, a group of middle-aged men talked about the murder on the sidelines. Longtime residents say they have developed a habit of looking up at the rocks above the DPW yard every time they drive by. Others, like Bedard's old girlfriend Cavallaro, can't help but wonder if the murderer is still living in town.

"How do I know that someone I went to school with wasn't involved or knows something?" she said. "In a town this small, everybody knows everybody's business. It's like a little Peyton Place. How can something like this be kept so long?"

While the Swampscott police never developed suspects, the town's principal investigators believe the murderer was someone who knew

Bedard.

"I think it was a friend of his. I think it was somebody very close to him," said Cassidy, who knew Bedard's family and continued to work on the case when he became police chief.

Hanley agrees with Cassidy. "I think it was someone in his circle of friends. I firmly believe that.... It's a logical conclusion to make," he said.

Bedard's closest friends scoff at the retired investigators and believe it's time to start the investigation from scratch.

"After 30 years it's time for them to think outside of the box," said Zuchero, who wants the police to re-interview everyone who knew Bedard.

A mile down the road from the cul-de-sac where he once lived and played stands a simple gravestone with the name Bedard. Unlike the smooth and ornate granite monuments that fill the Swampscott Cemetery, Bedard's is understated. Tufts of rock jut out from the front side, and on the back he's identified as a son who lived from 1959 to 1974. His friends aren't sure if they'll be coming today to the gravestone. "I'll light a candle and say a prayer for him," said Zuchero.

In Zuchero's kitchen the light will flicker on the picture on the refrigerator of the 15-year-old boy who is forever smiling.

December 16, 2004
The Boston Globe

She's Square With Life

Marilyn Coyne survived the Depression with little food and no heat in her parents' flat in Portland, Maine. She married and sent four children to college. She saw her husband and one of their children die. And, last fall, after three years of fighting breast cancer, she was told by a doctor that she had months to live.

In hospice care and losing weight in recent weeks as the cancer crept through her body, she confided to a hospice volunteer that she had a last wish, something that recalled summer nights of her childhood and joy with her husband. She wanted a final square dance.

Yesterday, her wish came true. Coyne donned a floral skirt, a crimson petticoat, and a red peasant shirt, and walked to the center of a nursing room social hall, where nine professional square-dancers, dressed in cowboy shirts and calico, waited for her.

It had been a decade since she last clasped hands with a partner, but as music played, the elfin Coyne deftly followed the dance caller's instructions of allemande left, promenade, and do-si-do. After five minutes of swinging her partner, and singing along with "She'll Be Coming 'Round the Mountain," Coyne let her thin, 82-year-old frame fall into a padded wooden chair and took a deep breath.

"That," she sighed, "was wonderful."

It may have been bittersweet, this scene, but it befitted the decades that led to it. For much of her life, Coyne had sought refuge on the square-dance floor. She learned the art as a child growing up on Portland's mostly-Irish Munjoy Hill, where she received the nickname Minty. The name stuck for life (she never liked Marilyn, she says) and still hints of a youth long past.

"I'm Minty McNeill Coyne, the girl who could steal any heart, anywhere, any time," she says.

As a teenager, she met Patrick Coyne. The two went to separate Catholic high schools in the city, but they became fast friends, brought together by poverty and hardship and, ultimately, by square-dancing. After their first square dance together, they realized there was more than friendship between them. "I just liked him from the very start. We were good friends and got along very well," she said. They married in 1947.

In Portland, Patrick worked as a foreman for the city water district, and Minty took a clerk job at a credit union. Minty says she lived a "simple life," working, taking care of her children, and putting her passion into baking apple pies and attending weekend square dances.

There, she found escape among people who, like her, reveled in music, dance, and small talk.

"I'd feel free when I danced, and it's nice if you have a husband who likes it. I have some friends and their husbands would never do anything like that," she said.

All of her children would graduate from college, fulfilling her dream for them. "I never could go. I wanted them to go so bad," said Minty, who is 4 feet, 10 inches tall, has sharp blue eyes, and short silver hair.

One son became a doctor, a daughter became a lawyer, another son went into real estate, and a third son, Danny, was an assistant secretary of state in Maine. At a family picnic in 1991, when Danny Coyne was 40, Minty watched as her son collapsed during a basketball game and died.

"I screamed 'Danny's dead, Danny's dead' over and over, and cried and cried," she said, adding that there is no such thing as closure when one loses a child.

Tired of Maine's frigid winters, the couple moved to Gulfport, Fla., in 1995, determined to square-dance as much as they could. She sewed all of her dresses and shirts and bought new petticoats and shoes.

Ten years into their retirement, Patrick died, and Minty moved north to be closer to her daughter, Carol. She settled into an assisted-living facility in Tewksbury and soon after, felt pain around her breast. After tests, she was told she had breast cancer and had a breast removed.

The cancer never went away.

After Coyne mentioned her desire for one last square dance, Camryn Walsh, of Care Alternatives Hospice, decided to bring the dance to Minty. Walsh arranged to bring the Riverside Squares, a Danvers square-dancing group, to Minty's floor at the Meadow View Care and Rehabilitation Center in North Reading.

"What we really try to provide is comfort and dignity when patients and families are faced with incurable disease," said Walsh.

For an hour yesterday, the music played and dancers danced while a small crowd of nursing home residents, and Minty's nurses and social workers, hooted and hollered in appreciation. Then the dancers packed up and were gone, and Minty sat in the dining room, talking about everything from the economy and technology to nature. She's waiting for a really warm day so she can take a walk outside. "I don't like sitting around," she said.

She does not fear death or dwell on the idea of not being around much longer. "I know I'm going to die one day, but it doesn't bother me. I don't think about dying," she said. "I believe in afterlife. I assume there's a heaven. . . . I'll let you know if I get there."

March 20, 2009
The Boston Globe

ACKNOWLEDGEMENTS

When I was a kid, I helped my friend Chucky Finger with his paper route. One of the perks of the job was reading the Boston Globe. Years later, I was lucky enough to fulfill my childhood dream of working at the Globe. Thanks to the Globe for permission to reprint these articles in this book. Also thanks to my editors at the Globe for their counsel: Marcia Dick, Kerry Drohan and Leslie Anderson.

Writers need feedback and I am grateful to my family and friends who have always been there to read my works. Thanks to my wife, Devorah, and my son, Aaron, for your support and patience while I was on deadline. Also, to my sisters Sheri Kelton and Phyllis Osher, for your advice. There are many others who have helped me along the way. They include David Townsend, David Shear, David Brooks, Neal Stamell, Chucky Finger, Fred Vainas, Bette Keva, Ramy Osher, Bernie Hyatt, Michael Eggert, John Fisher, Barry Rosenberg, Yossi Lipsker, Shmuel Posner, Phyllis Boris and Joe Feinbloom. Also to those relatives and friends who have passed on, I will be forever grateful for our time spent together: Sam and Ruby Rosenberg, Eddy and Judy Rosenberg, Esther and Murray Katz, Harry Brandwein, Joel Uchenick, Benjamin Entine, Alan Lupo, Eva Rosenberg, and Esther, Alexander and Sol Sandler.

Also, thanks go out to Globe readers for supporting journalism. And thanks to my sources, who were kind, patient and willing to tell their stories. I hope I've done them right.

Made in the USA
Middletown, DE
14 February 2017